Hanns Eisler Political Musician

1 Berlin, c. 1930

Hanns Eisler Political Musician

ALBRECHT BETZ

Translated by BILL HOPKINS

CAMBRIDGE UNIVERSITY PRESS

Cambridge
London New York New Rochelle
Melbourne Sydney

Published by the Press Syndicate of the University of Cambridge
The Pitt Building, Trumpington Street, Cambridge CB2 1RP
32 East 57th Street, New York, NY 10022, USA
296 Beaconsfield Parade, Middle Park, Melbourne 3206, Australia

Originally published in German as *Hanns Eisler: Musik einer Zeit, die sich eben bildet* by Edition text und kritik GmbH, Munich 1976 and © Edition text und kritik 1976

First published in English by Cambridge University Press 1982 as *Hanns Eisler Political Musician*
English edition © Cambridge University Press 1982

Printed in Great Britain at the University Press, Cambridge

Library of Congress catalogue card number: 81–12260

British Library Cataloguing in Publication Data

Betz, Albrecht
Hanns Eisler political musician.
1. Eisler, Hanns
I. Title   II. Hanns Eisler. *English*
780'.92'4   ML410.E37

ISBN 0 521 24022 0

Contents

vi   Contents

Acknowledgements

Between 1972 and 1975 I had a series of conversations with friends, acquaintances and colleagues of Eisler, who should be given special thanks. Most of the conversations were recorded: Kurt A. Adler (New York), Irmgard Arnold (Berlin), Mordecai Bauman (Stockbridge, Mass.), Alvah Bessie (San Rafael, Calif.), Ernst Bloch (Tübingen), Hans Bunge (Berlin), Harold Clurman (New York), Lester Cole (San Francisco), Louis Daquin (Paris), Max Deutsch (Paris), Georg Eisler (Vienna), Lou Eisler-Fischer (Vienna), Stephanie Eisler (Berlin), Paul A. Falkenberg (New York), Marta Feuchtwanger (Pacific Palisades), Irma Friedmann (New York), Robert Gilbert (Ascona), Jakob Gimpel (Los Angeles), Paul Henried (Pacific Palisades), Joris Ivens (Paris), Rudolf Kolisch (Boston), Fritz Lang (Beverly Hills), Katia Mann (Kilchberg bei Zurich), Ben Margolis (Los Angeles), Hans Mayer (Tübingen), Chris Marker (Paris), Vladimir Pozner (Paris), Erwin Ratz (Vienna), Jean Renoir (Beverly Hills), Alain Resnais (Paris), Harry Robin (Los Angeles), Earl Robinson (Los Angeles), Lolla Rosenfeld (New York), Joachim Schumacher (Woodbury, Conn.), Charles Seeger (Bridgewater, Conn.), Lee Strasburg (Los Angeles), Salka Viertel (Klosters bei Davos), Jean Wiener (Paris). I would like to thank the Deutsche Forschungsgemeinschaft (DFG), Bad Godesberg for a three-month stipendium for research in the USA in the autumn of 1973. The directors of the Hanns Eisler Archive and the Bertolt Brecht Archive in the Akademie der Künste der DDR in Berlin, Herr Grabs and Frau Ramthun, I thank for their kindness and helpfulness. The following archives were also used: Bundesarchiv Koblenz, Deutsche Bibliothek, Frankfurt am Main (Abteilung IX Exil-Literatur), Library of Congress (Music Department), Washington, Lincoln Center (Music Department), New York, ASCAP, New York, Los Angeles Times, New York Times, New York Public Library, San Francisco Chronicle, Academy of Motion Picture Arts and Sciences, Hollywood, Rockefeller Foundation Archives, New York. In addition the estates of: Lion Feuchtwanger, Pacific Palisades and Arnold Schoenberg, Brentwood, Los Angeles.

A. B.

Publisher's note

The publishers wish to acknowledge with thanks the help of Professor David Blake in the final editorial stages of the translation of the text after the death of Bill Hopkins.

Thanks are due to the following for permission to quote extracts from Eisler's works.

Exx. 1–6, 10, 11: © Universal Edition (Alfred A. Kalmus Ltd); Exx. 9, 12: © 1955 by Edition Peters; Exx. 7, 8, 13–18, 20–34: © VEB Deutscher Verlag für Musik, Leipzig; Ex. 19: © Verlag Neue Musik

The list of Eisler's works was originally prepared by Professor David Blake in 1973 for *The New Grove Dictionary of Music and Musicians* (London: Macmillan, 1980), where it appears in shorter form.

Photographs are reproduced from the following sources.

Kurt A. Adler (17); Akademie der Künste, Berlin–DDR (19, 21); Kurt Desch Verlag (5); Hanns Eisler Archive (7, 9, 10, 16, 18); Stephanie Eisler (1, 4, 6, 8, 12, 14, 23); Lion Feuchtwanger Archive (15); Irma Friedmann (2); Gerda Goedhardt (13, 20, 22); Arnold Schoenberg Archive (3); Joachim Schumacher (11)

Overture

Thus I believe that precisely Schoenberg's method can become extraordinarily important for a new social music if we can understand how to use it *critically*. It will be a matter of standing Schoenberg on his head somewhat, so that his feet are on the firm ground of our social links with the (historical) struggle of the masses for a new world.

Eisler on Schoenberg[1]

I openly acknowledged myself a pupil of that great thinker ... The mystification which dialectics was subject to in Hegel's hands in no way prevented him from being the first to represent its general modes of operation in a comprehensive and intelligent way. In him it is stood on its head. It has to be turned the right way up if we are to discover the rational kernel inside the mystical shell.

In its mystified form dialectics became a tool of Germanic philosophy because it seemed to transfigure the existent. In its rational form the bourgeoisie and their spokesmen find it a vexation and an abomination because, together with the positive understanding of the existent, it implies the understanding of its negation, its necessary decay, including all evolved forms in the flux of things and thus at the same time demonstrating their transience; it allows nothing to impose on it, and it is essentially critical and revolutionary.

Marx on Hegel[2]

His whole attitude is revolutionary in the highest sense. In both the listener and the executant this music develops the powerful impulses and insights of an age in which productivity of every kind is the source of all enjoyment and morality. It brings forth new tenderness and strength, endurance and versatility, impatience and foresight, challenge and self-sacrifice.

Brecht on Eisler[3]

Eisler's historical importance lies in the fact that he paved the way for a social art in a field which today is still considered rather as a refuge from politics; and this he did at a time of transition which had been initiated by the October Revolution.

Eisler's musical practice – and theory – is also a first answer to Schoenberg: he endeavoured to abolish bourgeois music, or more precisely, the bourgeois in music. This could be seen ultimately as a form of isolation, at a time when modern music and the public were very much growing apart from one another. Only in the perspective of a society no longer divided into classes would such an abolition be possible. Eisler's musical language achieved this not by going counter to the great tradition but entirely through and by means of it. It was precisely the formal innovations in his compositions that enable their social function to be fulfilled.

His saying to the effect that music was made 'by people for people'[4] draws attention to the unity of revolutionary and humanistic intentions. The current separation of feeling from understanding, the supposed unrelatedness of the claims of music to those of politics, those of private life to those of social action, have to be dispelled as false, if ingrained, alternatives, and this must be done by example and incitement through a dialectical art; or more precisely, an art of dialectical materialism.

Eisler worked throughout his life in an atmosphere of tension created by great social, political and aesthetic conflicts, which, for all their contradictions, gave a liberating strength to his music. Their roots are to be found, above all, in the actual course of history. Right from the start, the falterings in the development of socialism, for which he and his art campaigned, the set-backs and blind alleys of a historically young movement, brought about errors which on a number of occasions put an almost unbearable strain on his critical impatience and solidarity. After a while such conflicts die down. It remains valuable to study them for the political lessons they contain. That a man with such a sensitively organized mind and leading a frequently difficult existence should also be confronted by problems of a private nature goes without saying and is of lesser interest in connection with his work.

Four periods may be distinguished in Eisler's work and life. The first includes his education and his early Viennese works, extending up to 1925. The second, his early middle period in Berlin, coincides to some extent with the second phase of the Weimar Republic, from 1925 to 1933. The fifteen-year exile follows as a third, or later middle period, which Eisler largely spent in the USA (until 1948), followed by a fourth, his late period of creativity, from 1950 to 1962 in East Berlin.

The most important decade for Eisler's development was the 1920s since these years saw the onset of a threefold revolution to which he responded wholeheartedly: the major social upheavals brought about by the First World War and the October Revolution, the 'revolution of musical material' associated with Arnold Schoenberg (free atonality and twelve-note technique) and the arrival of the mass media (radio, the gramophone, sound films) which affected the standing and function of the arts.[5]

In the late 1920s there also occurred an event which augured well for cultural history both within and beyond Germany – Eisler's meeting with Brecht followed by their first work together. Differing characters of comparable calibre, both made use of the most advanced resources of their art and shared the same political perspective. In their music theatre and vocal works Eisler and Brecht succeeded in creating a synthesis which, being both geared to actual practice and 'relevant', won back the social impact that had long been played out by bourgeois art, and not least because it drew in a new public and its reactions in a new way.

The two great themes dictated by history – emancipation of the proletariat and the fight against fascism – were not the only ones. The 'purification of the emotions' (as well as their enrichment), involving the whole fabric of life, was inextricably bound up with political enlightenment and mobilization: the aim was to achieve a self-aware, lucid and benevolent rationality, appropriate to a scientific age that was freeing itself from the shackles of capitalist interests.

1

Early years in Vienna

Songs, piano music and chamber music

In the spring of 1923, Schoenberg launched the career of a pupil to whom he had been particularly attached – a pupil whose subsequent development was to take him a long way from anything his teacher could have anticipated.

After studying with him for four years (from 1919 to 1923),[1] Eisler presented his 'graduation exercise': already a masterly work, this was a piano sonata, and Schoenberg immediately decided it should be performed, even though – as Alban Berg was surprised to report – 'the third movement is nothing like completed yet'.[2] Only a week later, Schoenberg wrote this advice to his pupil:

Dear Eisler, As soon as you have this letter, go to Universal Edition,[3] say that I have recommended you to Mr Hertzka, the director, and ask when you can show him your works.

Naturally I can't promise that anything will come of it. He didn't take Webern until it was almost too late, and he still hasn't taken Berg! . . . Best regards. 6.IV.1923.[4]

Few letters of recommendation can have been couched in more sarcastic terms than those in which Schoenberg sought to get Eisler published:

Dear Mr. Hertzka, The bearer of this letter, who should already be known to you through the work he did in a humble capacity at UE,[5] is my former pupil Hanns Eisler. He will be trying to interest you in his Piano Sonata and in an opera which he has not yet quite completed. Unfortunately I am not sufficiently acquainted with your more recent composers to be able to plead effectively with you on his behalf, and so can only hope that my insignificant word will be of some use to you. Even so, I would like to mention that he recently played his Sonata for me, whereupon I spontaneously decided to put it on the programme for the next concert of

2   As a student of Schoenberg (c. 1922)

the Prague Society – an action for which I certainly deserve the censure of all sensible people (including the envious). Naturally I am not offering you any advice; the fact that I have previously recommended to you the works of Webern and Berg on any number of occasions has doubtless proved once and for all my lack of judgment and fallible instinct. So do whatever you want to. With best regards.[6]

The result was unexpected and immediate. On 12 April Eisler cabled his teacher from Vienna: 'My works accepted for publication by Hertzka. Sonata great success in Prague. Sincerest thanks – Eisler.'[7]

The success of Eisler's opus 1 had been given a helping hand two days previously by the pianist Eduard Steuermann,[8] whose performances of works by the Viennese group were regarded as definitive. The two items of news reached Eisler simultaneously. A euphoric letter, brimming over with gratitude (quite exceptional for the 'somewhat refractory fellow' he then was),[9] went to Schoenberg on 13 April:

Honoured Master, I can give you very pleasing news of myself (you will already have received my telegram). 1) *Hertzka has taken me on as a house composer.* This is a firm agreement. First he will publish my Sonata. My other things are to follow ... He was enormously amiable and insistently explained that I had only your recommendation to thank for it. 2) The Sonata went down very well in Prague ... The 3rd movement (Finale) seems to have made the most impact. 3) You may possibly remember that I submitted a cycle of (6) songs for the Salzburg Chamber Festival. Yesterday Pisk came to me (unprompted) to inform me that the committee had accepted it unanimously. It seems that Marx and Wellesz were very enthusiastic about these songs ...

Honoured Master, you can imagine how happy I feel about all this. For years I have caused you irritation and vexation. If anything worthwhile is going to come of me then I have *only you to thank for it!*

Of course I am still only a raw, blundering beginner, but who knows what sort of a botcher I would have become if you had not taken me on as your pupil!!! And it is not just in music that I owe everything to your teaching, your works and your example. I hope that I have indeed improved a little bit as a person too. You have weaned me from my excessive 'swanking' and from my pompous talk and untruths – any remnants of which I hope to get rid of completely.

In addition you have always concerned yourself about my material circumstances, and I shall never forget how you obtained a job for me

(UE) during that terrible winter of 1919–20. Without it I would literally have starved. The stay in Holland[10] too saved me from a physical breakdown, as my doctor has confirmed as well.

So I have you to thank for everything (perhaps even more than my poor parents) and in return I can only give you my promise that I shall try very hard to please you and to do credit to the name 'pupil of Schoenberg'.

I earnestly beg you to accept the dedication of the Piano Sonata op. 1.[11]

In sincerest respect and gratitude/Your most devoted pupil/Hanns Eisler.[12]

When he writes of the 'vexation' he has caused a teacher who has frequently enough been portrayed as authoritarian and tyrannical, Eisler is not just indulging in coy impudence. His fellow pupils confirm that he was the only one among them who dared to voice dissent openly. Rudolf Kolisch, who was later to become Schoenberg's brother-in-law and was already a violinist of note, reports that:

Of course his chief characteristic was rebelliousness. We could feel in the classes that this made for a special relationship between Schoenberg and Eisler. He was very fond of him. Above all he recognized and appreciated his considerable talent. Naturally Eisler annoyed him a great deal, particularly because of his independence, you know, which he simply couldn't bear – I mean his intellectual independence. In fact Eisler was never intellectually submissive. I must say that he was perhaps the only one of us to adopt this attitude quite consciously. He was always rebellious, and even contradicted, which was a mortal sin, of course – quite inconceivable. Not in matters of fact, naturally . . .[13]

Similarly, Max Deutsch:

Very soon Eisler began to criticize Schoenberg (not musically, for heaven's sake!); but his way of life, his adherence to middle-class precepts, his relationship to his wife and children, and above all his philosophy of life. His admiration for Swedenborg (with a strong element of religion), for Dostoievsky, and Strindberg too . . .[14]

From Schoenberg's point of view, Eisler's demonstrations of dissent were simply the rebellions of a pupil who was not materially well off, but who was a favourite of his, and he thought they would probably blow over with time. On the other hand, Eisler's relation to Schoenberg was from the very first complicated by dual standards. His admiration and respect for the composer and teacher to whom he owed a deep debt of gratitude were counter-balanced by an increasingly critical attitude towards his ideo-logical positions: Eisler later spoke of him as a 'political . . . petty bourgeois of a quite horrendous kind'.[15]

Even though there were times when the relative importance of these opposing judgments obviously shifted, their opposition remained present in Eisler's mind with striking constancy, neither pole ever entirely taking over from the other. These carefully weighed scruples were a prevailing feature of Eisler's relations with Schoenberg; he was, however, alone among Schoenberg's pupils in sharing three of his teacher's biographical phases: Vienna, Berlin and Los Angeles.[16]

When in 1924 the Viennese journal *Musikblätter des Anbruch* brought out a special issue to mark Schoenberg's fiftieth birthday, Eisler – at twenty-six the youngest contributor – wrote of his teacher in the following extremely precise terms, which call to mind the dialectician of later years:

> It is imperative for the musical world to rethink its ideas and to see in Schoenberg not a saboteur and revolutionary but a master. It is now clear that he created for himself a new kind of material so that he could make music that was as rich and self-contained as that of the Classical com-posers. *It is he who is the real conservative: he even created his own revolution in order that he could then be a reactionary.*[17]

This paradox, first formulated to account for the case of Schoenberg, was to become a fruitful challenge for Eisler: 'even in his most "radical" works, Schoenberg was . . . no more than a musician';[18] and the 'master's' innovations, mistaken for attempts at sabotage and revolution, remained within the realm of music; certainly the concepts used by Eisler in making this assertion – 'revolution', 'reactionary' – already point a long way beyond that realm.

The muted anticipation of his later criticisms (and their point of view) is camouflaged by the tone of homage. Eisler is still writing as a member of a 'school'. Its position is as yet by no means assured. The term 'musical reactionary' is intended to undermine the attacks of the conservative camp and refers in the first instance to the revival of classical forms in Schoenberg's most recent

3 Arnold Schoenberg the teacher (1922)

works, in which he has moved on to 'composition with twelve notes'.[19] Eisler shows solidarity in the campaign against the malicious distortions and narrow-mindedness of those who stand for every kind of musical tradition, the latter being – in Mahler's words – mere sloppiness. Schoenberg and his pupils alike are conscious of being the representatives of musical evolution, even if the pupils are less histrionic about it than their teacher. Only in the light of his conscientious conception of rigorous artistic labour is it possible to understand his scorn for many 'composers' and parasitic musical manipulators who are bogged down in the false security of worn-out clichés and who castigate all radical advances into virgin territory as anarchism or charlatanism.

Schoenberg's revolution in musical material and his new means of musical expression, which together represented a purification of musical language as he had found it, were not legislative acts imposed by a great individual merely according to his own requirements; rather, they corresponded, albeit in a somewhat indirect way, to the changing forms of awareness of the early twentieth century, as well as in their own turn contributing to them. We need not here examine how far this growing control over musical material paralleled increasing mastery over the natural world. In order to give adequate expression to the shift in social awareness (which in Schoenberg's as yet partially irrational outlook corresponded to changes occurring within himself) it was necessary to eliminate the late Romanticism that had now run its course; and at a purely technical level this required a fundamental rethinking of existing structural ideas.[20]

The rampant chromaticism of the nineteenth century had undermined major–minor diatonicism, leading to the breakdown of tonality's traditional role as a centre of gravity. Schoenberg, whose early links were with Wagner and Brahms, described how he had moved through various stages of extended and subsequently indeterminate and free tonality to arrive at his abandonment of tonal centres (in the Second String Quartet op. 10 of 1908).[21] This could be said to mark the beginning of his second period, the culmination of his first having been reached in the Chamber Symphony op. 9 with 'great progress in the direction of the emancipation of the dissonance'.

The renunciation of tonality and the hierarchical organization associated with it deprived traditional musical architecture of its meaning.[22] In order to avert the anarchy with which musical forms were threatened, a new kind of organization was necessary, one which would be that much more stable and 'with which it was possible once again to construct forms'.[23] In 1922, whether as a conscious or an unwitting response to this necessity, Schoenberg evolved his method of 'composition with twelve notes related only to one another'. After the atonal middle period – the works of which Eisler considered 'the most important that Schoenberg wrote. Yet . . . a magnificent cul-de-sac'[24] – Schoenberg had come up with a procedure which could replace the worn-out rules of musical syntax.

From the very first, its opponents saw the use of twelve-note series in composition as an abstract, intellectual device, a cerebral manner of construction which crippled spontaneous inspiration. There can be no doubt that the apparent lack of sensual appeal in many works of Schoenberg's third period can be attributed primarily to the persistence of old listening habits. The listener has to work extremely hard if he is to follow simultaneous processes in detail. And again, there is something academic and at times arbitrary about Schoenberg's wholesale application of the twelve-note method in all its rigour to music of every genre. Eisler's comparatively free handling of the new techniques of composition (he had no need to shoulder the responsibility of having invented them, of course) can be understood partly in terms of his greater detachment from the cultural and social context within which Schoenberg had discovered them.

Much has been written about the Vienna of the early years of the twentieth century, and about the unsettled talents it harboured under the declining Imperial monarchy and the infant Republic. The canonization of a few great names – Karl Kraus, Sigmund Freud, Adolf Loos, Peter Altenberg, Arnold Schoenberg – is apt to suggest to a later age the existence of a united intellectual 'opposition party'. But this was by no means the case. It would be truer to say that within a society still permeated with the relics of feudal order there existed, in a state of extreme (and largely mutual) isolation, a number of thoroughbred bourgeois specialists. Their individual intellectual and artistic rebellions are to be seen as expressions of social change concealed under cover of their various specialisms. The old system denied them the possibility of integration and they broke free of it as individuals having a claim to genius. Society, pledged to the old régime and perpetuating its surviving features, excluded them but offered some compensation in the form of recognition by small groups. (But during the 1920s the young Eisler fought against the idea that emancipation should always remain of this specialized sort.)

A common factor in the campaigns fought by these isolated individuals was their attack on degraded forms of artistic activity, and on the correspondingly flaccid life-styles[25] of a public entrenched in narrow-minded cosiness and deaf to all changes. The more trivial producers churned out the bitter-sweet cheeriness of operetta whilst composers of a 'higher' order were working the neo-romantic aesthetic of gloomy emotionalism sugared over with rhetoric and ornamentation. To counter all this it was legitimate to press the claim that serious art possessed an epistemological function and needed to get its message across.

In that situation the strongest new impetus was provided by the convulsive developments taking place in physics. From these a mathematical and logical concept of cognition was taken up by philosophy and extended into other disciplines. The suitability and scope of any proposed epistemological apparatus were subjected to close scrutiny, and similarly with theoretical data and artistic raw materials; whole areas were shown up as having been nothing more than a pseudo-knowledge hallowed by tradition.

If we consider the evolution of bourgeois thought from the neo-Kantianism of the turn of the century up to the neo-positivism of the 1920s, we can see that, as a consequence of the need for greater precision and more stringent methods, the entire cognitive process came to be reduced to principles of grammar, and philosophy to the theory of language. At the same time, when language had been broken down into its constituent elements and logical analysis had revealed the principles of combination underlying verbal propositions, real progress had been made towards cleaning up ideological thought. If all metaphysical thought was to be eliminated, it was first necessary to do away with definitions of 'being'; and, to achieve this, such hierarchies and relationships as were codified in the existing rules of grammar and syntax had to be dismantled. The task of analysis was then to examine the structure of any series of given (semantic) elements and to work out their syntax.

The way in which Schoenberg investigated the raw material of music was similarly analytical. He too dismantled the existing language of music. He sought ways of establishing a new logical organization now that the old one's stronghold of tonality was

being exploited to foster trivialized emotions. The state of composition as he found it, with all the portentousness of its inflated
symphonic forms and the bombastic orchestral forces associated
with them, was inadequate to his need for greater concentration
and intensity of expression.

Within the secluded confines of officially sanctioned music, the
increasingly murky subjectivity of late Romanticism might have
continued to pour forth indefinitely. In order to clear away its
decaying remains, new, constructive formal principles were
needed: their task would be to circumvent pompousness, bombast and arbitrary ornamentation whilst at the same time permit-
ting greater expressiveness.[26]

Yet Schoenberg's very 'need for expression' cut both ways. In
order to satisfy it he had undertaken the difficult (and thankless)
task of scouring away music's traditional materials so as to make
available more logical, purified ones. The concentration of complex musical matter into an extremely tight space – a characteristic which took into account the 'increasing analytical capabilities
of the human ear'[27] – implied a total avoidance of padding and a
stringent elimination of all that was not functionally essential to
the musical idea.

However, if the value of technique when composing in a new
idiom is overestimated, there can be a dangerous tendency to
regard the musical language as self-sufficient, to dissociate it from
objective requirements and in this way to idealize it for its own
sake. In the work of many of Schoenberg's disciples, this insistence on the absolute value of technique degenerated into a pure
fetish: and while they were acquiescing in a preordained syntax of
serial organization, claiming that the manipulation of musical
material was itself the whole purpose and aim of their art, the
truly social task – that of communication – was swept under the
carpet. Their 'expression' remained abstract, arbitrary, sometimes even random. (The selfsame problem in much new music is
countered by the assertion – itself pretty irresponsible – that the
'inexorable' development of music has brought it about.)

Yet this is not the only way in which illogicalities come into
play. In Schoenberg the tendency towards systematic, theoreti-
cally based organization – and not only in twelve-note music – is

combined with what appears to be a strikingly outdated, even if by no means entirely naïve aesthetic of intuition.

Schoenberg ascribed enormous importance to the role of the unconscious mind in artistic creation: he composed, as it were, under the compulsion of an 'inner necessity' and according to the dictates of an unconscious driving force which had to be obeyed intuitively. The insistent claims he made for the 'truth' of his art were part and parcel of a self-image not without elements of the cultural high priest. It was this attitude of intellectual aristocracy, the cult of his own personality and everything it stood for, that became the first target for Eisler's critique of his teacher. He also felt repelled by the latent religiosity underlying the motives for Schoenberg's attitude: this went deeper than a mere compensation for the outsider's role into which the musical world had forced him.

When Schoenberg composed 'intuitively', in a very rapid and spontaneous way, it could hardly be taken as indicative simply of a state of diminished intellectual control at the time of his creative activity. As a theoretician he was far too self-aware for that. His tenet that 'a mind that has been strictly trained in musical logic will function logically under any circumstances (in composition)'[28] refers to that precise mastery of technique without which no musical idea, however spontaneous, can achieve a structured form:

Ernst Bloch – in a highly metaphorical way – defined Schoenberg's position as one of 'excess in music':

This music, whose boldness and measure of total nihilism are already sufficient to set it apart, (is) full of the scars of a difficult period of transition that was anything but delightful . . ., and yet equally full of indefinite or still ill-defined flashes of portrayal. If the transition it portrayed had had its roots in society, then Schoenberg's art too would have been more intoxicated with beauty and more simple; but music of such a stamp would have needed to be anchored to a muscular morality of a quite different kind.[29]

As Alois Hába writes, Eisler had from the very start 'acquired a type of expression that was independent of Schoenberg's music and more energetic'. This was a concomitant of 'his livelier temperament and his fundamentally optimistic view of life, though

also of the fact that he was a born practical musician'.[30] But it was
assuredly more than this. Eisler's more comprehensible idiom, in
its way as logical and as bold as Schoenberg's, was motivated –
even if at first indistinctly so – by social considerations.

'The interesting thing about my parentage is . . . that I am the
product of two different social classes. My father was a philosopher . . . and my mother a worker',[31] as Eisler was later to
report. He thought it 'characteristic that two classes should thus
have come together to a certain extent'. The father having been
Viennese and the mother from Leipzig, it was also a union between Austria and Saxony – both of them lands of music *par
excellence*.

Though actually born in Leipzig (1898), Eisler grew up in
Vienna and always maintained that he was a Viennese at heart; on
the other hand, the class alliance which in retrospect – and with a
touch of self-mythologization – he saw himself as representing
appeared in his work in quite different ways.

The boy's most enduring impressions must have been of his
long years lived in material poverty; at the same time he watched
the arduous intellectual exertions that his father made in spite of
everything. The example of energy and self-discipline set by
Rudolf Eisler,[32] who as an autodidact almost without income
continued to write undeterred, must surely have left its mark.
Admittedly, it is not easy to determine to what extent the three
children – Elfriede, Gerhart and Hanns – saw this ascetic mode
of existence as an example fit to be followed. The association
between intellect and poverty seldom presents itself as being *a
priori* a worthy goal to strive towards. It is probable, too, that the
children, who very soon turned towards rebellion and emancipation, were hardly drawn to the necessarily sequestered nature of
such a life-style.

Looking back, Eisler reported that his mother, on the other
hand, paved the way for his emotional and moral identification
with the cause of the workers; she 'knew what it was to be poor,
and what it was to struggle too, and her influence was
enormous'.[33]

The youngest of the three children (his sister was three and his
brother one when he was born), Hanns Eisler attended a primary

school in Vienna from 1904 until 1908, thereafter going to the 'strictly Catholic'[34] Rasumovsky Gymnasium up to the time when he joined the army in 1916.

It was a natural outcome of his extremely friendly relationship with his brother that, while still a schoolboy, he came into contact with the progressive youth movement and the socialist school-children's organization in 1912. With this came early access to atheistic and socialist literature: Häckel and Kautsky, the easier writings of Marx, anarchistic texts and introductions to philosophy were not simply read; they were above all debated. Eisler's ready wit and repartee, later to become famous, the uncommon directness of his manner of thinking and speaking, his enjoyment of dispute and contradiction, these must all have been developed and honed in the 'Debating Club' of the socialist secondary-school pupils.

There were 'immensely vehement debates, and at times we also came into conflict with our excellent father: the sectarianism that we would preach at the age of thirteen appeared rather too facile to that earnest philosopher'.[35] One may easily imagine that the critical and 'objective' neo-Kantian is likely to have reacted dismissively towards the raw, vaulting enthusiasm of his children's radicalism. He had written, a few years previously, that 'prudent' social thinking should 'steer clear of two extremes': 'Anyone . . . familiar with human nature and able impartially to observe the historical process of social development must be convinced that the goal can be reached neither through a total "communism" nor through an "anarchic" individualism. Both these tendencies are one-sided . . .'[36]

The young Eisler's first attempts at composition likewise date back to his early years at secondary school. His brother tells us that in their youth they both received piano lessons for a short time, before these were discontinued for financial reasons. 'But we were a musical family to the extent that my father, who spent his days and nights sitting writing at his desk, had *one* recreation. At that time we possessed a piano, and my father would sing and play to us: Hugo Wolf, Schubert, folk songs of all kinds, operatic excerpts too.'[37]

As a boy, Eisler's grasp of the rudiments of music was self-taught. Since it was only in his childhood years that the family had the use of a hired piano, he had to learn elementary theory by himself and compose 'by ear'. By his own account, he acquired the knowledge necessary for reading scores at the age of ten or eleven by studying the Reclam edition of Wolff's *Allgemeine Musiklehre*. He was later to make use of the ability he developed at the time of rapidly mastering new fields by virtue of diligent reading, as equally he would of his facility in composing without the use of a musical instrument.

The young student was sensitive to the social conditions inseparable from the pursuance of a musical profession.

At that time I asked my more prosperous school-fellows to take me home with them to their piano, and requested those who could play to do so for me, or else I would bungle around on the piano myself. I recall . . . that the reluctant good ladies would let me into their draped best parlour as a poor schoolfriend of their son, and there I could for an hour try out my compositions in solitude. The impression of this somewhat condescending though not ill-natured attitude on the part of these bourgeoises whose homes I entered with the aid of my schoolfriends is truly unforgettable. Thus my musical life began under a strange kind of patronage.[38]

Like the majority of the composers of his generation, Eisler started with songs. He was at first noticeably more influenced by those of Mahler and Hugo Wolf than by those of Schubert or Brahms. His accompaniments are written for piano or for small chamber ensemble. In addition to texts drawn from plays by Büchner and Hauptmann, he turned for preference to poems of Morgenstern and Klabund. Rilke and Trakl make only passing appearances. As a student he was already well versed in literature. Music and literature were pre-eminent among his interests; and they met in vocal music, a field in which Eisler was later to open up new dimensions.

(He would doubtless have protested if we were here to omit mention of another interest – one which at that time was of almost equal importance to him: 'He may have been small, but he was a keen footballer, and would even cut school so as to play football in the Jesuits' Meadow in the Prater.'[39] There he got to know Jascha Horenstein, who recalled above all his comical appearance: '. . . at thirteen he already had a bald patch like a forty-year-old's. Imagine a compact body supporting a large head on whose moon-shaped cheerful face was a perpetual mischievous grin, and at every rapid movement this head would reveal its bald patch . . .'[40])

Eisler tells us that his first major work was an anti-war oratorio, written shortly after his call-up (1916); he took his text from a currently popular book in the Insel series containing poems of Li-Tai-Pe.[41] This was also his first attempt to 'make music useful'. It followed a confrontation with the then all-powerful Imperial authorities.

At the outbreak of the war, his brother, together with some other students at his school, had brought out a very short-lived cyclostyled anti-war magazine; this fell into the hands of the police, who promptly raided the house. Gerhart, who had already been called up in 1915, was dismissed from the officers' training college and ordered to the Italian front. Since Hanns too was mixed up in the affair, the two brothers were both listed as 'politically suspect' ('p.v.').[42]

After being wounded and hospitalized a number of times, Eisler returned to Vienna at the end of 1918. There he found the monarchy overthrown and revolution in the air. The hordes of home-coming soldiers favoured radical solutions. Spurred on by the workers' and soldiers' councils, the Red Guard was formed in Vienna. 'We had lost the war, were wounded, and had nothing to eat', as Max Deutsch has put it. 'Our only refuge was the ideal of a communist revolution.'[43]

Tendencies of this kind, however, were rapidly stifled in what was left of Germany and Austria. The machinery of administration and power had remained largely intact, and it was possible for Social Democrats and Conservatives alike to bring it to bear on the suppression of anything that might threaten the citizens' republic.

The situation was not, indeed, a foregone conclusion: the KPÖ [Communist Party of Austria], founded in Vienna in November 1918 by a dozen intellectuals (Eisler's sister playing a leading part, was able to develop rapidly for some months early in 1919.[44] Social revolution had been brought right to the doorstep by the October Revolution in Russia, the formation of two soviet republics in countries bordering on Austria – Hungary and Bavaria – and the catastrophic state of the economy and of the social services. It is true that the radicals of the Viennese Left were without any solid foundations in the masses: they believed it would be possible to seize power without long preparatory activity amongst the masses, and that it could be achieved by some sort of *putsch*. Since popular workers' leaders such as Friedrich Adler did not enter their ranks, and organized labour largely continued to vote Social Democrat, hopes for an Austrian Soviet disappeared with the collapse of the Bavarian and Hungarian Soviets in the summer of 1919. The beginnings of economic stability and a series of progressive socio-political moves by the SPÖ [Austrian Socialist Party] – at the time it adopted a far more forward-looking stance than the German Social Democrats – conjoined ultimately with internal disagreements within the KPÖ in contributing to the stagnation of the revolutionary movement.

In 1918–19 Eisler's brother and sister were setting out on careers as professional revolutionaries in Vienna, moving on to Berlin shortly afterwards (due to the diminishing prospects offered by the situation in Austria); Hanns meanwhile embarked on composition studies at the New Viennese Conservatory early in 1919.

Because his self-taught knowledge of harmony appeared to be adequate, he was immediately accepted for the counterpoint class. Very soon he began to find the instruction he received from Karl Weigl too undemanding and conventional; the traditional way in which the Conservatory was run, with its chronically outdated syllabus, seemed to him to suffer from fossilized routine and time-wasting. After all, he was already twenty: for a musician, his first regular training had not exactly come early.

Eisler was looking for a strict teacher. He found the strictest of all. When on leave from the front in 1917, he had already heard Schoenberg's Chamber Symphony in Vienna – conducted by the composer – and had been very impressed by it. It had even been rumoured among the young musicians of Vienna that the radically modern composer was the best teacher of counterpoint. When accepted into Schoenberg's master class, Eisler still had gaps and weaknesses in his education. His knowledge of musical history, for instance, was small. Lack of means prevented him from enrolling in Guido Adler's class in musical history at Vienna University. During his four years of study with Schoenberg (1919–23) Eisler had much else to catch up on. Moreover, great demands were made on him: as his fellow-students were to report, he worked with tremendous industry and application. There was a moral consideration to egg him on: as the most talented of his generation of students in Mödling, Schoenberg taught the penniless youth for no fee.

In order to live, he took on the job of conducting two workers' choirs in 1919: the 'Karl Liebknecht' and the 'Stahlklang' (from the Siemens–Schuckert works). In the winter of 1919/20, Schoenberg obtained part-time work for him as a reader for Universal Edition. His vocation benefited from both activities: 'In doing this', writes Alois Hába, who at that time was also working as a proofreader for Universal, 'we became acquainted with the works of contemporary composers and with the precision of the engravers' work, and from then on we endeavoured to write out our own manuscripts with still greater care.'[45] His contact with workers' choirs gave Eisler early insights into the listening habits of the masses and also into the particular receptivity and responsiveness of untrained singers. It is probable that already at that early date he felt that the current repertory of predominantly gratuitously sentimental songs was urgently in need of replacement.

At first Eisler lived in one of the military barracks in the Grinzing area of Vienna which had been unoccupied since the war – this was one of the few ways in which students and artists with a minimum of means were able to live in 'independence'. He lived with a girl friend, a young Viennese teacher, who was able to support him to some extent. She was later to recall that 'he was so poor that I gave him manuscript books so that he could write'.[46] His permanent hunger was blunted by cigarettes and alcohol. There were certainly light-hearted sides to Eisler's early bohemian period. Whole nights would be spent in discussion and drinking, and often in music-making. He would perform his songs in a high-pitched, wheezy voice, and his companion 'Muschi'

Friedmann would accompany him on the piano she had rented for him.

While he was still a student, Eisler began to teach, initially at the Verein für Volkstümliche Musikpflege [Society for the Promotion of Music among the People], where workers could become acquainted with music. As in Schoenberg's case, though with longer interruptions, he was to continue with his teaching activities alongside composition throughout his life. He later endeavoured to pass on to his composition pupils what he had learnt from Schoenberg. This was above all an intimate knowledge of the great tradition.

Schoenberg's teaching was centred on analysis of works by the classical masters, and never on instruction in 'modern' composition. Basically, music began with Bach. De facto, for purposes of teaching, he reduced the history of music to five classical names: Bach, Mozart, Beethoven, Schubert and Brahms. 'Thus these were the cornerstones of his teaching,'[47] according to Eisler.

It appears that it was during the Mödling years that Schoenberg most effectively combined group courses in which all his pupils took part (harmony and counterpoint in addition to 'analysis') with individual tuition (twice a week). There were few who persisted for more than a year under his severely critical eye. Before anyone was permitted to write in the 'modern' idiom, he had to have studied the great works right down to their finest technical detail and to be able to apply classical procedures of composition with assurance. Bach's Art of Fugue was studied for a whole year; Brahms' chamber music and Beethoven's keyboard variations were thoroughly and precisely analysed. Craftsmanship was considered a first priority: Schoenberg insisted on technical understanding; it is easy to see why this attitude – akin to the engineer's in its conjunction of the analytical with the constructive – was so well suited to Eisler's logical and mathematical propensities.

'I can say that it was really there that I first learnt musical understanding and thinking . . . Reason, imagination and feeling were not in conflict, but the one would produce the others.' It was Eisler's view that 'the strongest impact ever made on him' was by the fact that problems of form were answerable to moral principles, and that 'eloquence in music, responsibility . . . and the avoidance of all insincerity' were taught as prerequisites for incorruptible 'striving after musical truth'.

Honesty, objectivity, clarity and imaginativeness were also in evidence in the way Schoenberg performed music . . . How to phrase a particular passage in Beethoven, how to choose the right tempo. Thus there is no question of Schoenberg's having taught some sort of arid craftsmanship. What he taught ranged from the simplest technical information and a contempt for the commonplace, the trivial and empty musical formulae to the performance of masterpieces.[48]

Unlike many of his contemporaries, and also in contrast with Schoenberg himself, Eisler very soon adopted a critical attitude towards Wagner and Mahler. He accused both of 'formlessness', and Wagner of 'endless melodizing . . . inflated instrumentation', although 'no musician . . . could ever resist the magic of the score of *Tristan*'. 'Bombast in music' was contrary to his own striving for concision, for concentration and for tight-knit form. Still more was he irritated by Mahler's eclectic 'philosophical outlook'. On the choice of texts for the Third Symphony, for instance, and on the symphonic reworking of song themes in the First he pronounced harsh verdicts such as 'disagreeably pompous and over-sentimental'.[49] His verdict on Mahler's followers was even more cutting.

He was repelled by lack of precise articulation, excessive length, the expansive and the vague. He was bored by the indulgent excesses of morbid post-*Tristan* music and by the ethereal eccentricities of an *art nouveau* steeped in the ideology of renunciation. In place of the variegated spinning-out and breaking-up of themes, Eisler from the start had a penchant for laconic, epigrammatic abbreviation and concentration. He felt attracted more to Brahms' academic stringency: 'Here I found rounded form, shapely themes.'[50] As a student he was a notorious 'Brahmin', he says, and furthermore, Schoenberg had expressly drawn his attention to Brahms' piano writing.

Eisler's time as Schoenberg's pupil coincided exactly with the transition from atonal to twelve-note composition. After Webern and Berg, he was the first to write in the new technique.

Schoenberg's works – including the theoretical books, such as the *Harmonielehre* – provided Eisler with the point of reference closest to his own views in all matters of musical thinking, whether or not he acknowledged it in particular details. Thus his own independent work as a composer developed through a critique of his teacher (the earliest example being *Palmström* op. 5, which is related to *Pierrot lunaire*).

In compositional technique, Eisler's model was above all the music of Schoenberg's atonal middle period. Besides the early Chamber Symphony and the first two string quartets, the piano pieces and *Pierrot* exerted an influence on him. As for Webern, who taught Eisler during Schoenberg's absence, he took a great deal from that composer's op. 12 songs for his own Songs op. 2, which he dedicated to Webern.

His early works still chiefly inhabited this particular world. But already they laid stronger emphasis on the energetic, the transparent and the concrete. Lyrical tenderness too was straightforward, never merely a generalized effect. Thus there were real signposts to his future lines of development.

Works as early as the two piano sonatas opp. 1 and 6 are tauter,[51] as well as featuring greater contrast in their rhythmic organization than many piano works by the Viennese School. They are dominated by a refreshing motoric element (see ex. 1).

Ex.1   Sonata op. 1, first movement

The same applies to the Wind Quintet op. 4 and the String Duo op. 7 – pieces each of whose structure is very self evident and which demand a spirited performance.

In May 1925 the city of Vienna awarded Eisler its Art Prize for his freely atonal Sonata op. 1, the work which marked the termination of his period as a student. The last of his early Viennese works (according to its opus number), the Duo op. 7 for violin and cello, was performed at the Venice Music Festival in September of the same year. A favourable and very detailed report of it appeared in the journal *Musikblätter des Anbruch*. It begins: 'Hanns Eisler is the composer who represents Arnold Schoenberg's latest generation of students.' His ability to combine facility with an assured discipline is praised, as is 'the piece's abundance of internal relationships . . . (Here) Eisler proves himself master of a freedom which, following Mozart's example, enables him to pile novelty upon novelty and yet build a unified structure.' In conclusion, the review refers to

that imaginative talent of Eisler's, which may be very personal to him without being so overtly in evidence as his melodic inventiveness, his harmonic eloquence and his knowledge of his instruments. In the first place, the Duo will speak for itself, and at the same time it will bear witness to the teacher Schoenberg, under whose guidance Eisler's discipline as a composer grew and acquired the ability to fuse with the congenial charm of his musical nature.[52]

The author of this sensitive and highly illuminating appraisal was the pupil of Alban Berg, Theodor Wiesengrund-Adorno.

Meanwhile, Eisler was living, composing and teaching in Berlin. When, after 1925, he published his first essays and critical notices, in which he dealt with the social function of music, he attained – just like Schoenberg, though with an intent which was soon very different from his teacher's – that threefold activity of *composer, teacher* and *theoretician*, which was later to lay the foundations for the all-embracing *practical* usefulness of his work.

Eisler's distaste for the posture of 'art for art's sake' quickly began to assume a definite form. Whilst still a student he saw clearly that artistic technique ought not to remain an end in itself, but should be at the service of ideas that are relevant to humanity; however, at this stage he was not aware how this could be realized in music itself. There was a long road to travel from his lively mistrust of esoteric asceticism to writing 'politically useful' music. And though the revolutionary nature of that period demanded the latter, there was also an obligation to make use of the most advanced tools of the composer's craft. On the other hand, it was precisely by virtue of its 'autonomous' development that new music had so thoroughly cut itself off.

Those all-night discussions in Grinzing, Horenstein tells us, had been taken up 'on the one hand with the music of Schoenberg and Webern, and on the other hand with the consequences and prospects of the Russian revolution of 1917'. Eisler would become angry when speaking of 'the "splendid isolation" of those contemporary Viennese composers who were of any account, with respect to their attitude of "art for art's sake", and their disdain for the historical events which had literally revolutionized the world'.53

His diary for the years 1921–2 reveals that in this he exonerated his own teacher, though did not entirely spare him. 'Schoenberg possesses the most incredible abstraction of thought. He could talk of the technique of travelling in such a way that one would not want to send him a picture postcard', he noted angrily in 1922, adding: 'If he had become a politician, he would do everything in such a way that one could invert it.' On the subject of the unconditional discipleship that Schoenberg required of his followers, he writes: 'A.S. demands devotion to his cause as if to the Catholic religion.' The submissiveness of Schoenberg's entourage – Eisler makes an exception of himself – led him to observe: 'Schoenberg resembles Napoleon: he too would only tolerate blockheads in his entourage. If it includes anyone of intelligence, this is only because Schoenberg thinks him backward.'54

The earliest jottings (1921) have a far less assured ring to them. 'Escape from self, submission to a great personage. Dread of the future. Chimerical existence.' The preoccupation with himself is brief and restrained; one is aware of a shying-away from exhibitionistic self-glorification. 'An idiotic mood puts thoughts of consolation into the mind. (As if grief were present)'; thus begins the first entry. 'However, writing on white paper bound in leather is dirty sentimentality . . . The evening like a dog's bone sticking up out of the day's putrescence.' Irritation with attacks of melancholy – which he attributes to periods of sterility as a composer – combines with merciless sarcasms turned against himself: 'For someone who is high-spirited and conceited, it is often difficult not to do everything with an eye to self-advertisement. (Me, for instance.) . . . that immaturity, disorganization and ambitiousness associated with the will to create is a bundle of every conceivable coarseness, conceit and vulgarity. (Me, for instance.)' His dissatisfaction with the wretched purgatory of not yet being able to achieve clarity of vision was not alleviated by his comfortless material situation. '. . . Everything very gloomy. Salvation in work.'

Something which at that time afforded some support against subjective feelings of isolation, against poverty and against scorn, was the Schoenberg school's view of itself as unquestioningly identifiable with musical progress – a view still largely shared by Eisler. This made halts in production even more disturbing. 'When I have produced nothing for a few weeks and am leading a false existence (with my wit on the outside and what pain on the inside), I feel like creeping away somewhere.' This confession – rare among his writings – concludes: 'To be alone is the highest, most painful enjoyment'; this is a clue to Eisler's very secretive inner life – a life full of tensions – and to the extreme vulnerability which he later tried objectively to come to terms with.

Eisler's first musical protest – which likewise remained an internal one – was expressed in the conjunction of the lyrical with the grotesque in his autobiographical *Palmström*. This was probably originally conceived entirely in relation to the 'I' of the diary, between whose jottings it made its appearance in 1921. In point of fact, this op. 5 of 1924 is the most interesting of Eisler's early works; as 'studies on twelve-note rows' it is his first essay in the new technique; and in it Eisler simultaneously interweaves his admiration for and criticism of Schoenberg, who had urged him to undertake these studies,[55] in a mischievously ambivalent tone which brings out his objective detachment and heralds the transition to his own position.

His choice of texts provides a clue to this. The first idea noted in the diary is for 'Grotesques. For solo voice and chamber orchestra'. Of the three Morgenstern texts that Eisler selected (1. Palmström sometimes wishes he could dissolve, 2. Funnels wander through the night, 3. Palmström takes paper from his drawer) he used only two in the final version, adding instead three further ones which allowed him to parody not only Schoenberg's aesthetic but equally his own relationship to his teacher.

'L'art pour l'art', unambiguously enough occupying the central position in the five sections that make up the cycle, is followed by 'Galgenbruders Frühlingslied' [Spring Song of a Gallows-Bird] with its closing line: 'It is almost as if I were he who I no longer am.' If here Eisler speaks of the pupil–teacher relationship which he is beginning to move away from ('Spring too breaks in on our quarrel; O blessed time!'), he concludes in 'Couplet von der Tapetenblume' [Couplet of the Wallpaper Flower] by allowing his authoritarian teacher to warn him cryptically of the dangers of blind adherence (which in the case of the other pupils generally led to traumatization): 'You can never see enough of me, no matter how far you look into the chamber and pursue me round corners – you will go crazy, darling.'[56]

Palmström opens with a genuflexion towards Schoenberg – the first two notes of the row are his initials, A and E flat (A–Es), joined in the same bar by B and E (H–E); but at the end, in the 'Couplet von der Tapetenblume', the B–E interval whirls to and fro in crazy leaps in the *Sprechstimme* part (see ex. 2).

This couplet, which is sublime cabaret music, demonstrates – as indeed does *Palmström* as a whole – that Eisler used serial technique in a less academic way than Schoenberg; this can be seen for instance in the fact that it allows scope for frequent recourse to tonal relationships without any loss of tension.

What is new above all is the dialectical interaction between the

Ex.2   *Palmström*, 'Couplet von der Tapetenblume'

doch,   statt – im Mai'n ___ und Mon-den-schein auf   je-der der vier Wän – de.

music and the text. Here, Eisler's treatment of his text further develops the 'speech-song' of Schoenberg's *Pierrot*; its most significant gain was that it permitted 'the text to be woven into the musical structure without the need to renounce its grammatical and semantic structure'.[57] At the same time, Eisler had reservations about *Pierrot* precisely because he was concerned with exact articulation, and, instead of using a text simply as an excuse for composing, he wanted to use music to increase the impact of a text.

When he first heard it in 1921, what initially impressed him was the 'nature of the chamber music . . .; although even at that time I had little patience . . . with the text, I considered this way of making music magnificent . . . what I called a continuation of the filigree chamber-music sound, of which I was very fond from Mozart onwards'.[58] Subsequently, Eisler's criticisms were harsher:

The relationship of Schoenberg's music to these poems, which, even to one of naïve tastes, can barely feign any artistic worth, is one of conforming, illustrating and empathizing. By virtue of the exaggerated emotional identification characteristic of speech-song as a mode of performance, as prescribed and rhythmically precisely defined by Schoenberg, Giraud's absurd village-green demonicism has an embarrassing effect and detracts from the music.[59]

If we consider the differences that were already apparent at an early date between Eisler's and Schoenberg's vocal compositions, the most prominent is in their choice of texts: in addition to Giraud, Eisler rejected George as being disagreeably slanted towards psychology and aimlessly overcharged with emotion. Hothouse esotericism seemed to him wayward, anachronistic and absurd. He often found such poetry still further 'overheated' by the manner in which it was set to music.

In contrast, the young Eisler cultivated an attitude of anti-subjectivism. He judged that personal emotions were basically valued too highly. 'Mood' alienated him. What he felt should be resisted first and foremost was a conception of music as a 'comforter' by which people forced into self-denial could be reconciled with their fate. Music must above all not remain contemplative. (A few years later, he was to find agreement on all

4   On the outskirts of Vienna (c. 1924)

these viewpoints from Brecht, who consequently was to become the author who had the greatest importance for Eisler.) The aim of much of Eisler's vocal music is to lend intensity to the clarity of a text, and to present it in such a way that its meaning – especially when it operates on different levels – is unmistakable, and sensual and intellectual enjoyment are united. The invigorating power of that music is something we shall be considering later.

The first requisite is clarity. This involves converting speech intonations and rhythms precisely into notes and neither disfiguring words and sentences nor stretching them to the limits of comprehensibility. The accompaniment should never mask the flow of the voice. In later years, Eisler was himself enough of a man of letters never to treat texts as having secondary importance.

Ideological disagreements with Schoenberg doubtless contributed to the very timely development of his own manner of composition. He saw the act of writing music as being in no way separable from political awareness. A diary entry of autumn 1922 is instructive: 'I am now beginning to understand that it is no good studying the theory of composition with Schopenhauer, nor even with Kant, and certainly not with Hegel: how easy to become a Marxist.'

Twisted mockingly into a paradox, this aphorism fastens on the difference between an aesthetic (Schoenberg's) which goes back to Kant and Schopenhauer and one that is – or is to be – founded on Hegel and Marx. Kant's name stands for his teacher's idealistic conception of art, which Eisler was beginning to criticize as being undialectical and limited: Kant's aesthetic was the first to formulate the extreme attitude of 'art for art's sake'.

In and after 1917 needs and possibilities were coming into view which suddenly made ideas of aesthetic autonomy appear out of date; Eisler's initial attitude was one of instinctual opposition, since he not so much saw as felt how things stood. Schoenberg's position no longer satisfied him, because it left no room for real protest against the prevailing circumstances – even though it never made its peace with them.

He always found subjective idealism untrustworthy. Eisler turned his back on an enjoyment of art which had floated free of any social function, a pure act of contemplation, an artistic ideal of the immaculate work as far as possible unsullied by concrete content. (Schoenberg disapproved of Berg's choice of text in *Wozzeck*: angels, not batmen, ought to be set to music . . .)[60] His teacher's swimming against the stream remained within the confines of music, was immanent to the system. 'Schoenberg's chief quarrel was directed against bourgeois fraudulence . . . in the music industry – against the shoddy work of star conductors, against highly coloured, superficially composed scores . . .'[61]

Schoenberg's commitment was by no means solely to his own cause: he stood up, subjectively as ever, for the evolution of music. Eisler saw this very well; at that time, his own problem was that of uniting artistic activity with political activism. This led him to ask questions about the composer's public.

For Schoenberg, 'the listener was the listener, and he had few thoughts about the class structure of bourgeois society'.[62] In other words, it was enough simply to postulate an aesthetic consensus (that of an educated musical élite), and its historical and social situation did not enter into the question. Short-lived attempts to attract a new public changed little: their circle was still extremely narrow.

Only after years of transition was Eisler to discover the broadest circle: the masses.

2

Berlin – music and politics

The move to the German capital

As soon as he had completed his training, Eisler felt that Vienna was a dead end. Despite the early recognition he had received there – backed up by a very concrete ten-year contract with UE – he must have sensed that the Viennese scene made any further development difficult and that there 'the path of the serious modern artist . . . amounts to an incredibly sensitive, over-refined intellectuality'.[1]

It seemed impossible to get away from the laboratory conditions under which radically modern music continued to be produced. The size and scope of its public remained stagnant. Eisler's alienation was reinforced by the virtually private nature of its institutions, its audiences' proneness to snobbery and the lack of any genuine social communication. Furthermore, it was now important that he should earn money. And for this the prospects in Vienna, where his teacher had never really established himself, were inauspicious.

In autumn 1924, apparently in order to investigate the possibilities there, he went to Berlin for a short while. A young pupil of Artur Schnabel, the pianist Else C. Kraus, was anxious to study the First Piano Sonata with him. The impact of her concert – one of the first in Berlin to feature exclusively new works – was powerful and double-edged. So too was the response to Eisler, whom Berlin was now hearing of for the first time. Adolf Weissmann, at that time the doyen of German music criticism, wrote in praise:

. . . a man who heads straight for his goal with all the forces at his command. His three-movement op. 1 is . . . polyphonically conceived and executed, yet it is a piece of extreme artistic economy and individual construction. The second movement's passacaglia is exemplary . . . It is already possible to imagine that one day Eisler will blossom into a powerful composer . . .[2]

Favourable judgments of this kind were counterbalanced by remarks in the conservative press, which even then was not afraid to publish malignities reeking of ideological prejudice: thus, 'a product of chaotic trends of an all-too familiar kind'.[3] An important consequence for Eisler was that in the following year he came into contact with Schnabel, who invited him to write piano music for his pupils, and he also managed to obtain a teaching post at the Klindworth–Scharwenka Conservatory.

When Eisler settled in Berlin in 1925, it had already overtaken Vienna in importance as a musical centre and exercised an extraordinary attraction for talented musicians; culturally and politically, it was the most multifaceted of European metropolises. Above all, Berlin was the focal point of the German workers' movement, towards which Eisler was now beginning consciously to move. It was not easy for him to adjust.

Coming from an Austria where, some years after the First World War, capitalism had not yet become thoroughly entrenched, and belonging to a group of avant-garde musicians whose aesthetic revolution had only reached an audience of connoisseurs, Eisler found in Berlin a public which had already largely been taken over by the culture industry. The rapid spread of broadcasting from 1924 on was already having its effect on musical life. The technological revolution which swept through the channels of public communication,[4] affecting its tempo and its efficiency, and the pervasive commercialization which was not confined to the field of entertainment, were here conspicuous to a striking degree.

Whereas in Austria the attitude of a Schoenberg as an 'intellectual leader' – surrounded by faithful pupils serving as the apostles of the new theory – was still a meaningful form of intellectual opposition, in the Berlin of the 1920s it would have seemed absurd. How out of date as an esoteric phenomenon the Schoenberg school was, contrasted with its extreme progressiveness in the treatment of musical material and performance – completely free from commercial pressures – must for Eisler, once he was in Berlin, have seemed an irreconcilable contradiction. And it was not the only one.

In Vienna Eisler had devoted all his energies to the mastery of his craft: apart from studying a number of texts of Marx and Lenin, he had no time left for politics except for political discussions with his fellow students. His contacts in practical music-making had not extended further than his temporary directorship of two workers' choruses. True, his brother and sister must occasionally have kept him informed about the latest position vis-à-vis the revolutionary movements, but it seems probable that only in Berlin did he feel that the considerable disproportion between music and politics in his own mind could no longer be justified.

His aesthetic experience was based on an intimate knowledge of traditional and modern music (in the Viennese and Prague Society for Private Performances, in addition to works by his own school, Schoenberg had rehearsed and performed music by Stravinsky and Bartók, Reger and Strauss, and also by French composers from Debussy to Milhaud and Honegger); in Berlin this was overshadowed by bitter social struggles, strikes, mass unemployment and the most brutal exploitation. He was confronted by concrete examples of what he had read about in political texts, in the *Communist Manifesto* and Marx' *Eighteenth Brumaire of Louis Napoleon*. To respond immediately to this in his art – even if he wished to – was impossible for Eisler: the two worlds were too far apart.

Thus it was that the start of Eisler's second, Berlin period was marked by his realization of the fact that his previous artistic interests were incompatible with his new-found political ones. The same discovery was made by not a few of his generation – and not only composers. They internalized the conflict, claiming that under the prevailing circumstances this was inevitable: a classic case of the divided consciousness of the bourgeoisie. For Eisler there were several reasons why this did not come into question, precisely because of the prevailing circumstances. To act dialectically (and practically) could only mean to seek to resolve this contradiction – at the same time one of the most difficult and one of the most fruitful – without compromise of any sort. In other words: he must politicize what was supposedly the least political of all the arts, music.

It is worth tracing in some detail Eisler's not uncomplicated development as an 'organic intellectual' of the up-and-coming revolutionary class (in Gramsci's sense),[5] distinguishing its representative and its individual features, and also observing the historical phase in which it took shape.

The second period of the Weimar Republic began in 1924 with its 'relative stabilization', meaning that of capitalism: after the suppression of the workers' rebellion of 1923, and following the end of inflation, the Dawes Plan brought about a considerable resurgence of the German economy. The United States, the world's foremost financial and military power after the war, launched international loans from Wall Street with a view to stimulating German industry to the point where Germany could meet the costs of reparations. At the same time, the recently 'stabilized' Reich constituted a highly 'interesting' market for capital exports, as vast industrial capacity was conjoined with marked shortage of funds. 'Germany', wrote Arthur Rosenberg, 'had now become a sort of colony of the New York stock exchange . . . Stresemann was only able to achieve all his successes for as long as he . . . kept in line with the financial capital of the West . . . The destiny of Germany as a whole was dependent on every fluctuation of America's prosperity.'[6]

This 'apparent economic prosperity' led to a temporary weakening of the workers' movement and for the time being consolidated the parliamentary system; indeed, a mere six years after the end of the monarchy, the bourgeois middle classes were by no means republican or democrat in their outlook. It would be truer to say that they simply tolerated the Weimar Republic – so long as it appeared to be functioning adequately. The collapse of the New York stock exchange in October 1929 necessarily brought about a crisis in this system too, permeated as it was by American capital. It was built on sand.

Even so, public awareness of the enmity between capital and labour had been clouded over by the pooling and correlative rationalization of industry which had been forced on the economy since 1925, and which nourished illusions about the permanence of the new stability. In fact the merging of entire branches of the economy into giant monopolies (such as IG-Farben, Stahlverein [the German steel trust] etc.) led to massive concentrations of economic – and, by extension, political – power. The change to conveyor-belt technology meant greater socialization of labour for workers in industry; increased division of labour (Taylorism, Fordism) entailed comprehensive training programmes for workers involved in the labour process. A decrease in the number of jobs available was a further consequence of rationalization.

The two political parties in contention for the votes of the working masses, the SPD [German Socialist Party] and the KPD [German Communist Party], had co-existed uneasily all along, and in 1924 were pursuing conflicting policies. Whereas the SPD sought to come to terms with the 'stabilization', supporting the Dawes Plan and the policies of Stresemann, the youthful KPD campaigned against both. Led from its left flank, it assessed the German situation as being henceforth a revolutionary one, despite the bloody defeats of 1923. With its slogan of 'Organize the Revolution',[7] coming just as the economy was beginning to be consolidated, it alienated the masses right from the word go. The left wing of the KPD was hostile to any policy of a united front and collaboration with the trade unions.

The chief representative of this policy was Eisler's sister. As Ruth Fischer,[8] she and Arkadij Maslow were at the head of the Party in 1924–5. Her meteoric rise (and fall) within the KPD – from 1924 she was also a member of the Reichstag – culminated during the period when Eisler was moving to Berlin.

It was also under her and Maslow's leadership that the re-organization of the Party – its 'Bolshevization' – got under way. This remodelling on the basis of the Russian Communist Party, in accordance with a resolution of the Fifth World Congress of the Comintern in July 1924, meant the building up of the Leninist people's party according to the principles of democratic central-ization and the creation of activist cells. The radical, and sub-sequently inconsistent course taken by the Fischer–Maslow group, which could only end by weakening the KPD, the election defeats it brought about[9] and its insistence on independence brought the group into conflict with the Comintern. In November 1925 Ruth Fischer and Maslow were suspended from the Politburo. Their chairmanship was handed over to Ernst Thälmann, who thus became effectively the Party's leader.[10]

It is difficult to judge whether and to what extent Ruth Fischer at that time had any influence over her younger brother, who was seeking his own political orientation in Berlin. Hanns Eisler had always been closer to his brother Gerhart. Nevertheless, he shared certain traits of political intransigence with his sister, a brilliant intellectual and an orator in the grand style. Gerhart Eisler moved to Berlin from Vienna at the end of 1920, a year after his sister, and was subsequently active for the Party as a journalist, political educator and information officer; from 1921 he was a member of the regional committee of the KPD in Berlin (presided over by Ruth Fischer as political secretary). In 1925 he belonged to the moderate 'middle group', later to be the 'conciliators', who, together with other groups, were already opposed to the Fischer–Maslow programme.

It was natural that Hanns Eisler's attitude to the Party at a time when its factional struggles over policy extended as far as his own family should be somewhat reticent and temporizing. Early in 1926 he did indeed apply for membership; but this went no further than formal registration. Not the slightest hint of it can be found in his music; the two worlds remained poles apart, and Eisler himself in an interim phase on the Bourgeois Left.

A further reason for this is that hitherto the Party, which in 1925 had been in existence for seven years, had hardly evolved any realistic solutions to the problems of cultural work. In bourgeois circles there seems to have still been a persistent mistrust of the political reliability of artists sympathizing with or affiliated to the workers' movement. And clearly not without reason.

Walter Benjamin's friend Asja Lacis, for instance, tells us:

At that time there could be no question of a permanent revolutionary professional theatre. The revolutionary tide had turned, and the artistic intelligentsia had for the most part moved over uncritically to the side of the bourgeoisie . . . A theatre of this sort could only count on the most dependable and progressive elements of the working classes as its audience. But these elements did not have the means to maintain a permanent revolutionary theatre.[11]

The low standard of living of the masses (still no higher than it had been before the war), their wage demands, and the need for political adjustment to the recently 'stabilized' Republic took up almost all their energies; even the demand for more Agitprop work barely went beyond proclamations; clearly it was necessary to trust to the proletarian subculture that had originally been initiated by the educational work of the Social Democrats, and to the belief that the socialist tradition was still alive.

One exception was Piscator. Asja Lacis says of him:

Piscator was one of the few people in theatre to remain true to the revolutionary movement. In this he certainly took up an isolated position as far as professional theatrical circles were concerned. His creation of a revolutionary theatre at that time took effect in two areas: in the staging of individual political campaigns . . . and in his work as a producer at the Volksbühne [People's Theatre].

When Eisler arrived in Berlin, the name of Piscator was synonymous with political theatre, indeed with political art pure and simple. His second political revue (*Trotz alledem* – Despite Everything), which he staged for the Tenth Party Conference of the KPD in Berlin in July 1925, may have been Eisler's first radically new experience in the arts in Berlin.

What was new was that the historical material [1914–19] . . . was handled without reference to the personal experience of the hero; the way in which documentary material was used – to far stronger effect in those days than any number of poetic conceptions of art or sophistries clothed in iambic metre – was also novel, as was finally the inclusion of film for the first time in the sequence of scenes . . . The documentary chronicle became the forerunner of many scenic ventures of the *Agitprop* type which were to present staged historical panoramas using documentary material.[12]

Its extraordinary effectiveness and its unusually direct communication with entire audiences were the results of a conjunction of political content with innovation in theatrical technique. 'The whole performance', as Piscator commented, 'was a single immense montage of actual speeches, articles, newspaper cuttings, appeals, broadsheets, photographs and films of the war, of the revolution, and of historical personages and scenes.'[13] The decor and the blending of the visual elements were by John Heartfield. Two years later, Eisler was to collaborate with Piscator and Heartfield when he wrote his first music for the stage.[14]

There were no immediate successors to Piscator's experiment. The Party had too little contact with artists to make them politically productive, or to propose specific roles and tasks for them. Individuals were unable to bridge this gap on their own initiative alone. Rapprochement was made extremely difficult by the perpetuation of certain attitudes by many artists who had been active during the Expressionistic period following the war – attitudes such as the demand for leadership, intellectual patronage, and a condescending and doctrinaire approach to the workers' movement.

As late as 1927 – the year in which the way was being paved for change – Johannes R. Becher noted that a programme of demands alone was not sufficient (even for such artistic activity as was to evolve from within the masses themselves: the workers' musical movement, for instance, or proletarian–revolutionary literature): 'The controlling sectors of our party had not yet realized that it was necessary to support this literature if we wanted to demand any real effectiveness of it.'[15]

The aim of achieving collective communication that would be politically stimulating required not only new content and new forms, but also new types of organization for the 'producers'.[16] In music – as we shall see – this was at the same time more difficult and simpler.

The break with Schoenberg

Eisler's final emancipation began when, in March 1926, Schoenberg – who had done more for him than for others – accused him of 'betrayal',[17] and broke with him for many years; and that emancipation very quickly made its mark on Eisler's work as a composer. At the root of the conflict there was a misunderstanding that throws some light on the incompatibility of two diametrically opposed conceptions of music and art – an incompatibility that had become apparent in the guise of aesthetic and technical differences.

The facts are as follows. In January 1926 Schoenberg had been able to take over a composition master-class in Berlin as Ferruccio Busoni's successor[18] – a token of recognition that had been denied him in Vienna. From this new and strategically favourable position he was able to make more friends for the new twelve-note music, and in general to consolidate his standing. Now it was no longer a matter of 'establishing new forms in the face of the guardians of a common tradition, but of open squabbles between the various factions within modern music, with Schoenberg reacting particularly irritably to the charge that he had long been overtaken by the most recent developments in musical history'.[19]

Meanwhile Eisler's first successes at international music festivals had gone a very long way towards proving the fruitfulness of the 'school'. In the previous year, however, a shadow had fallen over the teacher–pupil relationship when Zemlinsky, formerly Schoenberg's brother-in-law, reported to the latter – not, it seems, without satisfaction – certain critical remarks of Eisler concerning, amongst other things, the compositional possibilities and potential of the twelve-note technique.

Shortly after settling in Berlin, Schoenberg had completed his Three Satires op. 28, strict twelve-note choruses in which he settled his accounts with rival factions in contemporary music. Here he poured scorn on the 'new classicism', above all ridiculing Stravinsky for his clever versatility, referring to him as 'little Modernsky' who had his baroque wig on at that time. As well as his inability to countenance other gods alongside him, it was probably also the need to make sure of his followers that moved him to take Eisler to task. He immediately checked his memory in a letter to Zemlinsky:

I. Did Mr E. say that he was getting away from all these modern things? II. that he did not understand twelve-note music? III. that he did not consider it to be music at all? This is what you told me he said, and since E. disputes it, it remains for me to ascertain the truth. You perhaps also remember the praise you bestowed on him: that he was the only one of my pupils with a mind of his own, and who didn't blindly adhere to everything.[20]

A few days later, Eisler responded with an indignant letter. He had felt himself denounced by the indiscretion, and unjustly so, since his criticisms had been aimed not at Schoenberg so much as at 'music festival music', which in his eyes was devoid of all social relevance, and at its parasitic public. The tone of Eisler's letter must have struck Schoenberg as quite unjustifiably arrogant and wounding. Eisler wrote:

I am bored by modern music, it is of no interest to me; much of it I even hate and despise. If possible I avoid hearing or reading it. (Alas, I must also include my own efforts of recent years with this.) Having just come from a *music festival,* I certainly expressed this disgust in the strongest of terms.

He makes an exception of his teacher, then continues:

What amazed me still further was your opinion of me as a person. Namely (with some exaggerations): A 'dernier-cri' middle-class youth stuffed full of the latest vogue words, totally fascinated by every new tendency, capable of every kind of shabbiness in his consuming ambition, 'scratching the back' of people who can be of use to him, etc. etc.

If time and my state of health permitted me to complete a little article I have begun, I could lay before you the clearest proof that it is not such a simple matter as that. But I may perhaps finish it yet. You will then certainly totally reject what little I have to say, but on the other hand you could be assured in it of my utter loyalty to your person and your cause. Even without this, however, I have the fullest confidence in what the next few years will bring . . . In conclusion may I ask you, if it is possible, to forget this matter.[21]

Schoenberg's angry reply does not dwell long on the reproach that mere 'loyalty' is not enough for him. And he stops assuming that Eisler's criticisms were just something mischievously spoken on the spur of the moment:

I was anxious to convince myself that it was only the cynicism and nihilism you find so successful in coffee houses that had tempted you to fall in easily with the opinions of those in whose company you found yourself – a view of the matter which would have allowed me to be lenient, since I do not consider this mental state as a disease of the skin but at worst a shabbiness of clothing which it is possible to change.

With the relentless exactitude of the pedagogue he seizes upon Eisler's weak point in the following argument:

You . . . were not able to keep your opinion of me to yourself, but had to blaze it abroad even though a change of allegiance is *not yet* perceptible in your works, even though you only *had it in mind* to manifest this change of allegiance (which was consequently not a creative act) in your future works; even though, therefore, the manner of composition which should document the change did not yet exist.

The letter concludes in terms of a formal separation; Schoenberg adds a gesture of magnanimity which may give some idea of the greatness of this unique character: 'May things go well with you and may the future bring you much good fortune. And if it should chance that I might be able to help you in any way, you know full well that it would be a further unjustice on your part not to let me know.'[22]

Eisler thought it proper to reply once more – and not the slightest bit more judiciously than before: 'Finally, permit me the following remarks', he says towards the end of his letter;

there has been no 'change of allegiance', nor any attempt to establish one. Neither am I striving to achieve or abandon any particular manner of composition. Questions of musical style and other kinds of problem are foreign to me, indeed they barely interest me at all. I write what I hear, as well as I can. The fact that people change is an inescapable fact of life from which no one can be immune. But I do not change allegiances or points of view like old clothes.[23]

Schoenberg's 'last word in this affair', in which he cannot allow Eisler 'even the smallest loophole through which you would escape', remorselessly insists on what seems to him Eisler's tactless and unethical behaviour, since

at a point when there was no necessity for it (for I could perhaps have found your opinion interesting, approved of it, indeed possibly even accepted it!) . . . (you aired your views) to a person by whom you could expect them to be received with approbation . . . and since your disagreement with me need not necessarily have been absolute opposition if by your behaviour you had not made it so. I have composed in a different way from Mahler and Zemlinsky, but I never felt the need to place myself in opposition to them. And only in cases of opposition are such prompt and open declarations necessary.[24]

Schoenberg had not wanted the rupture, nor in the first instance had Eisler, but he left his teacher no other choice. The latter must have felt that he had been deliberately provoked into it: an unmotivated desertion at the worst conceivable time, and a thoroughly incomprehensible one, since Eisler had not (yet) produced anything that might indicate a divergence and could perhaps have been tolerated as such. In fact it was a matter of genuine opposition, and it was only because Eisler's political motivation still remained hidden that Schoenberg mistook it for a simple difference of attitude.

Aesthetic and moral considerations – largely identical in Schoenberg's mind – furnished the criteria by which he made his judgments. According to these Eisler, in base ingratitude, had committed a breach of confidence. The reference to his own relationship with Mahler is illuminating; he, Schoenberg, had indeed composed in a different way, but had never sought to move away from the older composer. What this means is quite simply that Schoenberg was aware of being entrenched in a tradition which permitted progress and evolution without any sense of discontinuity as a consequence.

Although we admittedly have no concrete evidence for saying so, it was Eisler's conviction that the time was ripe for such a schism: the flow of tradition must be diverted from its bed (read: 'reproductive network') and into the stony tracts of social experience so that it can help to alter the conditions of the latter.

His political criticisms of new music were initially focussed on its *isolation*, and on the fact that although its hermeticism and inaccessibility were supposed to be proof of real quality, it was actually transparently lacking in content. He then turned his attention to the atmosphere of élitism in which it existed, and finally to the nature of its public, which worried him from early on. In short, it was the fact that music 'turned a deaf ear'[25] to the conflicts of its times, its social confrontations, that disturbed him and made him want to break away from it.

Looking back thirty years later to this crossroads in his development, Eisler noted:

. . . Schoenberg had a high opinion of me. Of a hundred talented students, I was the third of his pupils whom he recognized as a master. Now, (he) thought, I would sit in the saddle and ride with him. And my communism was just a youthful folly; it would soon pass (just a consequence of my hunger) . . . I did what no one expected: I broke with him. I did this crudely, ungratefully, rebelliously, irritably, despising his petty-bourgeois attitudes, withdrawing from him insultingly. He behaved with generosity of spirit. The letters he wrote to me during those weeks are magnificent documents of this unique man.[26]

Eisler accepted the blame for the separation, the ending of this almost filial relationship, citing Schoenberg's 'petty-bourgeois attitudes' as the cause – that is to say, both his apolitical stance (for all his nostalgia for monarchy) and his heroic awareness of his mission as an artist; they found expression at that time (1925) in texts he was writing himself, as for instance the second of the Four Pieces for Mixed Chorus op. 27: '. . . Thou must believe in the spirit!/Immediate, emotionless/and selfless./Thou must, O chosen one, must, if thou wishest to remain chosen.'[27]

Late in life, too, Schoenberg was to write: 'We, who live in *music*, have no place in politics and must regard it as foreign to our being. We are a-political, at best able to aspire to remain silently in the background.'[28] Seen in this perspective, Eisler's political convictions could only meet with this verdict: 'I have indeed never taken him seriously, but always considered these tirades as attempts to make himself interesting.'[29]

Interim on the Bourgeois Left:
three transitional works

Schoenberg's challenge (and to have interpreted his behaviour in any other way would have brought Eisler to a crisis) could only be taken up by producing such artistic 'evidence' as could justify an opposite point of view, the absence of which, somewhat paradoxically, had caused his teacher to react so implacably. For, five years earlier, Schoenberg himself had hardly been in a position to point to new artistic results when in 1921 he told Rufer of the newly discovered laws of twelve-note technique: 'I have made a discovery which will ensure the supremacy of German music for the next hundred years.'[30] It was only later that his proof – and even then less perhaps of his theory than of the applicability of the technique – was to follow, and when it did it was by no means without traces of earlier methods of composition.

And so it was with Eisler. Indeed the only difference that began to emerge at that time consisted in the aim to change, not primarily the *technique* of music (for any given specific expressive purpose), but its *function* in society: in other words, to give pride of place to its social evolution rather than the intrinsically musical, which was to be made to serve the former.

With his first steps in this direction, Eisler was not yet able to address a new public: this had first to be created. The existing one was above all intent on the fascinations of new art. Consequently the task presented itself as follows: not to fall short of the compositional standards of the Viennese School, but at the same time to make an open declaration of his protest against musical culture. Initially this could only be achieved in one way: through the *text*.

Thus Eisler attacked new music at its most vulnerable point. Its choice of 'poetic' texts, generally originating in threadbare emotional worlds, necessarily hampered the liberating impulses of advanced composition, channelling it into retrogressive paths. They withdrew from reality instead of bearing down on it. The three transitional works dating from 1925 and 1926 – *Tagebuch* [Diary] op. 9, *Heine-Chöre* [Heine Choruses] op. 10 and *Zeitungsausschnitte [Newspaper Cuttings]* op. 11 – have a satirical, at times also grotesque mien. They keep within the bounds of traditional forms and at the same time criticize them: *Tagebuch* unmasks the pompous solemnity of chamber cantatas, the Heine Choruses pour scorn on the petty-bourgeois mentality of glee-clubs, and *Zeitungsausschnitte* wishes good riddance to the lyricism of the concert hall. First and foremost, what is common to all is an attack on conventional patterns of *musical consumption*. Launched from the left flank of the bourgeoisie, they renounce bourgeois art while using bourgeois methods. At this point he was moving forwards from criticizing Schoenberg to taking up positions of his own.

The very title of *Zeitungsausschnitte* indicates the move towards new content.[31] The form of concert lieder 'for voice and piano' is now used to project documentary material instead of lyrical esotericism. But it is not a matter of 'vulgar' texts set against the music's backcloth of a more elevated style. Instead of the harmless squibs that could easily be fabricated from the contrast between the two genres, Eisler's aim is to denounce the times by means of newspaper clippings – a literary procedure he took from Karl Kraus.[32] The task of interpreting these clippings, which Kraus had entrusted to special techniques of quotation and commentary, now falls to the music.

Within the cycle, two groups of texts are highlighted: wedding announcements, which take the place of love songs, and children's songs – these being overtly proletarian, without a trace of the innocent naïvety of those watched over by nannies. The performing directions for the wedding announcement of a petty-bourgeois girl read: 'to be performed without any parody, humour, wit etc.', sung 'very plainly and simply'. This means without sarcastic winks, but also without the irony which would indicate a secret sympathy with its object.

In a completely serious way the documents tell of what had become of love and family relationships during and after the war. The damage done to human feelings through the inflation, the oppression and sadism felt in the rhymes of children and gutter-snipes, the misery of back yards and the aspirations reflected in the hypocritical phrases of those better off: what these 'big-city songs' record is the emotions of reduced circumstances.[33] It is the very grotesqueness of their effect that betrays the suffering hidden beneath their surface. Eisler portrays it without any touches of the picturesque, without any tone of overt lamentation. The skill with which, often in a very short space, he points up sentences and phrases, casting doubt on them or conveying their falseness, and his technique of musical quotation are here geared to a denunciation of post-war misery. Both the carefully handled piano accompaniment and the melodic line (which by no means spurns attractive ideas) only serve to drive home the corruptness of the prevailing conditions. On the other hand, the hollow ring of their words reveals the people conjured up by these newspaper cuttings as victims of circumstances, hostages to fortune; and in just this way they regain something of their real worth.

The demand to bring about change, nowhere explicitly stated, is nonetheless present throughout the cycle. It concludes outspokenly with a politically slanted observation of nature written by Eisler himself, the 'Frühlingsrede an einen Baum im Hintershaushof' [Springtime address to a tree in the back yard]:

> I earnestly request you to blossom, Mr Tree; do not forget: it is Spring! Are you on strike because of the terrible courtyard? Are you on strike because of the frightful rented barracks? You are surely not being so impossible as to dream of green forests. Adapt to your surroundings, if you don't mind! Perhaps you think that it is superfluous to blossom in our day and age? What are tender young leaves to do on the barricades? You would not be at all wrong, Mr Tree! Forget: it is Spring.

Under these conditions it is impossible to blossom, even though that would be 'natural' – just as one has no business to evince lyricism in the face of social need, at a time of strikes and barricades.

Indignation, grief and the hope of revolt all find their place in Eisler's *Zeitungsausschnitte*, which have nothing in common with sarcastic fun. Even their ambivalences are turned destructively against the surviving social order. This is done by the music: while the text retreats into the background, the meaning of the text is simultaneously brought out. Here Eisler achieves a process of musical alienation which permits him to undermine the conventional view of circumstances and to bring problems clearly into view.

Zeitungsausschnitte was his first approach (as a composer) to current reality and – even if still very much from the outside – to that of the proletariat. Bourgeois attitudes to the subject – complacency or fatalism – are excluded *a priori* as being incompatible with the desire for social change. Although inspired by motives of humanism rather than of class struggle, the cycle is a key work in Eisler's vocal output. It heralds a breakthrough to new possibilities in relating music to social reality, combined with an important shift of emphasis in favour of the text.

The composition is characterized by concentration and concision: written in a free atonal style, it also makes good use of procedures derived from serial technique. The diction is exemplary: the melodic line never detracts from the meaning of the text; the harmonic articulation is always aimed at transparency, and the brevity of the individual pieces prevents any autonomy of 'expression' (see ex. 3).

Eisler must have felt the success of *Zeitungsausschnitte* as a mixed blessing. On the one hand he could take satisfaction from the praise of Anton Webern, who wrote to him that 'on studying the score [the impression it made on me] became even stronger',[34] or from detailed reviews such as that of T. W. Adorno, which ended: '. . . all things considered, the songs are so extraordinary, their rage has such power, their identity such distinctness, their tone such living substance, that they must be emphatically commended';[35] on the other hand, there was little sign that they had had the desired effect on the concert-going public. Bewilderment, or even shock, were not in evidence: *Zeitungsausschnitte*, first performed in Berlin in December 1927, was applauded and accepted as a successful work – one, perhaps, which had an unusual, exotically interesting text.

Ex.3   *Zeitungsausschnitte*, 'Aus einer Enquête: Der Tod'

After a still more 'successful' performance in Vienna in the summer of 1928, a success to which the singer had contributed greatly, Heinrich Kralik wrote in *Die Musik*:

Zeitungsausschnitte was received with pleasure and enjoyment. . . Sharp atonal invention on banal or silly pomposities which otherwise are not exactly common material for composers to set. To have peeled away the crust of . . . these little musical jokes . . . and presented them as choice delicacies redounded to the credit of the charming singer Margot Hinnenberg-Lefebre. As if with a cajoling tenderness on her lips, she shaped these *gamin*-like compositions with a sweet voice and a compelling smile; and what started as cruel malice ended by being docile miniatures which the audience encored in their entirety.[36]

For Eisler, who had meanwhile taken up position on quite different terrain, such misunderstandings confirmed that criticism which does not abandon traditional forms and their context will be absorbed without any bother.

No other work seems so far removed from the interests of the young composer as his opus 9, completed late in 1926, the *Tagebuch des Hanns Eisler*. The title promises something we would least expect from Eisler: subjective confessions. In fact, by its inclusion of the composer's name, the title is already given a slightly exhibitionist twist. It announces a self-portrait of a special kind.

Written half a year after his dispute with Schoenberg, the diary is above all a counter-provocation addressed to his teacher. What it amounts to is that Hanns Eisler is henceforth no longer 'the pupil of . . .', but is himself.

The 'Little Cantata for three female voices, tenor, violin and piano', falling into three parts, opens with a clear reference to the 'old man's' move to Berlin, shortly after Eisler's own. The key sentences of the prologue, performed by the female trio, read: 'The old man is right, is right!'/'It is impossible to be all alone in a strange town.' The subsequent reply, performed simple-mindedly and childishly protesting good will: 'But if there are two of us, how much more we can enjoy ourselves!' is knocked on the head by a final: 'It is impossible! Impossible!'

This 'Impossible!' casts its shadow over the ill-humoured reflection of himself in verses of grotesque stupidity which follow after a wayward violin solo. 'The whole world is a cold shower/Before which I crouch miserably! . . . What should I do in order not to explode?/The damp is dripping from my bald spot.' Discontent and malaise with the world merge with that directed towards himself: in a tenor solo headed 'Depression' Eisler takes a passage from the letters which sealed his break with Schoenberg: 'If one is a stupid, base, middle-class lad:/Oh, how ugly everything is!/If I ever go to my eternal rest,/Bury me wrapped in manuscript paper!'

The answer to this cheerlessly morose confession is provided by the soprano with some 'Guter Rat' [Good Advice]. 'Dear child, do not be so downcast!/Do not sorrow with so much pleasure;/Do not speak so much of your grief/In these damnably interesting times!' Here, at the climax of the cantata, with a cheery repetition of 'Verdammt' (damnably) counterbalancing the 'Impossible' of the first piece, the piano interrupts with a quotation from the *Internationale* (see ex. 4). We hear the first bars (fitting the text 'Awake, ye damned (*Verdammte*) of this earth!'), after which the soprano concludes her good advice in a vein of encouragement: 'Be alert! With eyes open, not closed!/Or else we shall bury you in manuscript paper today' – a summons which even overshadows the ending, with its sceptical biding of time: 'In three and a half years/we'll be glad to hear of it . . .'

At the heart of Eisler's *Tagebuch*, the only openly autobiographical statement in his entire musical output, there is a sort of translation into music of a moment from the composer's life in 1926. He has recorded the instant at which he overcame his melancholy, which he had disguised with a veneer of the grotesque. The way out which he now saw was neither psychological nor aesthetic, but political. At the same time, it would be an oversimplification to see in this merely an emancipation from Schoenberg under the banner of the *Internationale*.

If this had been so, and the new direction so simple, Eisler would have selected an affirmative, bellicose text and not one of multilayered comic pathos. The vein of self-mockery running through the *Tagebuch* is directed not so much at himself as an individual and his private mental processes as, with social intent, at the son of the bourgeoisie in him. It is a critique of his own class conducted through himself – only this spotlighting of the bourgeois in himself and in his art is more than a passing concern.

After the first performance at the Baden-Baden Music Festival in the summer of 1927, the reviews, without troubling over the way in which it travesties the cantata genre, praised the 'grotesque intensity' of the *Tagebuch*.[37] Features of its grotesque mode of expression included its passion and simultaneous ability to hold

Ex.4   *Tagebuch des Hanns Eisler*, 'Guter Rat'

passion at arm's length. Criticism, even rage, is expressed in such a way that it can be laughed at. It is a halting mode of expression which withdraws emotion whilst retaining its attitudes. With the grotesquerie of opus 9, Eisler is still afflicted by the persisting uncertainty of whether and how the compositional methods he has learnt and mastered can be adapted to his new aims.

His experiences on a visit to Paris in the summer of 1926 (during which he had begun work on the *Tagebuch*) reinforced his lack of confidence in the destiny of a music which was consciously indebted to nothing more than the originality of its idiom.

In the salon of Marya Freund, the great interpreter of *Pierrot lunaire* and Schoenberg's representative in Paris, he got to know the French composers and their work. A lot of music was performed. Marya Freund, who knew and still sang Mahler's music and was a friend of Ravel, had had her attention drawn to Eisler by Schoenberg in Vienna, and took an interest in his songs.

Among the composers who frequented her house were Milhaud and Poulenc, Ibert and Roussel, Desormière, Jean Wiener and others. Stefan Priacel, Marya Freund's son, was a young journalist who spoke German well and acted as Eisler's interpreter; of these soirées he reports:

Without doubt the majority of these artists were revolutionaries only within the limited bounds of their professional techniques. Certainly differences of political opinion would have arisen between them and Eisler if the talk at these evenings had been about anything other than music . . . (He) went away from these soirées firmly convinced of the rightness of his aims. He would not admit of any musical language, even the most intelligent, if it was the privilege of a small band of devotees.[38]

On top of this was added Eisler's aversion to the neo-religious trend in vocal music that was just beginning at that time (two years later he was to write of its relation to the political crisis);[39] he also disliked the image his French colleagues presented to the world. Priacel tells us: 'He had a sort of physical resistance to these somewhat fashion-conscious musicians, and he instinctively rejected the world of dinner-jackets . . . his witticisms and epigrams were less "gratuitous" than theirs, more thought-out, and at the same time more satirical and serious.'

In Paris, even more conspicuously than in Vienna or Berlin, Eisler must have found it a source of irritation that composing appeared to be the prerogative of tasteful and elegant gentlemen who satisfied the aesthetic requirements of the bourgeois public with cultured, moderately modern concert music or inconsequential, witty *jeux d'esprit*. 'Perfumed with the praises of high society'[40] was what Heine had called such music a hundred years previously, with Chopin in mind. In the Paris of 1926, works which had brought a breath of fresh air into the musical scene –

such as early Stravinsky or Milhaud's *Le Boeuf sur le toit* – were already things of the past. Artistic discussions were now much more likely to be concerned with Surrealism and psychoanalysis, and with the methods by which the poetry of the unconscious could be liberated and the language of dreams communicated. All this was at the opposite extreme from what Eisler was looking for at the time.

Becher, in Berlin in 1926, described German literature as having reached a point of 'stagnation'.[41] The apathy and cynicism of bourgeois authors were the obverse of their inability to raise any serious problem, let alone to contribute to its solution. Becher's reproach also implies a criticism of the revolutionary intelligentsia, who so far had not succeeded in making any contact with the proletarian masses, since that cannot be achieved through mere contemplation.

Eisler's first attempt to make contact of this sort was in his Three Male Choruses op. 10. The current state of workers' choral societies did not speak at all well for the choral medium as being rich in potential for political communication. Most of the societies had degenerated into narrow-minded glee-clubs; their atmosphere of moist sentimentality – which Eisler found particularly deplorable – was the result of their members' conversion to the petty bourgeoisie. Set against the immediate ills of this deterioration, however, there was the possibility of linking up with what was numerically the most powerful cultural organization of the workers' movement[42] in the hope of transforming collective singing into a relevant community art with a strong impact on the masses.

As the only kind of music-making which did not depend on financial necessities (instruments, tuition, etc.), choral singing allowed the most widespread active participation. Its disadvantage was that for many their lack of musical education made it difficult to learn unfamiliar new music and it was not easy to nurture interest in it. It cannot be said that in his op. 10 Eisler had taken account of the technical standards of amateur choirs. It remains a transitional work in that, in keeping with its political content, it addresses itself to the audience of the workers' choirs and to the choirs themselves but can scarcely be performed by them. It consists of complicated structures, packed with allusions, and composed with all the polyphonic arts of the Schoenberg school. His hitherto limited experience of the proletariat's way of life and requirements as well as the contradictions in political development around 1925 and 1926 prevented Eisler at this stage from putting over his ideas in a simpler, more concrete form.

For his op. 10, a forerunner of the later militant choruses and intended to be absolutely relevant, he chose, surprisingly enough, texts from Heine's *Zeitgedichten* [Poems of the Times].[43] They were written before and after the abortive revolution of 1848. They serve as a reminder that historical misery projects forward into the present (the similarly abortive November Revolution of 1918, still a recent experience, was the latest link in the chain). In Eisler's choruses this is not made the pretext for a lament, but a challenge to make the struggle more intensive in the future. The aggressive methods of satire are directed precisely against self-pity and refuge in resignation. The 'cheer'-ful, unpolitical attitude of working-class singers and their repertory of moth-eaten songs of nature and love are as much in need of scourging as is the increasingly strong movement to the Right in German internal politics.

In order to adapt the Heine poems to his own ends, Eisler combined fragments of text, completed and assembled linking passages, changed or replaced titles. He built up a sequence in three parts: 'Tendenz – Utopie – "Demokratie"' [Tendentious-ness – Utopia – 'Democracy'], which is given inner coherence by means of parallel relationships.

Heine's derision of empty generality in the painstaking, yet helplessly committed poetry of his time, entitled 'Die Tendenz', becomes in Eisler's version (minus the definite article), despite its sprinkling of satire, a positive tool in the form of a sung motto which points the way: to engage in political struggle. Heine's question about the non-appearance of a German revolution which, following the earlier English and French Revolutions, had to remain on the agenda for a very long time ('1649–1793–???'), is answered in a challenging way by Eisler in 'Utopia': the decisive step of getting rid of monarchs and princes through revolutionary justice still founders on sentimental reverence and the inability to act. Heine's satire 'Der Wechselbalg' [The Changeling], originally directed at Friedrich Wilhelm IV of Prussia, is brought up to date by Eisler's insertion in the middle of the text, relating it to the bourgeois type of 'formal' democracy.

He is able to observe the 'relative stabilization' and above all the retrogressive developments which accompany it. Early in 1925 the Republic acquired a monarchist president in Paul von Hindenburg.[44] In the autumn it became known that a settlement was being negotiated with the Hohenzollerns – seven years after the Kaiser's abdication – with a view to restoring their family estates and awarding them compensation out of public funds. The princes were making similar demands. For bourgeois and Social Democratic governments to engage in such transactions[45] must have seemed to Eisler an absurd historical anachronism, and must have confirmed him in his radical opposition. The Choruses op. 10 bear unmistakable traces of this.

Shortly after the beginning of the first, there occurs a revealing superimposition: the words '. . . (sing in . . .) the manner of the "Marseillaise" ' are set by Eisler to the opening bars of the 'Internationale'. This draws attention to the diachronic nature of co-existent conflicts. Whilst at a national level the confrontations between the bourgeoisie and the nobility persist ('Marseillaise'), at an international level the proletariat has to fight both.

The 'German bard' is satirically reminded to be 'no longer the sensitive flute, the idyllic soul', a weakness that is made the theme of the second chorus. This begins: 'Only the German has soul; he will still be a good soul even when staging a rebellion.' And it ends with a musical idea which gives fresh emphasis to Heine's closing lines. 'In a six-horse court barouche mottled with black, its chargers bedecked with wreaths,/the weeping coachman high on the box with his funeral whip;/thus will the German monarch/one day be led to the place of execution/and most humbly guillotined.'

As we know, the attitude of servility never went that far; Heine was mistaken. The appearance of humility must remain illusory – this is the only way that Eisler could interpret the text. He achieves this in musical terms by adding two bars in which the conflict – the climax of the satire – resolves itself in pianissimo:

over the word 'guillotined', as it fades away on a falling line, the word 'soul' is heard, sung falsetto, as the equally feeble victor over the intended deed (see ex. 5).

In the mid-1920s, 'democracy' was for Eisler at the most so-called 'democracy'; it was a word in inverted commas. In his view it was primarily adapted to the interests of the bourgeoisie, and was permeated with residues of monarchism. This is indicated in the opening words of the third chorus: 'A child with a great pumpkin of a head,/a blond moustache and a venerable pigtail . . .'

Ex.5   Three Male Choruses op. 10, 'Utopie'

Eisler wrote the central part of the text himself. Heine, seeing a monarch as a person and as a representative, had used moral denunciation – very much in the Enlightenment tradition. At the heart of his text he had introduced a satirical picture of degenerate sexuality in the upper classes: 'A changeling, which a corporal/ secretly laid in our cradle/in place of the suckling child, which he stole, –/The monster which with falsehood,/With his favourite whippet perhaps,/The old Sodomite fathered . . .'

Eisler replaced this text with a more general one relating to 'economic democracy' and its attempts to integrate the workers: '. . . the finest opportunity for betrayal!/The changeling that has cast its spell on us,/The monstrosity born of filth and fire,/To every bourgeois fatally dear, dear, (dear) . . .' After this substitution he was able to revert to Heine's concluding lines without alteration: 'I need not name the monstrosity! You should drown it! You should burn it!'

This very broad challenge concludes the first work of Eisler's to show an overt political alignment. However, composed as they are in a richly varied style of four-part writing, condensing a complex web of interrelationships – the performance time is barely more than five minutes – the op. 10 Choruses cannot yet be expected to penetrate the popular consciousness. Although the work is undoubtedly successful from the formal point of view as well as being extremely clever, it could hardly be totally comprehensible to a mass audience. At the same time the Choruses are the first forceful step of a young, radical artist along the road to abandoning his class. With these Choruses Eisler came closer to his goal of placing the acquisitions of new music at the service of politically unambiguous texts.

Approaching this goal seriously as a composer meant establishing different conditions of artistic production and a new relationship with the public. In his determination to make his art useful and to give it as broad a social base as possible, Eisler took up a position quite the opposite of his teacher's. Schoenberg, who thought of the antithesis between the artist and society as immutable, was a typical product of a restricted development – that of the latter-day bourgeoisie. For Eisler this was effectually a thing of the past, even though it continued to exist. If the isolation of the artist could not be removed simply by waiting for better conditions, it necessarily followed that he must make his own efforts to break through.

The October Revolution held out to the younger generation of artists the hope that they might be able to attempt this in alliance with the workers' movement. Eisler saw this as the only meaningful possibility. But for an artist to identify with the cause of the proletarian class did not mean that the latter had already accepted him and adopted him as its own. That required more than merely writing *for* the proletariat.

Militant music

The Baden-Baden Music Festival (1927), at which Eisler was represented by his *Tagebuch* op. 9 and also by his first music for film (composed for Ruttmann's *Opus III*), was slanted towards new forms of *angewandte Musik* [applied music]. Whilst Hindemith also produced a piece of film music,[46] the première of *Mahagonny* by Brecht and Weill introduced a Songspiel which conspicuously departed from the neutral zone of 'applied music'. As Brecht commented in his programme note, 'The little epic play *Mahagonny* simply draws the consequences of the irreversible collapse of the existing social strata.'[47] The critical type of music theatre which here arose on the basis of the Mahagonny songs in the *Hauspostille* [Family Devotional] develops above all a destructive power. The halting élan of Weill's melodies, the melancholy cynicism which veils the anti-bourgeois attitude, the conjunction of sport and technology in the concert hall (the stage is a boxing ring, with projections providing the background): all this produced a combination which simultaneously attracted, provoked, and instilled doubts in its audience. The style of Weill's songs, with their rhythmic inspiration drawn from Stravinsky and from jazz, and their instrumentation deriving from the same sources, fascinated young composers as a means by which serious use could be made of modern American folk art.

This collaboration between Weill and Brecht must have impressed Eisler not only by the way in which the text was set, but also by the latter's own special quality: the eminent suitability of Brecht's verses for musical setting.

At that time, in common with Kurt Weill, Stefan Wolpe, H. H. Stuckenschmidt and others, Eisler was a member of the music section of the leftist-bourgeois 'Novembergruppe'.[48] This seems to have been an unsatisfactory interlude, as with Brecht's membership of the 'Gruppe 1925' (together with Becher, Döblin,

Kisch, Tucholsky and others). The opposition represented by the attitude of these artists was too politically indeterminate for Eisler. When Egon Erwin Kisch introduced to Eisler the poet Robert Gilbert,[49] a sympathizer with the KPD who wrote for its official organ *Die Rote Fahne* [The Red Flag] as well as for *Die Weltbühne* [The World Stage], edited by Ossietzky and Tucholsky, the outcome was a fruitful collaboration. A joint satirical opera, begun early in 1927, was, however, taken no further by Eisler; the strong impression made by the new form of Songspiel, and on the other hand the deterrent example of the impression made by 'modern opera', an example of which he saw a few months later in Krenek's *Jonny spielt auf*,[50] must both have been factors in this. Also, he probably felt that the subject was not sufficiently broad to fill such a large-scale form: it was a critique of the bourgeois welfare ideology, including its Salvation Army, and of its whitewashing of a class-ridden society. The political circumstances of the year 1927 were extremely suitable for accelerating Eisler's move to a position of enlightened militancy. News of the blood-bath of the Viennese workers[51] must have reached him while he was still at the Baden-Baden Festival in July. In Berlin the summer was marked by protest demonstrations against the threatened execution of Sacco and Vanzetti, the American trade-unionists.[52] The massive move towards the Right in the bourgeois block government under its central leadership, scandals over secret arms production and so forth sharpened the climate within Germany.

The KPD and SPD Party conferences, both taking place early in 1927,[53] showed up very different ideas about the state of the workers' movement. For the Social Democrats, Rudolf Hilferding evolved his thesis of systematic 'organized capitalism'. This was to be the outcome of the formation of combines and the pooling of major industries, and from it would come a peaceful, evolutionary route to socialism. For the KPD this kind of reformism and denial of Marxist principles represented an abandonment of the class struggle. Their Party conference was conducted entirely in the context of the tenth anniversary of the October Revolution and 'in the spirit of Lenin'. The accent was on systematic Marxist training, the publication of the writings of Lenin: in short, laying the theoretical foundations which would serve as a basis for future actions.

Its lack of experience in the application of Marxist principles was one of the chief weaknesses of the young Party, which had lost its outstanding leaders Liebknecht and Luxemburg only a short time after its foundation.[54] To try to make good this setback by training and by utilizing the resources of publicity and of art seemed to be a first priority: it was vital to propagate the knowledge about social relationships and historical processes which alone could make it possible to evaluate the current balance of power and thereby to work out appropriate strategies and tactics.

For the first time questions about cultural policy were given an important place. The demand for a tangible revolutionary culture and art made it important to obtain the services of sympathetic artists as active collaborators in the proletarian cultural organizations. Even the least significant of them had had some experience in this field. Consequently they turned their attention to the Soviet Union.

'As the tournaments in the arena of aesthetics came to an end it was necessary to shape the living flesh . . . The revolution placed practical tasks in the foreground – to influence the psyche of the masses, to organize the will of the working class.'[55] Sergei Tretiakov, one of the pioneers among the young Soviet writers and later to be a friend of both Eisler and Brecht, penned these words as a retrospective glance at the early years after 1917. What was required was to abolish the schism between art and life. This did not mean pressing forward as individuals in their respective artistic disciplines, independently of each other, but, on a broadly organized basis, using artistic resources to help to articulate and unify the needs and political interests of the masses.

Conscious calculation of the necessary effect of a work as opposed to purely intuitive 'autonomous growth', and consideration of the totality of what is usable in place of the earlier 'bringing-into-the-world' of the work of art, 'for the use of all humanity' – that is the new form of organized influence exercised by our manufacturers of art.[56]

The experiences of the Soviet avant-garde, and their collaboration with political mass organizations, were only taken up on a broader basis in Germany in the late 1920s. It was still to be learned that political activity itself could lead to the discovery of new artistic realms. Also, that revolutionary art arises in collaborative work, on a collective basis. As an instance, Eisenstein's *Battleship Potemkin*, which was shown in Berlin in 1926 and from which dates the popularity of Russian films among Berlin workers (and not only them), is at the same time, with its bold montage technique, a demonstration of how new findings in the media can be pressed into the service of political aims.

A year later, on the tenth anniversary of the October Revolution, a further influential genre of political cultural work arrived in Germany with the Blaue Blusen [Blue Tunics], an Agitprop theatrical group markedly inspired by Tretiakov. The time was propitious. At its Party conference in March 1927 the KPD had appealed for the formation of a 'red militant cultural front',[57] in other words for the unification of the workers' cultural and educational organizations. The task would be to support their social demands and their political struggle by means of attractive and compelling productions: to reach the vast masses whilst at the same time broadening the circle of sympathizers.

Rather than the frequently verbose and abstruse language of the Party press with its abstract theoretical jargon which tended to act as a barrier to communication, current problems were to be made tangible by means of directly corresponding art forms, whetted by lively, clear and frequently satirical language.

A campaign for the increased acceptance and popularization of new media such as photography, film and radio was launched (and this even before the Party conference in question) by one of the ablest organizers and agitators of the German workers' movement, Willi Münzenberg.[58] The successes attributable to his Roter Konzern [Red Combine], which embraced journals, periodicals, book publishers and a book club, were also founded on his quick responses to technical innovations in the communications media and to the changing requirements of purchasers. Thus, just as in 1926 he succeeded in breaking the monopoly of the Berlin gutter press – the *Welt am Abend* [Evening World] became the widest-read socialist daily newspaper[59] – he also built up with the *Arbeiter-Illustrierte-Zeitung* (AIZ) [Workers' Illustrated News] an attractive counterpart to the commercial illustrated press. This was achieved partly by a systematic and original introduction of pictures and photomontage; but above all Münzenberg's papers took into account the interest of the masses in sport, cinema, entertainment and everyday life. One of its main objectives was to establish the political relevance of this sphere, and to show its links with the history and outlook of the workers' movement.

Münzenberg's combine was itself part of an all-party people's organization with strong KPD connections: Internationale Arbeiterhilfe [International Workers' Aid] (IAH).[60] This undertook social relief work for strikebound and locked-out workers and supported or instigated political campaigns. Not so much a charitable institution as an organization to reinforce the militant power of the workers, IAH increasingly complemented its work through political and cultural institutions which encouraged activism and partisanship. It was vitally concerned with resisting the exploitation and division of the working class, warning against reformism, and appealing for vigilance against policies of isolation directed against the Soviet Union, the 'Heart of the Revolution' and the 'Fatherland of the Working Man'.

The tour of the Moscow Blaue Blusen in the autumn of 1927 was also organized by IAH. In the wake of its success, Agitprop groups arose in numerous German towns, generally formed from proletarian amateur theatrical groups. According to their own definition, the Blaue Blusen were 'a newspaper brought to life in drama . . . a real-life stage born of the Revolution . . . a montage of political and everyday manifestations from the point of view of the proletarian class ideology'.[61] 'The living newspaper should, like a film, have a fast tempo . . .'[62] Short, succinct scenes, full of ideas and performed aggressively and with élan, frequently cabaret-like in their impact, and with a musical accompaniment provided by a piano or a jazz band: this was the new formula for a dynamic and popular political art which could have a chance of developing its persuasive power over the working community.

Their Berlin appearance at Piscator's theatre in the Nollendorf-platz, which had been opened four weeks previously, also moved the bourgeois critics to enthusiasm. Alfred Kerr wrote: 'Everything was bang up-to-date, attractive, entertaining, competent.'[63]

Rote Fahne described the reactions of a public assembled from a wide variety of backgrounds:

The *class identification* excited the workers: this was *their* troupe, and it was their life that was up there on the stage. The sympathetic intellectuals were amazed by its 'novelty', 'freshness' and 'originality'. Both the artistry and the factuality of its presentation of the Russia of the workers and peasants elicited their tumultuous approbation. Soviet Russia was instantly brought right home to them. All obfuscations and misrepresentations were swept away. There stood revealed the spirit and the strength, the *conviction* and the will of the world's first workers' and peasants' state.

And the first-nighters, the clever set who are sated with 'the culture of the West', came from the Renaissance Theatre and its play of 'The Italian Dusa', from the Gramatica, or from the legal comedy of the Englishman Galsworthy at the Artists' Theatre not exactly bubbling over with the problems of their bourgeois society. – In the Blaue Blusen they discovered a respect for the 'naïve'. (This is how the class-will of the working people is 'artistically' described.) Here there was nothing dead, nothing over-refined or insoluble. With mute or voiced recognition, the representatives of the society of yesterday followed the bright beginning, the first surges, the sparks and flares of a *new society*.[64]

The enthusiasm of this description is accounted for by the feeling of certainty that a new historical phase had begun to assume vital shape. Every success of the young Soviet Union must at that time have given impetus to the almost contemporary KPD. The enthusiastic identification of the cause of the proletariat with that of the Soviet Union was at this stage shared too by numerous workers in Social Democrat organizations. It was important for the KPD to make contact with these: compared with the much older SPD it was a party representing a minority of workers, in many regions it appeared merely sectarian, and in order to counter the accusation that it pursued illusory ends it needed a concrete demonstration to the contrary: namely that the theories of Lenin were capable of being realized in practice, were necessary, and were in the interests of all working men.

To the extent that they too based their work on aesthetic innovation, sympathetic artists were increasingly impressed by the breakthrough achieved by Soviet art in its combination of Futurism, Constructivism and elements of Proletkult in their 'production-line art'.[65] In it they discovered models and suggestions of how to abolish traditional aesthetics and to work out new and precise programmes for the social tasks to be undertaken.

Even though this held true for film and the graphic arts, for theatre and for literature, Soviet music largely continued to run on nineteenth-century lines. It held few attractions for the composers of Western Europe. For the politically motivated amongst them, revolutionary mass songs provided an exception. In addition they made use of certain methods of performance which had been developed in entertainments involving ideological agitation: inserted spoken choruses, linking texts, slogans read out to the accompaniment of percussion. These were didactic procedures which at the same time provided contrast. They made it possible to bring out and consolidate political content.

When, late in 1927, Eisler joined the Berlin Agitprop group Das Rote Sprachrohr [The Red Mouthpiece][66] – as its composer, pianist and conductor – he subjected his work to new conditions. He no longer relied on the old forms of publication. The critique of official musical life which he had taken over from Schoenberg was not sufficiently far-reaching: to persist in an attitude of opposition meant to succumb to certain terms and conditions of the bourgeois world which had to be fought against. Eisler's new form of activity was his first step in helping to create for music the counterpublicity that the Party was aiming for in its cultural work. It came into competition with conservatively directed commercial culture and entertainment which was using technological innovations the more effectively to play upon the ingrained habits of its public.

In writing music for the Agitprop group, Eisler learnt how to express himself 'in a way that the workers could understand'[67] and with musical precision. Here, in direct collaboration and constant discussion with them, he gained a more secure knowledge of the requirements and points of view of the proletariat, their patterns of behaviour and emotional outlook. To make contact with their level of musical experience meant, in practical terms, to adopt accessible and 'low' genres, or at least elements of them, and – with the resources of modern music – to fuse them into new forms. Through these, far more thoroughly than through the mere patching of political texts on to melodic clichés, awareness could be stimulated, sharpened, and pointed in a specific direction.

As the first Agitprop troupe of the Communist Youth League (KJVD), Das Rote Sprachrohr addressed itself first and foremost to a public of working youth, from which it was itself predominantly drawn. For them Eisler composed incidental music, songs and militant ballads, including one of his best-known, the 'Kominternlied' [Comintern Song].[68] Under the leadership of Maxim Vallentin, the theatrical producer and actor, it soon became the most important German Agitprop group. Over and above satirical and sharply focussed minor forms (used for agitating about everyday demands and immediate goals), it sought to open up larger forms which had much in common with proletarian theatre. These were to accord greater importance and time to propaganda for the historic aims of the workers' movement. Themes such as strikes, strikebreaking, solidarity and (later) the united front demanded serious representation on stage.

Music, if intelligently used, was in a position effectively to indicate the relationship between the various topics and to intimate the emotional level. The task of making such complexities clear through the correct application of compositional methods was one which Eisler developed to a fine art: his later music for theatre and film owed much of its dramatic qualities to his experience with Agitprop.

At the same time Eisler complemented his practical musical work with activities as a critic: for *Rote Fahne* he wrote essays and reviews of major operatic and concert performances – generally sharply critical, with unconcealed rage at the typical Berlin musical life into which subsidies were poured. These essays were always kept at a level which could be easily understood, and were intended to awaken interest in social aspects of music. One of the first of them, published in October 1927, ends in the following strong terms:

Along with the crisis of the bourgeoisie and the general crisis of capitalism, a new kind of crisis in music is dawning and we are witnessing the beginning of a new chapter: Modern Music.

The most significant thing about modern music is this: in the years following the war, in nearly all the arts, a number . . . of revolutionary artists have appeared who in their works have drawn genuinely revolutionary conclusions from the social situation. *In music this has not happened and is not happening* . . . Among musicians the only thing to have spread has been a slushily petty-bourgeois attitude or else worldly-wise nihilism . . .

From 1918 to 1923, during the period of inflation, of the Spartacist struggles, of the Soviet republics of Munich and Budapest, and of the Red Army of Warsaw, the only things that musicians were bothering themselves about were matters of technique. There was not a single one who felt even the slightest waft from the winds of the time.

The result of this 'timelessness' and restrictedness of music is that modern music has no public – no one wants it. As a private concern of well-educated people, it leaves the proletariat cold. The bourgeoisie hankers after stronger stuff for their diversion and entertainment. Like virtually no other art, modern art is leading an illusory existence which can only be maintained by artificial means.

The disintegration of bourgeois culture is expressed more markedly by music than by any other of the arts. Despite all its technical refinements it is an empty vessel, for it is devoid of ideas and of a common language. An art which loses its sense of community thereby loses itself.

The final sentence makes a demand which might have been taken from a manifesto: 'First the proletariat most forge for itself a new music out of the expertise and artistic methods of the bourgeoisie.'[69]

Eisler was searching, in a rudimentary way, for a theory to support his intention to lead new music out of its isolation and to indicate the direction it should take. We can briefly state the principles he was to adopt: the first requisite is to analyse the present: the rejection of what already exists means at the same time recognizing that it provides the foundations of the future. It follows from this that musical evolution is embedded in social history. As a preserve of the bourgeoisie, music mirrors the latter's subjectivity: whether in a slushy or a sophisticated way – the autonomy granted to technique has enabled this music to manoeuvre itself into a position of isolation. Both ideas and common language have fallen by the wayside.

Eisler, who at that time was more than usually preoccupied with Marxist theory and questions of musical history, meant neither an abstract community of language or just any ideas. If it were to be possible to establish the new human collectivity in which art could again have a comprehensive significance, the dominance of the class system had first to be abolished. The immediate task of the artist was to apply his resources so that they would be instrumental in creating a sharper awareness of this. At a time of transition the chief aim of revolutionary art must be in its 'militant and educational character.'[70]

First of all music's autonomy had to be relinquished. It was necessary to forge a different relationship with the public than would be possible in a bourgeois context. For Eisler bourgeois music was discredited by its insistence on isolating composition from social reality. It had become impotent to handle big contemporary subjects which could capture the attention of the masses.

This was precisely the job envisaged for *angewandte Musik*. It had its roots in social considerations. It started out from the question: *for whom*, under what conditions, and from what perspective is it necessary to compose? In practical terms, it involved deciding on subject matter and artistic method *according to functional requirements*. This reversal of the traditional attitude, in which the expressive needs of the individual were the alpha and the omega, brought with it a reappraisal of aesthetic values.

The hierarchy of conventional priorities was overturned: 'beauty', aesthetic charm and enjoyment were no longer the highest aim, but were pressed into its service. Their job was to help to make social and political ideas clear and attractive, and to speed their realization. 'Consummate form' and precise structuring were not to be used in the interests of a closed, self-contained work, but to establish and strengthen the power emanating from the music and to give greater cogency to those impulses which were directed towards action. 'Entertainment' and enjoyment would no longer remain superficial distractions, finished and done with once the performance had come to an end. The need for entertainment was harnessed in a positive way to the overriding interests.

The new reciprocal relationship of knowledge and perception, emotion and action, takes on the guise of an *extension* of the traditional concept of music. The shift in the relationship is

5   Eisler with (from left) Paul Hindemith, Bertolt Brecht and heads of broadcasting Ernst Hardt and Hans Flesch at the German Chamber Music Festival in Baden-Baden (1927)

accountable to Marxist findings: the artist's task is to infuse it with vitality and fertility. The inclusion and integration of documentary material[71] give concrete form to the new content; at the same time it strikes a blow against introspective and psychological interpretative reactions to music. Text and composition come into a fresh relationship with each other: music is to derive its fullness and complexity from the text and, in its role as a political art with a special capacity for reaching the emotions, convey it precisely.

It is his urge towards *musical practice* – the union of theoretical awareness with practical activity – that from this time on distinguishes Eisler from other composers. The ideal to which his compositions aspired might suggest a concept of *new objectivity*. It is dynamic and not at all 'free from ideology'. It takes a stand against all pseudo-neutral ambivalence. Its characteristic feature is that the *point of view* from which its judgments are pronounced is openly confessed and proclaimed. As a Marxist one it was not yet universal, but it aspired to universality. His most important project was to give concrete musical expression to the new vision of the world and the hopes of the working class. To use the language of the time: to bring about, through the self-emancipation of the proletariat, the liberation of mankind, a true humanism.

Eisler kept his distance from the fashionable *Neue Sachlichkeit*,[72] which reacted in a stringently formal and emotionally atrophied way to the changes wrought by the rapid onslaught of technology. His self-awareness as an artist of a time of transition did indeed enable him to give pride of place to objective social relationships, but he always sought to refer them back to their human aspects.[73]

He was keenly aware of the inhuman conditions of life shared by a large part of the population: he saw here a living indictment of the apolitical attitude of many German composers, and felt that the latter showed the same human impoverishment whose obverse side was seen in material wretchedness. The low standards imposed on the aesthetic appetites of wage slaves were in his view related to capitalist *exploitation*. Only when this was combatted could the standards be raised.

This was how, from 1927 on, Eisler approached the task of analysing the current social position of music. Between the proliferating splinter-groups of the bourgeois modern composers on the one hand and the as yet ideologically confused movement for workers' music on the other, he observed the steady growth of that type of music which, thanks to its resolute conquest of the media of broadcasting and the gramophone, threatened to submerge all others: light music.

Eisler showed himself realistic enough not to condemn and ignore light music as being, aesthetically speaking, commercial trash; instead of reacting with the horror of the uncompromising musician, he understood it as mass music – even if of a depraved kind[74] – which penetrated to virtually every social level.

Any political music which wishes to reach the masses, and particularly the young, can ill afford not to begin with light music. Eisler was to make use of those elements he considered viable (in particular those of jazz), transforming them and placing them in a politically slanted context.

The aggressive and protesting character of contemporary militant music was not to rest on the text alone: it had to be contained in the musical ideas themselves, infiltrate the composer's attitude, and permeate every cell of the music. Eisler took pains to invent individual musical characteristics derived from the text[75] which would then provide a maximum of polemical acuity in close conjunction with it. Eisler's stance as an agitator in the later years of the Weimar Republic blended totally with his purely musical forms, as is shown by his instrumental music of this period, to create *a tone of aggression*.

Eisler's revolutionary temperament enters fully into this music's specifically motoric, tingling character, which takes violent contrasts in its stride and is both sharp and flowing at once. Just as dialectics has 'its centre of unrest in the antithesis',[76] Eisler speaks of music as 'antitheses turned into sound'.[77] These reflect not only social tensions but also the will to intervene in them and to strip away the fatalism of consolation. The intention is to go beyond the text as it is generally perceived by the reasoning faculties alone and penetrate into the emotional world of the masses in order to alter its physical structure.

It was also important for the workers' movement to emerge from its isolation, to break down the barriers of communication and to win over other classes as allies. Artists and intellectuals could, as representatives of its members, help the workers' movement give expression to its own living conditions, to its tasks and aims, to give these the *form* that would enable them to reach the outside world without falsification, and to find sympathy and support there.

At this time Eisler saw his social task as being to give musical strength and an active character to the workers' movement. The more he engaged in practical collaboration with the organizations of the workers' musical movement, the more their members tended to give him a direct mandate. This was fundamentally different from the purely intellectual initiative of an individual: in situations of real conflict, the latter, lacking genuine class responsibility, tends to retreat into a Utopian idealism. This is the anachronistic attitude of the apostle of Enlightenment; it is not far from here to an undoubtedly comfortable position not infrequently met with amongst intellectuals: that of arbitrator in current disputes.

Marxism developed as a critique and attack on bourgeois ideology; only in militancy can it develop further. Its historical aim is universal emancipation. The process leading to this must be set in motion from the most advanced outposts: the avant-garde of the workers' movement. At that time the optimism of the young KPD was backed up by the conviction of its leaders that within a short time there would arise a revolutionary situation in which they would be required to take over the initiative.

To what extent and at what date Eisler may have shared this view is difficult to discern from our present perspective. His was a critical optimism, not of the flag-waving kind. To make art answerable to a political movement is not the same as ignoring the latter's inconsistencies and difficulties; much rather, indeed, it is to direct attention to them – showing them as superable, but not yet overcome.

When Eisler placed both his compositional talents and his political brains, ready to learn and adapt, at the service of the workers' musical movement, he was seizing a historic opportunity to create a new art that would have a new effectiveness: an art which would draw its content from the masses and use new techniques to bring it home to the masses.

Political choruses

The rabble-rousing choral document 'Vorspruch' [Epigram] op. 13 marked the start of Eisler's period of militant music like a signal flare. The text, written by Eisler himself, culminates in a sentence which was to become a byword of anti-establishment workers' choruses: 'Our singing too must be a fight!'[78] Concise and direct, an accessible and lapidary slogan, these words pronounce the pointlessness of any attempt to fight which seeks to break away from the bourgeois routine of concert life without acknowledging its political colours.

During the 1920s such attempts included the revival of 'community singing', the musical youth movement together with musical youth leagues, amateur choral groups and school choirs, etc. Eisler felt that their use of folk music with its glorification of pre-capitalist conditions was dangerous because it caused people to forget politics. The vague ideal of a popular community supposedly transcending all class conflicts made it susceptible to fascism. Of the musical youth movement of Jöde, 'who declared he had given the German people back their folk songs', he was later to observe: 'Its chief ideal was for its choral brigade ever to be singing "Maria ging durch den Dornenwald" together with the militants of the Red Front.'[79]

The desire to take refuge in mood evocation, in subjectivity or in unmotivated levity was no less widespread with workers' choruses, having been reinforced by traditional styles of performance. Late in 1927 Eisler wrote for the first time about the workers' musical movement, which ought 'under no circumstances to rest content with allowing singing to lull them into neutrality', and pinpointed their weakness: 'Programme planning cannot be eliminated simply by pressure on the directors from the class-conscious members of choral societies. There is a lack of works that are truly irreproachable from the ideological and musical points of view.'[80]

As Eisler saw it, just as the social democracy of the Right had adapted itself to bourgeois ideals, so the workers' choral societies had, under its influence, increasingly moved towards petty-bourgeois choral singing. From a musical point of view everything he had yet heard seemed to him intolerably outdated; politically he was scandalized that workers' choirs were singing within a context which had been provided in advance by the opposing side. He felt it was misguided to make their performances poorer copies of formal concerts. On such hostile terrain it was only possible to achieve *succès d'estime* – within the bounds permitted by their opponents.

The 'Vorspruch' op. 13, built entirely on antitheses, promises in its introduction something 'out of the ordinary'. In anticipation of this 'quite different thing', suspense is created by a theme with variations, a parody of what was usual in glee-clubs – the sanctimonious mood, the songs of nature and of love. The chorus sums this up as 'a turning-away from reality'. After a massive build-up, the last of the song's three parts brings an abrupt change: in a coda Eisler links the motto 'Our singing too must be a fight' to two quotations from standard works. He positions them in such a way that they constitute not just a political appeal, but can be related by the singers to their previous, reformist performing practice: 'We have nothing to lose but our chains . . .' and, finally, the 'Awake . . .' from the 'Internationale' (see ex. 6).

At the same time, the 'Vorspruch' is an introduction to three subsequent choruses. In each of these a critical counterpart[81] to what has been parodied in the 'Vorspruch' is evolved: the extremely serious 'Gesang der Besiegten' [Song of the Vanquished] expresses mourning for the numerous victims among the militant comrades who have not died in vain – the very opposite of pretentious church-bell religiosity. 'Naturbetrachtung' [Contemplation of Nature] seeks to dispel illusions in establishing a direct link between suppressed capacities for enjoyment and the class system: 'Only when we have won will there be a constant blue in the sky.' Finally 'Kurfürstendamm', a montage of snatches of conversation heard on the fashionable boulevard of that name, reduces love to random reflexes on the periphery of the pursuit of amusement; in uncanny contrast to this: the match-sellers 'of our class'.

With the Four Pieces for Mixed Chorus op. 13 Eisler succeeded for the first time in bringing his political concerns into line with his artistic ones. When they received their first performance in 1929, their impact was felt just as strongly in the working classes as in the reviews of the bourgeois press. In the meantime half a dozen such choruses had appeared: 'Kurze Anfrage (Lied der Arbeits-losen)' [Brief Enquiry – Song of the Unemployed] and – an arrangement – 'Bauernrevolution' [Peasants' Revolution] op. 14, 'Auf den Strassen zu singen' [To be sung on the streets] op. 15, a march-like chorus of agitation, followed by 'Der Streikbrecher'

Ex.6   'Vorspruch' (Four Pieces for mixed chorus op. 13)

Ex.6 *continued*

[The Strikebreaker] and 'An Stelle einer Grabrede' [In Place of a Funeral Oration] op. 17.

'The best proletarian revolutionary music that has yet been produced in Germany' was the praise bestowed by Durus (A. Keményi), the critic of *Rote Fahne*. Allowance had to be made for the technical demands on account of the effect: 'The *boldness* of the choral works met with success.' They 'are of uncommon value for us, since they have brilliantly fulfilled the requirements which have to be laid down by the class-conscious proletariat for a proletarian music *for our times* which will take its place in today's front line'.[82]

The conductor Klaus Pringsheim expressed his enthusiasm in *Vorwärts*:

This is a song of the 'Small Question' of the unemployed. I doubt whether such words, such a text, speaking from the souls of hundreds of thousands, has ever been set to such music or sung in such a way. Never have poet, musician, singer and listener been so at one, as it were. But they are here, because the musician's language convinces everyone.[83]

The opinion of Hans F. Redlich may be taken as representative of the progressive bourgeois critics; this appeared in the autumn of 1929 in *Anbruch*. It shows a characteristic vacillation between admiration for the music's quality and, if not repulsion, then at least strong reservations about its unambiguous political content: at times this is deplored, and at times played down by being given a psychological slant.

These pieces nearly all appeared in the context of a collection of proletarian choruses entitled 'Der Arbeiterchor' [The Workers' Chorus], and at no point is their party-political origin not in evidence. Indeed, more than that, they make the fact of their clearly defined class background the subject of their art: Tendenz, Utopie, Der Streikbrecher, 'Demokratie' – Gesang der Besiegten, Kurfürstendamm – thus the now pathetic, now ironic titles deter any attempt to observe this art objectively. Hanns Eisler would be the first to concede that these extraordinarily concentrated choruses, constructed with unerring assurance, are permeated by a raging demagogy, a power of suprapersonal harangue. It is up to everyone to decide whether the force of politically doctrinaire tendentiousness here exceeds the bounds of what is aesthetically admissible. Everyone should know that these pieces contain a clear revelation of astonishing mastery; it may thus be regretted that the composer has deliberately

endeavoured to limit the sphere of his music's effectiveness, thus depriv-
ing those unable to accept Eisler's party-political limitations, or rather his
fusion of higher art with the demands of the day and of the hour. On
closer inspection of the pieces (I have before me opp. 10, 13 and 17), one
is impressed by the rich formal invention of each single number, and the
technique of choral writing, which goes far beyond anything that the
choral style of recent decades is generally taken to refer to.

   . . . These pieces reveal a collectivist pathos which today should require
no comment, a demagogic rage of political commitment mounting to a
state of ecstasy, and an oratorical persuasiveness of stunning impetus.
And all this is achieved by the simplest four-part writing with undivided
tenors and basses, though it is also sustained by extreme precision of
declamation, passion of dynamic and rhythmic pointing, and total merging of the form with the content, which is incomparable! The subject
matter of the pieces in op. 13 and op. 17 is in general drawn from the
realms of class conflict. The 'Vorspruch' has a polemic against the
amateurishness of the existing choral style and for this purpose uses, in
addition to a mixed chorus, a speaker with a megaphone who gives out a
programmatically explanatory text, and finally a percussion group which
makes a stirring entry. 'Gesang der Besiegten' and 'Naturbetrachtung' –
whose calm and mighty flow ultimately gathers into powerful chordal
writing – are kept both simple and affecting. 'Kurfürstendamm' brings
the polyphonic principle into play. The many voices of a Berlin boulevard
by night are mirrored in the virtuosic intricacies of a witty counterpoint.
The negative pay-off which juxtaposes the ghouls and ghosts of the upper
classes with the matchseller of the lower classes is horribly effective. The
'Streikbrecher' from op. 17 introduces black humour in its treatment for
three-part chorus of the eternal theme of class justice, and 'An Stelle einer
Grabrede' – perhaps the finest of all the pieces – combines simple words
of farewell at a worker's graveside with a gripping polyphonic structure
of an extremely individual kind. The music of these choruses is as unique
as the naturalness of their technique. One thing is certain: the hand that
penned these bars has been tempered in the best of schools. The way in
which musical lines are combined with each other, thematic relationships
elevated into a formal principle, and the whole achieved with the infinite
freedom and delimitation of a music totally emancipated from the figured
bass (though by no means merely atonal) – this is just as remarkable as
the fact that here twelve-tone technique, which forms the basis of Eisler's
technical evolution as a composer, seems to have been completely sub-
sumed in a creation evincing the greatest free play of artistic emotion. In
contrast to other contemporary contrapuntists, Eisler practises a system
of prudent economy in such a way that the happy result is a totally
transparent choral writing, easily manageable from the vocal point of
view and never straying for a single moment into instrumental writing. A

DIE PRESSE UBER HANNS EISLERS CHÖRE

Die Sätze wurden fast der Reihe nach da capo verlangt ... Über die Chöre ist zu sagen, daß sie von glücklicher, ja schlagender Prägnanz sind und deshalb ihren Erfolg ehrlich verdient haben.

Berliner Tageblatt.

Seine Stücke haben einen starken melodischen Impuls, eine Sinnfälligkeit, die doch nicht in Banalität hinüberschlägt. Im „Streikbrecher" ergibt sich ohne Zwang eine originelle Form und das „Auf den Straßen zu singen" ist mit sicherem Griff hingesetzt. Es muß unter dröhnendem Beifall wiederholt werden.

Die Musik hat eine außerordentliche Kraft, sie ist in der melodischen Führung plastisch, im Harmonischen neuartig und interessant. D i e s e S t ü c k e g e h ö r e n i n j e d e n A r b e i t e r c h o r.

Berliner Börsen-Courier.

Ein Stück neue Welt ist Hanns Eislers „Musik für Arbeiter". Kühn sprengen diese Chöre die Fesseln alter Chortradition. Sie sind mehr als billige Stimmungsmache. Im „Lied der Arbeitslosen" und der „Bauernrevolution" hämmert leidenschaftliche Erregung, die ein Künstler mit fliegender Hand aber hellwachem Gehirn zu Gesängen geformt hat; Gesängen, die einen Appell bedeuten.

Vossische Zeitung.

Chormusik für Arbeiter ... die den Stil einer neuen Primitivität mit g e n i a l e r S i c h e r h e i t trifft.

Frankfurter Zeitung.

Eine besondere Arbeitermusik zu schaffen, die aus dem geistigen Horizont des Arbeiters erwachsen wäre und seine bestimmenden Erlebnisse zum Inhalte hätte, sind die sozialistischen Kulturorganisationen in Deutschland lebhaft bemüht ... Eine Sonderstellung unter diesen Kompositionen für Arbeiter nehmen die Chöre von Hanns Eisler ein. ... Sie sind melodisch und harmonisch im allereinfachsten Stil gehalten, für den Vortrag durch wenig geschulte Arbeitergesangvereine, gelegentlich auch durch ungeschulte Menge berechnet (so der eindruckvollste dieser Chöre „Auf den Straßen zu singen"). Doch es liegt Charakter in dieser Einfachheit. Miterleben steht hinter dieser Musik und spricht sich in ihr ohne jede „künstlerische" Prätention unmittelbar aus.

Neue Freie Presse, Wien.

Etwas vollkommen Neues, ein glänzender Wurf, textlich wie musikalisch. Ungewohnte Klangfarben für einen Text, der uns das Gewohntste unverhofft zu Gehör. bringt. Ohne Zweifel ist in Hanns Eisler für den modernen Arbeiter-Chorgesang ein Bahnbrecher entstanden.

Welt am Abend.

Wie ein Blitz schlägt die „Bauernrevolution" ein, sie zeigt Eislers spezifisch - chorische Gestaltungskraft schon auf dem Wege zum Monumentalen hin. Dieser Chor verdiente einen musikalischen Kleist-Preis, gäbe es einen.

Berliner Morgenpost.

Gewaltig, mitreißend sind die Eislerschen Chöre, die durch Worte und den suggestiven Aufmarsch der Stimmen zum musikalischen und menschlichen Erlebnis werden.

Tempo.

Eine ungemein lebendige, glänzend gearbeitete und wirkungsvolle Musik, deren Schlagkraft sich auch diesmal wieder so bewährte, daß eine Zugabe bewilligt werden mußte.

Deutsche Allgemeine Zeitung.

Eisler erreicht den hier zu fordernden Stil einer neuen Primitivität mit schlagender Sicherheit.

Deutsche Tageszeitung.

Bei aller Freiheit der harmonischen Grundierung und Stimmführung stellen sie keine abnormen Schwierigkeiten hin, sind formal einfach und werben mit einer h e r z h a f t e n , e i n d r i n g l i c h e n M e l o d i k — sind nicht Musik nur für ausgewählte Kenner, sondern wenden sich an das Volksempfinden in ihrer Textgestaltung und in ihrem b r e i t e n u n d f r i s c h e n M u s i z i e r e n ... N e u e M u s i k v o n e i n e m K ö n n e r , s a n g b a r u n d w i r k u n g s v o l l.

Leipziger Volkszeitung.

. . . . Eisler schafft aus der Arbeiterseele, aus dem Drange tiefsten eigenen Verstehens. In diesen Werken einen sich künstlerisches und menschliches Empfinden auf das engste.

Volkswille, Hannover.

... wirken die Chorsätze d u r c h F o r m w i e d u r c h I n h a l t s o m ä c h t i g , d a ß s i e d i e S e n s a t i o n d e s A b e n d s bildeten.

8-Uhr-Abendblatt, Berlin.

J e d e s L o b ü b e r d i e k ü n s t l e r i s c h e n F e i n h e i t e n , j e d e A n e r k e n n u n g d e r m u s i k a l i s c h e n G e s t a l t u n g muten ärmlich an.

Arbeiter-Zeitung, Wien.

Als Höhepunkt ein proletarisches Kampflied „Auf den Straßen zu singen", eine Komposition von unerhörter Kraft des Ausdrucks, elementar, von unwiderstehlicher Gewalt.

Diese „Bauernrevolution" hat nun auch vor einer Hörerschaft der Musikfachwelt als Elementarereignis eingeschlagen; es war der große Erfolg des Abends. Dieses Chorstück, echt und stark inspiriert, ist ein ganz großer Wurf von unerhörter Wirkung. Der Bach-Saal tobte.

Vorwärts.

Von einer bis jetzt unerreichten Wucht und Konzentration der künstlerischen Gestaltung sind die neuen Chöre von Hanns Eisler ... Chöre unserer Zeit.

Rote Fahne, Berlin.

Am leichtesten kann man sich bereits vorstellen, an welchen Hörerkreis Hanns Eislers Kantate für den Rundfunk „Tempo der Zeit" denkt, nämlich an die Schichten, die „das schöne Tempo schaffen, aber kaum haben können". Wie alles aus Eislers jüngster Zeit, wird die Musik in den Dienst scharfer sozialer Anklagen gegen diese Zeit gestellt. In seiner lebendigen, eindringlichen Form wendet sich diese Kantate an den Hörer, vermeidet alle billigen Effekte und musiziert gegen Tempo und gesellschaftlichen Schlager. Hanns Eisler, eine der größten Hoffnungen der jungen Volksmusik kann es sich leisten, das Lied vom Tempo nicht im Tempo der Zeit zu schreiben.

Die Musik.

peculiar penchant for bare fourths and fifths, occasional recourse to the
convention of bygone cadential formulae and a highly personal technique
of imitation, avoiding all the mechanisms of academic fugue, frequently
give the pieces a delicate archaic sheen which, together with the calm,
overtone-related harmonization of many sections and the lucidly placed
architecture possibly distracts the listener from the seamier side of
polemical actuality rather more than the composer would care to
admit.[84]

Eisler, then, was by no means isolated from the musical cur-
rents of his time. His recourse to earlier forms of church music, his
penchant for simpler writing and the tendency towards 'utility
music' – all these were trends which corresponded to his attempts
to make his music more and more suitable to the practical demands of workers' choral traditions. In keeping with this, his
evolution towards a more transparent texture with fewer voices
led yet further to monodic, rhythmically accompanied male
choruses. The impression of an often dramatic immediacy was
furthered by the fact that Eisler sometimes juxtaposed and sometimes combined speech-like with sung sections. Naturally, he
'bore in mind smaller choral societies in major cities and the
provinces', as he noted in his op. 19; here, in 'Ferner streiken:
50 000 Holzarbeiter' [Further Strike: of 50 000 woodworkers],
and in the later chorus to a text by Brecht, 'Kohlen für Mike' [Coal
for Mike] op. 35, he probably had his most impressive successes in
achieving intensity through simplification (which also extended
to the music's harmonic style; see ex. 7).

Redlich's reference to 'older cadential formulae', meaning
above all Phrygian cadences, points to Eisler's revival of modal
elements. Schoenberg had drawn his pupils' attention to these as
making it possible 'to introduce variety into the harmony'.
Already in his *Harmonielehre* he had pointed out that major–
minor tonality corresponded to the predominance of the Ionian
and the Aeolian modes, which for practical reasons had ousted all
the others, and yet still harboured 'possibilities other than the
scale': 'These fell into oblivion. Yet they are there, and hence
do not need any preliminary introduction as special cases; they
simply need to be brought out.'[85]

In fact, Eisler did not seize on modal elements in order to enrich

Ex.7 'Kohlen für Mike' (Two Male Choruses op. 35)

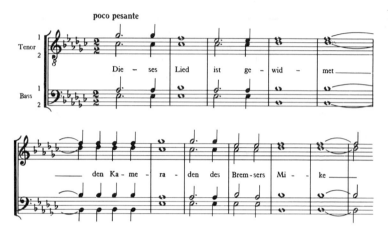

his palette with an unusual (because forgotten) harmonic colour. They rather seemed to him a useful means of recalling what was associated with them: *pre-individual collective consciousness.* Removed from their ecclesiastical context and purified of irrational residues, they were intended to give emotional re-inforcement to what had long been a political need: *class consciousness.*

This marks the essential distinction between Eisler's intentions and the aimless efforts which at that time, inspired by the petty bourgeoisie, sought to give expression to a vague community need by reviving *a cappella* singing. (Their anti-bourgeois pretensions fell on stony ground – until the National Socialists demagogically monopolized them.)

The ascetic function of church music consisted in inspiring a state of devotion and penitent regret, with hope offered as a compensation. For Eisler hope was the driving force of social interaction, and discipline and constructiveness were a *sine qua non* of revolutionary consciousness: this was the opposite of both anarchical individualism and pseudo-religious self-abnegation. Thus his response to the Bach revival of the late 1920s had nothing of the believer's absorption in retrospective contemplation. Tretiakov, who visited him in Berlin in about 1930, reports: 'Eisler leafed through some music on his piano and praised Bach. In him he sought an ally in the fight for the sort of chorus in which the whole public takes part, as opposed to the present-day schism between performers and passive listeners. The high culture of the chorus which unites people, brings them together, conduces to concerted rhythm and concerted movement'[86] – this was to be used politically, and the choruses, in their own interests, were to be transformed into militant organizations.

In his practical realization of this Eisler was helped by a friend who had previously been a fellow student under Schoenberg, and who was one of the most able choral conductors of the time: Karl Rankl. Working as the musical director of the Kroll Opera, he also conducted the Greater Berlin Chorus. His force as both a Marxist and a musical educator can be gauged from the phrasing of a lecture which he gave in 1931 at a course for choral conductors in Berlin. Their task, he said, was 'to collaborate in a new proletarian musical culture which was only now being born'. The chorusmaster must be not only a highly qualified professional, but equally a political functionary. It was necessary to combat clichés of 'sociability', and above all 'patriotic phrases and prattle about "sacred German art"'. He urged the 'cultivation of the pre-classical choral literature', since 'a great proportion of bourgeois music . . . was born of an individualistic consciousness that we reject'. An extreme sense of responsibility is demanded of the chorusmaster of a workers' chorus. For, Rankl concludes, 'he has to deal with the proletariat who, according to Marxist doctrine, must fulfil enormous political tasks within the next decades and will become the pillars of a new human culture'.[87]

Current performing practice was measured against historical demands: this reflected which political prospects were at that time considered either present or imminent. First, knowledge had to be acquired and propagated. For the creation of a new culture meant not only that individuals were to make and share discoveries; it also meant that ideas already discovered were to be worked over critically, 'socialized', and brought into new contexts. The popularization of the ideas of Lenin and Marx was given the highest priority. These formed a binding intellectual and moral tissue, and needed to become living rules of conduct. One possible way of assimilating them – and a particularly effective one – was for the masses to engage in their own artistic activities: choral singing as a collective exercise with emancipation as its aim.

Eisler's attempt to 'Agitpropize'[88] the workers' choruses came during a period of struggle. The singers were no longer to take up attitudes at odds with their own interests. The task of artistic articulation was to gather together their various individual experiences and integrate them as a single class experience. For the composer this 'delegated', controlled task was comparable to political and technological work.[89] It was creative in a new way. Renouncing the outmoded stance of basking in originality, it aspired to the greatest possible *transparency*. Whilst the political intent permeated and rejuvenated the musical form, the music itself acquired an inexhaustible charm.

Militant songs and political ballads

The vigorous circulation achieved by Eisler's *militant songs* from 1929 onwards was directly connected with the great *crisis*. This genre, produced by the desire to intervene in day-to-day political struggles, acquired at that time a disruptive power such as forms of art rarely develop. Response was international – as was the crisis of world economy – and also – on the other side of the coin – the hope that socialism could soon be established on an international basis. The militant songs gave expression to this hope.

The crisis, initially one of overproduction, rapidly assumed political dimensions in Germany after the collapse of the New York stock exchange. The situation became increasingly polarized: impoverished masses on the one hand, financiers and big property owners on the other. The traditional power groups found themselves compromised to a degree that they were no longer able convincingly to justify. A *coup* by the workers' movement seemed possible. But for that it would be necessary to overcome its chief weakness: it was divided.

The controversy between the two workers' parties became acute at just the time when the crisis came out into the open. The grand coalition into which the SPD had entered with the bourgeois parties after the elections of 1928 had already made them official allies of capitalism in the eyes of the KPD. Their consent to the building of battleships, which they had opposed before the elections, added to the picture of militaristic orientation. The ban on demonstrations imposed by the Berlin chief of police Zörgiebel (SPD) was seen by the KPD as being directed above all against themselves.

The leaders of the SPD, on the other hand, considered that since its new leftist line of 1928 the KPD had been following directives from Moscow. They felt that the struggle for dictatorship of the proletariat to which the Comintern was turning as its next strategic objective was an unrealistic venture. They must have construed the thesis of 'Social Fascism', according to which the Social Democrats must be resisted above other parties as the chief support of capitalistic régimes, as a declaration of war. And the establishment by the KPD of the Revolutionary Trade Union Opposition (RGO) seemed to them openly divisive.

In addition there were differences between the right-wing SPD leadership and powerful movements at the grass roots level of the party as well as between the two principal factions within the KPD. The leftist swing of the Thälmann group in 1928, to some extent redolent of a return to the Fischer–Maslow policies of 1924,[90] met with opposition from the 'conciliators' who were largely drawn from the earlier moderates of the KPD. They included Ernst Meyer and Arthur Ewert, Hugo Eberlein and Eisler's brother Gerhart. They were dubbed 'conciliators' because, in the interests of a broad party unity, they opposed the exclusion of the right wing (Brandler/Thalheimer). Above all they stood out against the establishment of trade union opposition groups: this seemed to them indefensible in view of the growth of fascism.

A number of artists sympathized with this group, which was supported within the Comintern by Bukharin, without however allowing themselves to be drawn into factional squabbles. Among them were Hanns Eisler and John Heartfield as well as Robert Gilbert, who wrote the first political song texts for Eisler and was a friend of the editor-in-chief of Rote Fahne, Kurt H. Neusüss. They also shared a common distinct dissociation from the SPD.

However, even at this stage the demand to make socialist art for and with the working masses was hardly reconcilable with precise party-political demarcations.

Eisler, who, though not *de jure* a member of the KPD, campaigned loyally for it *de facto*, wanted, like many artists, to broaden the mass basis of the workers' revolutionary movement. One possible way of overcoming causes of division and schism was to introduce what was common ground in the collective memory: this would constitute a unifying experience from which common interests and goals would emerge. As a composer, Eisler drew from this a consequence whose effectiveness transcended his transformation of workers' choruses: he attempted to replace the traditional *partisan song* by the *militant song*.

It could be held against the partisan songs of the nineteenth century ('Freiheit, wir warten dein' [Freedom, we await thee]) not only that they had been dulled by use: their feeling remained general, politically vague. Their combination of idealism with isolated naturalistic features appealed to sensibilities long past. In the meantime these songs had acquired the effect of an inferior Utopia. Their mission was fulfilled, and they belonged to history.

Militant songs, on the other hand, were distinguished by topicality, concrete and precise political content whose impact was heightened by the music. Their usefulness consisted largely in their adaptable viability: at demonstrations, mass meetings, rallies. A variety of compositional methods was needed in order to establish in a clear and comprehensible way the connections between current events and the ideas of the working class, and to add a dimension of emotional impact. An increase in actual complexity was not compatible with simplicity of musical language. What was necessary was versatility of methods, more concentrated and varied handling of the material.

Eisler wrote his militant songs for the proletariat of the great cities. These people lived in a complex web of industrial relations. Their experiences were dictated by modern industry and the varying forms of capitalist production. Exposure to a multiplicity of simultaneous visual and acoustic impressions affected their responses. Eisler countered the neutralizing flood of stimuli with succinct and forceful concentrated forms. They had of necessity to contend with the new light music, but also with the old workers' songs whose expressive content plumbed the depths of sentimentality.

The sense of immediacy which the militant songs generally achieved with their very opening bars, and the power of organization which they deployed, cannot be dissociated from Eisler's technique of *montage*. Here old and new resources came together in a new kind of association. This applied just as much to songs which rapidly crossed national barriers such as the 'Solidaritätslied' [Solidarity Song] and the 'Einheitsfrontlied' [United Front Song] to texts by Brecht, as to 'Der rote Wedding' [Red Wedding]* and 'Der heimliche Aufmarsch' [The Secret Troopgathering] written by Erich Weinert. The specific 'drive', acceleration and impetus that can be felt in these songs is due above all, from the rhythmic point of view, to their combination of marchlike and jazz elements. Unexpected syncopations are set off against the 'walking crotchets' in the bass of the accompaniment. This feature adds a special elasticity and a bracing springiness to the works' aggressive energy (see ex. 8).

From the early German songs of the sixteenth and seventeenth centuries Eisler took over an asymmetrical manner of constructing his melodies (e.g. 'Solidaritätslied') and changes of metre (see ex. 9). He used modal elements at least as much as in his choruses. And from the Russian revolutionary funeral march he frequently borrowed the alternation of major and minor between verse and refrain. The precisely planned juxtaposition of small contrasting units enabled him to give tangible form to the text's various lines of force. 'Eisler applies and handles his musical material in such a way that he can use it to bring out the greatest possible number of relationships that are of relevance in the text. This applies to the montage of single fragments as well as to his melodies, harmonies, rhythms, scoring and detailed performance indications.'[91] It is from this precision in their emphasis that the militant songs derive their militancy.

The texts of the militant songs revolve around the polarization of friend and foe. Existing evil is seen to be associated with

---

* *Translator's note.* Wedding is a district of Berlin.

7   Eisler conducts a recording session (1931) with Ernst Busch

exploitation, economic crisis and bad management. It is this that must be fought. The necessity – and possibility – for the workers to free themselves depends on solidarity and organization. Action by the greatest number, massive and politically meaningful participation require common thinking and an understanding of the class conflict and its development. The militant songs lend their weight to the difficult process of enlightening the workers about their own interests: they must become aware of themselves in

Ex.8   'Der rote Wedding' (Six Lieder op. 28)

Ex.9   'Solidaritätslied' (*Kuhle Wampe*)

class terms; only then will they be able to conduct themselves politically in an appropriate way.

It is in the text, with its rhyming verses and refrains, rather than in the music that reference is made to established song and ballad forms. This makes the songs easier to retain in the memory. Clear diction is of importance: the texts must be comprehensible on their own and must be adapted to the workers' mental horizons. The authors must deal with topicalities of the day before they can present content of a more far-reaching and general character. The variants to Brecht's text for the 'Solidaritätslied' make this clear. Only the original version of the refrain remains: 'Forward and never forget where our strength lies!/In hungering and in eating,/ Forward, do not forget!/Solidarity!' It was only in the final version that Brecht achieved the larger scale; here the first verse reads: 'Arise, peoples of this earth,/Unite with this thought:/That now she is becoming yours/And the great nourisher.'[92]

The 'Workers' Marches'[93] are closest in their content to the *political ballads*. Eisler did not conceive them as mass songs but for performance by a single singer at mass meetings. Ernst Busch[94] was their unrivalled interpreter from 1929 on. His experience on the stage and in cabaret stood him in good stead for giving point to sarcastic reports whose harsh social criticism often enough blends amazingly well with ballad form. As an example of this we may take Tucholsky's 'Bürgerliche Wohltatigkeit' [Bourgeois Charity] of 1929. In this warning about opportunism and illusion, which Eisler has set particularly stridently, Tucholsky combines aggressive satire with a call to arms:

Look! There is the convalescent home/of a group of joint-stock companies;/in the morning there is oatmeal gruel/and in the evening barley soup./And the workers are also permitted in the park . . ./(Refrain) Fine. That is the Pfennig. But where is the Mark–? II. They hand you down plenty of alms/with pious Christian prayers;/they tend the suffering woman in childbirth,/for they certainly need the proles./They also provide a pauper's coffin . . ./That is the Pfennig. But where is the Mark–? III. The Mark, in its thousands and thousands, has poured into foreign pockets; with a great to-do, the dividends have/been decided by the board of directors./For you the broth. For them the Mark./For you the Pfennig. For them the Mark./IV. Proletarians!/Do not completely fall for the swindle!/They owe you more than they give./They owe you everything! The estates,/the mines and the dyeing works . . ./They owe you happiness and life./Take what you get. But don't give a damn./Think of your class!/ And make it strong!/For you the Pfennig! For you the Mark!/Fight–![95]

Eisler assembled six such works in his *Balladenbuch* [Book of Ballads] op. 18 which was published in 1932 by Universal Edition of Vienna. All the texts take the bull by the horns, from the proletarian point of view. Brecht's 'Ballade zum §218' [Ballad of ¶218], for instance, denounces, along with the paragraph on abortion, the circumstance that it is above all working men's wives that are subject to it. Gilbert's 'Ballade von der Krüppelgarde' [Ballad of the Regiment of Cripples] urges war victims to join a resistance movement against remilitarization. His 'Ballade vom Nigger Jim' [Ballad of Jim the Nigger] depicts racism in the USA in such a light that a German worker can identify it with class antagonism in his own country.

For the ballads Eisler wrote an accompaniment scored for small orchestra. The sharpness of his scoring is new: he used the 'Paris instrumentation'[96] which was akin to classic Dixieland. The sharp, stabbing sounds are produced by the winds: two clarinets, saxophone, two trumpets and trombone; the rhythmic backing is taken care of by banjo, percussion, piano and string bass. Other strings are excluded.

Eisler's political ballads are an adaptable genre: they can be performed before a large or a small audience, either with orchestral accompaniment or simply with a piano to replace it, so that they can be staged anywhere. Often enough Busch appeared with only Eisler to accompany him. His metallic, penetrating voice and his talent for parody made him popular among the Berlin workers. A particular favourite of theirs was Eisler–Gilbert's 'Stempellied' [Song of the Rubber Stamp], which dealt with the worst effect of the economic crisis: mass unemployment. The text, written in Berlin dialect, has this refrain: 'If you're queuing for the rubber stamp/Your troubles won't go away. – Poor man, who is it,/so high up there, who's given you the sack?'

The dividing lines between the ballads and militant songs on the one hand and the 'songs' and political chansons on the other are fluid; and many of them were performed not only at political gatherings but at leftist-bourgeois cabarets and political revues. Authors like Tucholksy, Weinert, Gilbert and Walter Mehring generally wrote with both audiences in mind. The reason for this was the financial situation. For politically committed metropolitan artists, work in cabarets, in the theatre and in film was, along with printed publications, one of the few possible sources of income; for they made available the militant part of their work for nothing, asking no fees or rewards.

Such an attitude, in the absence of any firm point of reference in political practice, can prove extremely two-edged. On the one hand it is thoroughly legitimate. Tucholsky said: 'I cannot join in the game that consists in reproaching someone as follows: he writes verses for proletarians and earns his living as a theatrical producer . . . The communists too live in a capitalistic world.'[97]

On the other hand, an attitude of sitting on the fence can develop into a permanent condition which merely commercializes this very tension. In 1931, in a review of poems by Erich Kästner, Walter Benjamin diagnosed this phenomenon as 'left-wing melancholy'. He does less than justice, not so much to Kästner and Mehring, as to Tucholsky, when he describes it as 'literary mimicry of the disintegrating bourgeoisie':

Politically viewed, its function is not that of parties but of cliques; from the literary point of view not schools but manners; economically not producers but agents. And indeed this left-wing intelligentsia has for fifteen years without interruption been the agent of every intellectual trend, from activism by way of Expressionism up to the *Neue Sachlichkeit*. But its political significance ended with the transformation of revolutionary reflexes, as they appeared to the bourgeoisie, into objects of distraction and amusement which lent themselves to the consumer market.[98]

This 'radicalism', Benjamin continued, was 'precisely the one attitude that no longer corresponded to any action at all'. It was 'in general to the left of what was feasible. For from the start it had no other objective than to enjoy itself in negativistic peace and quiet.' In this way 'political struggle' was transformed 'from an obligation to decide into an object of pleasure'.

Eisler played a decisive part in reversing this process in Brecht's case – from Kurt Weill's 'culinary' librettist into the author of didactic political plays – 'The fact that the mature Brecht begins precisely at the point when his collaboration with Weill abruptly ceased, namely with *Die Massnahme* [The Measures Taken]'[99] of 1930 signifies the split with sparkling leftist-bourgeois radicalism and the embracing of the practice of the workers' movement. Eisler acted as the latter's 'emissary'.[100] He brought the organizational connection and his practical experiences with it to his association with Brecht.

Up till that date, Brecht, who for some years had already been following the 'icy path' of theoretical studies of Marx, had not progressed beyond anarchistic criticism of bourgeois society either in the *Dreigroschenoper* [Threepenny Opera] or in *Mahagonny*. It was from that society that his and Weill's audiences were recruited; with snobbish masochism they applauded what was intended to be destructive as the insolent eccentricities of two young stars.

Tucholsky satirized this state of affairs in his 'Lied der Cowboys' [Song of the Cowboys]: 'Exoticism as a literary programme:/That is comfortable and gets nobody wet/And harms no capitalist./Remington abaft.'[101]

The ineffectualness of such labours which simply provided the great machinery of entertainment with work of better quality, followed by the failure of *Happy End* in the autumn of 1929,[102] strengthened Brecht's conviction that bourgeois art was 'finished'[103] and progressive work needed to take a different direction.

Eisler had seen this three years earlier. In Brecht's eyes he was probably the living proof that new art had 'arrived' with the working masses. He offered the assurance both of the highest technical standards as a musician and conversely of practical feasibility – thanks to his experience with Agitprop, his mass songs and choruses, and his association with the party and the major workers' cultural organizations. In turn, Eisler wanted to win over Brecht, as the most talented poet of his generation, both for the cause of the workers' movement and as the author of the texts of his future compositions. Artistically they had in common an anti-romantic attitude, a rejection of the psychological and the autobiographical, as of artistic metaphysics, and, briefly, the aim of annihilating the bourgeois aesthetic.

Both had in view the 'avoidance of the narcotic effects' of art, the aim to conduct experiments so as to bring it to the height of rationality which would correspond to the scientific age in which they lived, and above all to arm it with a theory which would rationalize the functions of this art. The area in which Brecht was lacking, and in which Eisler had a start on him over and above his association with the workers' movement, was in reflection on revolutionary categories in Leninist thinking such as organization, class conflict and material power. These first became central topics in the didactic plays, *Die Massnahme* and *Die Mutter* [The Mother], on which the two collaborated.

The way was probably paved for Eisler's association with Brecht as early as 1927.[104] Already at the beginning of 1928 Brecht was introducing Eisler to Lion Feuchtwanger and proposing him as the composer for the latter's play *Kalkutta, 4, Mai* [Calcutta, 4 May];[105] to this Brecht had contributed his 'Ballade vom Weib und dem Soldaten' [Ballad of the Wife and the Soldier]; this was Eisler's first (and unquestionably one of his most successful) settings of Brecht.

At this time there was still a vast difference between the positions of the two men, as is clear, for instance, from the Baden-Baden Music Festivals. In 1929 Brecht, Weill and Hindemith offered the didactic play *Der Flug der Lindberghs* [The Lindberghs' Flight], whose adulation of technical progress showed how uncritical Brecht was towards trends of the *Neue Sachlichkeit*.[106] Eisler wrote a radio cantata with Robert Gilbert, *Tempo der Zeit* [Tempo of the Time] op. 16, which exposes in detail where the camouflage in the ideology of *Neue Sachlichkeit* lies: in the supposed neutrality of changes wrought by technology which embraces all classes and brings them closer together through a common goal. Eisler and Gilbert pose the question of *who* is producing the new technological achievements and *whom* will they benefit.

A topical example was the recently inaugurated traffic in civil aviation. The cantata begins with an announcement from a lecturer: '. . . At this time, when the speed of aeroplanes is beginning to rival the speed of the earth's rotation, it is necessary to check up on whether technical progress is being made useful to all and sundry . . .' The answer, given before the closing chorus, is as follows (spoken 'coldly and harshly'):

Who is creating this tempo of the time to make others so comfortable? All of you! With the work of your hands it is created! Make sure that for the others, that is, for the ruling class, it becomes damned uncomfortable! Abolish exploitation! Only then will technical progress serve those who create it. Change the world: it needs it![107]

It may certainly be doubted whether Eisler's adoption of Bachian cantata form was well suited to this subject. The new musical language and Gilbert's topical and in parts parodistic text do produce a stark contrast with the solemnity of the form, though do not entirely contradict it. *Tempo der Zeit*, composed as an experiment for radio, was Eisler's final preparatory step before embarking on his large-scale vocal works.

The great syntheses
Die Massnahme – Kuhle Wampe – Die Mutter

Die Massnahme is the most advanced outpost of political art of the late Weimar Republic. In it, Eisler and Brecht fused the genre each had evolved in his own field into a synthesis which possesses

a lasting power to disturb. A critique of false revolutionary attitudes is here deployed with inexorable logic; it is precisely this
that imbues the conflicts with an impelling and potentially productive power. Perhaps unwittingly the authors took up a challenge of major German theoretical thought: from Kant to Marx,
this has been critical in two respects – it liberated criticism and
reflected on itself (in a critical way).

In his series of didactic plays – a special form of epic theatre –
Brecht arrived at the culminating point in *Die Massnahme*. For
Eisler it was 'only in this new form that an appropriate function'
was given to 'the types of new music which had already come into
existence (such as: complicated polyphonic choruses, monodic
militant songs, speaking choruses, aggressive chansons and ballads)'. This form meant the 'transformation of a concert into a
political meeting' by the combined effect of Agitprop groups,
workers' choruses, orchestras and projected texts. The work was
aimed primarily at the singers themselves: for *Die Massnahme*
'has as its intention to teach not only the audience but also the
performers revolutionary conduct whilst depicting false political
conduct'.[108]

The fact that Eisler's 'monodic militant songs . . . were even
rehearsed with their audiences by particularly courageous
conductors'[109] must have been one of the sources of inspiration
for Brecht's conception of his didactic plays: as a model for
the revolutionary collective's self-understanding and self-
education.[110] Intended as exercises in dialectical method and its
verification, they are distinguished by particularly scanty stage
apparatus. As Benjamin has written, this simplifies 'the interchange between the audience and the actors and between the
actors and the audience . . . Each spectator will be able to become
a participant on stage.'[111]

This was the task facing Eisler and Brecht in 1930: how was
the theory (Lenin's) to be implanted in the awareness of the
proletariat (in teachable form), and, in doing so, what experiences, ideas and feelings could be brought into play? Where
the text had to take into account the current state of political
knowledge, the music had to bear in mind the reminiscences
which were gaining in value through the widespread musical

practices of the time. The 'large-scale form' to which many workers' choruses were devoting themselves at the time was the sacred genre of oratorio and cantata; works of this type were painstakingly rehearsed in keeping with the bourgeois concept of art as a transcendence over the everyday – a substitute for religion.

Eisler and Brecht adopted a dialectical attitude to this subject matter itself, by both rejecting it and using it. In his later theoretical observations on the didactic play, Brecht wrote: 'The imitation of a highly suitable model plays an important role, as does the criticism that must be directed on that model by means of a superimposed counter-play.'[112] The model for *Der Ja-Sager* [The Yea-Sayer], to which *Die Massnahme* originated as an antithesis, was a feudal Japanese play. Its weakness lay in the fact that it might be misinterpreted as a religious play. Brecht, for whom this had been a nasty surprise, appears subsequently to have watched out for this point with especial care. In his theoretical observations, already referring to *Die Massnahme*, he continued: 'It is by no means necessary to deal only with the representation of socially positive and worthwhile actions and attitudes; an educative effect can also be expected from the representation (in as grandiose a way as possible) of asocial actions and attitudes.'

The model that serves as the precedent for *Die Massnahme* is the Christian oratorio: its function is transformed into a political one. This can be detected in a series of direct reversals, both in the music and in the text. '*Die Massnahme* depicts a Party tribunal. The examining committee, represented by the chorus, sits in judgment over four illegal agitators who have been obliged, in the interests of the cause, to kill their fifth companion (a young comrade), who had been too soft-hearted and undisciplined and posed the threat to the Party of a possible catastrophe.'[113] In fact the courtroom setting is merely an external framework which allows objective observation, reporting, presentation and associated commentary. The internal structure, on the other hand – the sequence of scenes – adapts parts of the Christian Passion, reversing its content as well as its message.

Belief, idealism and mortal sacrifice reveal themselves as wrong. Christ's sufferings, held up as an example to be imitated, have their corresponding negative image in the erroneous career of the Young Comrade. The stages of his politically incorrect behaviour are presented in exemplary style. The 'burial', the final scene of *Die Massnahme*, quotes Christian references, particularly as the Young Comrade declares his consent to his death at the hands of the agitators. However, by showing that the shooting of the Young Comrade was a necessary measure – the *ultima ratio* of a desperate situation into which he had manoeuvred himself and his comrades – the reasoning behind this death is laid open to criticism. An *avoidable* fatality – in the context of *correct* political behaviour: this is one of the insights that must be gained, and it retrospectively throws fresh and clear light on the actual moves that add up to incorrect behaviour.

Whereas the Passion presents Christ's suffering as paradigmatic – the divine individual acts rightly, yet is misjudged by the others – *Die Massnahme* criticizes this model as being forbidding, whilst translating it into its own terms. By reason of the fact that the Young Comrade becomes the individual, the one who isolates himself from his anonymous fellow militants, at an inopportune moment, he is in the wrong: he has misjudged while the others have judged correctly.

The relationship of the individual to the collective appears as a reversal of the model and its hierarchy of values. The three levels of the old Passion with Christ at the top, the mass of the people at the bottom and the narrating Evangelist as the intermediary, are matched in *Die Massnahme* by inverted priorities: the masses (the examining chorus) as the highest, the Young Comrade the lowest (ultimately blotted out in the lime-pit), and the agitators in the middle as a small collective and as commentators.

In Eisler's composition, therefore, the detached choruses are given the most weight. Their collective pathos is intended to emerge objectively and untragically. They attempt to replace spontaneous psychological responses to the fate of the Young Comrade with a purified mode of feeling associated with political insight. Every detail of Eisler's suggestions for rehearsal are aimed at countering the ingrained manner of performing oratorios themselves. Above all it is necessary to break with the sort of 'beautiful performance' that relies on identification. 'What should be aimed at is extremely taut, rhythmical and precise singing', as expressionless as possible, 'that is, one must not feel one's way into the music . . . but should present one's notes as if reading a report – like a speaker at a mass rally – hence coldly, sharply and incisively . . . It is of great importance that the singers do not just accept the texts as being self-sufficient, but discuss . . . and criticize them at rehearsals'; the chorus is 'a report for the masses, which conveys to the masses a particular political content.'[114]

In addition to a male chorus and a mixed chorus, Eisler manages with a single tenor and an instrumental group consisting of only brass and percussion. The homophonic writing and the 'almost exclusively modal diatonicism'[115] produce an archaic atmosphere. The rich variety of possible combinations in the deployment of these economical resources and the artificial simplicity give rise to an impetus and a tensile strength which are perfectly suited to Brecht's biblical-sounding language (see ex. 10).

The oratorio as a model represents the enemy position to which they both relate in a polemical manner. It is a vehicle for that religiously slanted emotional residue behind the politically incorrect behaviour of the young revolutionary. Their joint overthrow of the model in music and text, while preserving a continuity with it, creates a complex interplay of the old and the new – form, manner of feeling and rationality – laying them open to a reciprocal critique. Once thus established as an investigative process, the conflict is able to become productive and fertile, to open up the mind to new doctrine and to produce a lasting change in awareness. In *Die Massnahme* the emotional spur – the Young Comrade's death, shown as avoidable – keeps this process in motion. This gets over the problem of using violence as concrete politcal didactic content.

The central piece in *Die Massnahme*, entitled 'What actually is a person?', opens with a report of the four agitators arriving from Moscow on their revolutionary mission in China. 'Every day we fought with the old allegiances, with hopelessness and resignation; we taught the workers to transform the fight for better pay into the struggle for power. We taught them the use of arms and how to fight in the streets.'[116]

8   With friend Karl Rankl, conductor of *Die Massnahme* (1931)

Ex.10   *Die Massnahme*, 'Lob der UdSSR'

Three main points are brought together: a campaign against old ways of feeling and behaving, a shifting of everyday experience into a political perspective, and the need for counter-violence wherever violence rules. It is what the Marxist classics teach about these that the didactic piece aims to present 'in broad images, removed from real life, but having their effect on it'.[117] This was even more urgent at a time when 'the working class' was, as Eisler wrote in 1931, 'in one of the most difficult and complicated periods of its class history, full of conflicts within its own ranks'.[118] His definition of 'art as an educator in class conflict'[119]

envisages its task as that of helping to overcome political confusion and division in a situation seen as revolutionary. In didactical terms: to provide practice in dialectical thought and behaviour. Only in this way can the masses see for themselves the rightness or wrongness of the strategies and tactics practised by their political leaders.

The 'radicalism of the Left', to which Lenin, with West European revolutionaries in mind, had devoted an essay,[120] remained a permanent danger to proletarian movements in the Weimar Republic too. *Die Massnahme* warns of such tendencies, and in doing so expounds passages from Lenin's essay. In connection with the actions of the Young Comrade, to be performed in turn by the agitators themselves, Lenin's analysis of 'petty-bourgeois revolutionism' is referred to. This is characterized by sectarianism which leads to the isolation of the masses, often combined with a resistance to forming a political army out of those who have been deformed by capitalism. The rejection of any politics of realism or of compromise and above all of Party discipline means that this attitude becomes not only useless but damaging too. It fails to comply with that maxim for political action which requires a combination of firmly held principles with flexibility of methods.[121]

In order to exploit the conflict amongst the ruling classes to the advantage of the ruled, in the case of *Die Massnahme* that between the Chinese merchants and the English colonialists, the Young Comrade should have been ready to make compromises. He refused, denying that he was endangering the movement. Incidentally, in this scene, and this scene only, is the bourgeois camp actually depicted, represented by the merchant; in his song about supply and demand he reduces man to 'his price'. The logic of capital is focussed and illustrated by montage – and the music does the same for its characteristic manifestations. Eisler quotes from bourgeois entertainment music. The merchant is caricatured (in a wicked parody of Weill) by squeaking wind instruments in jazz style as he conducts his conversation with the Young Comrade, an arioso of knockabout comedy. The cynicism of his aggressive song is palpably fashioned by Eisler as a perversion of his own militant song style. However for the accompaniment of this solo Eisler calls on a piano as well, a piece of bourgeois furniture *par excellence*.

The music of *Die Massnahme* backs up what is demanded by the text: *abstraction* from what is depicted on stage and, in turn, its *application* – the assimilation of what is understood as the message alongside one's own experience. It is on this account that 'discussion' plays such an important part. To keep it constantly on the move is an essential requirement for a transformation of awareness that is not merely to be superficial. At one point Eisler lays particularly clear stress on this by etching on the memory a Lenin quotation set as a strict canon: 'Cleverness is not making no mistakes, but/knowing how to remedy them quickly'[122] (see ex. 11).

With its first performance in December 1930 in the Berlin Philharmonic Hall, *Die Massnahme* immediately became the 'central topic of proletarian cultural discussions'.[123] As a challenge to political opinion it had an unprecedented effect on both workers and intellectuals. It gave rise to public controversies both within and outside the KPD, and in the bourgeois press as well. There, judgments ranged from 'a work of a prophetic nature'

Ex.11 *Die Massnahme*, 'Lenin-Zitat'

Ex.11   *continued*

(Stuckenschmidt in the *Berliner Zeitung*) to 'intellectual anti-music' (sic! Fechter in the *Deutsche Allgemeine Zeitung*). In the Viennese musical papers of the *Anbruch* we read: 'It is one of the few masterpieces in that area of the avant-garde in which the separation of artistic from political thought is no longer seen as admissible.'[124]

Die Rote Fahne spoke of 'epoch-making significance' and of what was, to date, 'the most mature and artistically perfect choral

work for working men to sing'.[125] Brecht's text was less favour-
ably received in the Party press. He was reproached with a charge
of idealism by those critics who were aware of the antithesis to
naturalism but were unable to grasp what was new in *Die Massnahme*. The piece's 'formal construction' was criticized, as if
Brecht – and his collaborator Eisler – had not expressly constructed a model which could facilitate criticism. The predominant feelings were of mistrust of an author from a different camp,
shot through with admiration for the brilliance of the text.
The association with Eisler, who had already proved himself
in the workers' movement, must have softened some of the
attacks.

The later course of history has imposed an apocryphal existence on this, Eisler's and Brecht's most advanced work. Only
if this course is changed can the work be meaningfully freed from
it.

In *Die Massnahme* artistic work *with* the masses consisted firstly
in bringing together amateur and professional artists, then in
questioning the audience and subsequently holding discussions
with it[126] with the intention of evaluating its criticisms in practical
terms; that is, producing one or more new versions in which the
experiences of the masses would be used even more positively.

In this, Eisler's activities as an organizer were of benefit. In
March 1930, when he was working with Brecht on the text of *Die
Massnahme*, he was already a member of the praesidium of the
IfA,[127] the Interessengemeinschaft für Arbeiterkultur [Com-
munity of Interests for Workers' Culture]. This was the overall
administrative body for this field. Since January 1929 Eisler had
given courses for workers in MASCH, the Marxistische
Arbeiterschule [Marxist Workers' School] (directed by Hermann
Duncker): these had been on the relationship of music to the
proletariat, the social history of music, and the possibility of using
dialectical materialism in analysing the relationship of music to
society. Eisler also collaborated in the BPRS, the Union of Proletarian and Revolutionary Writers, and indeed had done so since its
inception in autumn 1928.[128] Only this dense infrastructure of
workers' organizations in the late Weimar Republic can account

for the immediate strong impact of the new ventures – new in both technique and content – undertaken by Eisler in his militant music and his joint productions with Brecht.

The IfA, founded on the initiative of the KPD, had as its foremost aim the task of overcoming the compartmentalization of cultural work in the individual associations in order to be able to reach the masses outside the context of the organizations as well. Politicization and training appeared all the more urgent as, with increasing unemployment, there was a greater spread of resignation as a behaviour pattern, its products being described by Brecht as 'characteristic of petty-bourgeois riff-raff'.

The abandonment of personal interests, 'the tired and passive assimilation of certain levels of workers into the "quagmire"',[129] these are the warning themes of the first film on which Brecht and Eisler worked jointly:*Kuhle Wampe*. It dates from 1931–2, about the same time as *Die Mutter* which Brecht arranged for the 'epic theatre' from Gorky's novel. As with *Die Massnahme*, the production was by Slatan Dudow; it is marked by film montages of a distinctly documentary type, in the manner of Eisenstein and Pudovkin.

Kuhle Wampe tells first of the fruitless search for work and the (socially motivated) suicide of an unemployed youth 'who cannot make contact with the militant workers'. The second part shows the evacuation of a worker's family to an area of allotments and lays bare the destructive streak in petty-bourgeois behaviour, which goes against their own interests. This is contrasted in the third section with a sports festival and the preparations for it, in which thousands of young workers are united in conflict in the name of solidarity. In the fourth section there is a discussion amongst homeward-bound travellers in a tramcar about a newspaper report of the destruction of the Brazilian coffee harvest in order to maintain prices.

The film juxtaposes the difficulty of solidarity in behaviour under conditions of wretchedness (first half) with the necessity for solidarity in order to be freed from such conditions. It is obvious that changes can only be achieved collectively and in an organized way by people who are united and aware of their own interests. The delicate mental jolt at the end – the destruction of crops for reasons of market stability – is provocative: one's own hunger is seen to be the result of this system.

Self-contained pieces of music separate the four sections of the film as interludes and help to group the episodes. With the opening credits there is rapid, sharp music, 'a polyphonic prelude of *marcato* character',[130] which neutralizes sentimentality right from the start. (In *Kuhle Wampe* the working-class milieu is only referred to and not expanded on, so that social contexts can be recognized and understood in political terms.) With great caution, lyrical content is concentrated in one passage: Eisler's and Brecht's ballad 'Das Frühjahr' [The Spring] is set against shots of the young lovers out walking – 'The play of the sexes is renewed'.[131] However, the most important musical role is given to the 'Solidaritätslied', which helps to structure and sustain the entire second half of the film and with which it ends. Ernst Busch and the chorus of sportsmen workers take turns in singing the verses and refrains with the final challenge expressed as a question: 'Whose world is the world?' (see ex. 12).

In *Kuhle Wampe* the mass effect of the sound film is calculated to combine with that of the militant song.[132] The solidarity to which the film appeals must be one that can provide resistance, can struggle, and will not let the revolutionary goals out of its sights. For the worker-singers this attitude would at that time already mean a stance of opposition and exclusion from the DASB (German Union of Worker-Singers).[133] The latter's executive, by

Ex.12   *Kuhle Wampe*, 'Solidaritätslied'

rejecting a performance of *Die Massnahme* at the Berlin Federal Festival of 1931, had created a climate in which the revolutionary opposition felt it urgent to break away and constitute themselves as a separate group: the Kampfgemeinschaft der Arbeitersänger [Militant Community of Worker-Singers] (KdAS). Eisler and Rankl were its leaders, and the periodical *Kampfmusik* [Militant Music] was published. Here Eisler acquired a direct forum, though admittedly at the cost of communicating RGO [Revolutionary Trade Union Opposition] policies to the singers' front: some years later he was to write self-critically about this.[134]

In 1931, when the situation in the job market was undergoing a further rapid deterioration, there was indeed an increasing demoralization among working men. Their subjective readiness to fight abated. The effect of the split was devastating. Whilst the SPD felt obliged to adopt a policy of the 'lesser evil', giving up more and more ground to the bourgeois parties of the Right, the KPD took up a radical stance. Under the leadership of Neumann and Remmele it steered an adventurous course for a time. Its position was complicated by the fact that it attempted to fight both the bourgeois parties and the expanding NSDAP [German National Socialist Workers' Party] as well as reformism in the SPD, whilst its influence in industry and the trade unions waned more and more after 1930 and it became a party of the unemployed. Despite major victories at the parliamentary elections, it remained in the minority as a workers' party, and in practice had little opportunity for intervention. There was a danger that the connection between economic and political struggle would be severed.

It was this connection that Brecht and Eisler were concerned with in *Die Mutter*. For this reason, in their version of Gorky's novel the portrayal of Russian affairs is played down in favour of those relevant to the immediate requirements of the German workers' movement. What is shown is the importance of learning. The play insists – not without humour – on the untiring efforts that are necessary to acquire for oneself sufficient knowledge for political action. The Mother of the title, Pelagea Vlassova, goes through a process of learning. As the widow of a worker and the mother of a worker she is 'doubly exploited: as a member of the working class in the first place, and a second time as a wife and mother'.[135] The worsening situation drives her to develop political awareness (the historical background is the years 1905–17 in Russia). At last, with satisfaction, she understands that the process which is revolutionizing herself is a necessary one.

When many years ago I was worried at seeing that my son was no longer satisfied, I merely lamented it at first. That changed nothing. Then I helped him in his struggle for kopeks. At that time we went out on little strikes for better pay. Now we are going out on a massive strike at the armaments factory and struggling for political power.[136]

The Mother comes to the party 'only secondarily . . . as a result of theory'.[137] It is precisely her qualities of kindness and humanity that are turned into militancy and solidarity. With the 'third topic', class consciousness, which she comes to master, the mother–son relationship too breaks out of its narrow confines and acquires broader dimensions. In an unusually 'positive' way for a Brecht heroine, the Mother learns correct behaviour through her own example. Her common sense and tenacity, cunning and patience make her a positive antithesis to the Young Comrade of *Die Massnahme*, whose revolutionary impatience and radical spontaneity endangered the movement. In a more traditional way than *Die Massnahme*, *Die Mutter* contains only certain features of the didactic play and does not exclude emotional identification.

For the first performance in January 1932 Eisler wrote nine songs, ballads and choruses, which are today among his best known. They include 'Lob des Lernens' [In Praise of Learning], 'Lob des Kommunismus' [In Praise of Communism][138] and 'Grabrede über einen Genossen' [Funeral Oration for a Comrade], which are not only extremely precise in their thematic and contrapuntal composition,[139] but musically condense the teachings of the play at decisive points and augment the dramatic action.

The music for *Die Mutter* is not theatre music in the usual sense. It develops its own individual gestural quality. For Brecht gesture meant 'specific attitudes of the speaker . . . which he adopts when confronted by others'.[140] Eisler's music goes against the text. It expounds it, displays it objectively, and guards its authentic identity against metaphors and 'mood'. Instead of illustrating it, it takes up a position of contrast towards the text: or, more precisely, to the conventional response the latter might awaken (see ex. 13). Simply because specific images and scenes have so much evolved their own worlds of association, independent of their intended effect, music is able, as it were, to rescue the text from

Ex.13   *Die Mutter*, 'Lob der dritten Sache'

'theatre'. Instead of adding a further, emotional layer, it insists on detachment and allows the listener the pleasure of additional discoveries. This heightens his interest in the proceedings and makes him critically alert. He can find criticism thoroughly pleasurable. Music awakens the appetite for understanding, at the same time retaining its independent role in the partnership; initially it draws attention to itself as being more sensually attractive, and only then permits (specific) access to the text.

Without music it would hardly be possible to fulfil the exalted demand of writers to show everyday things as historically significant. Brecht writes:

> More consciously than in any other play for the epic theatre, in *Die Mutter* the music was calculated to instil in the spectator [a]. . . critically observant attitude. Eisler's music is by no means what one would call simple. As music it is fairly complicated, and I know none other of such seriousness. It admirably facilitates certain simplifications of the most difficult political problems which it is of vital importance to the proletariat to solve. In the little piece where the charges that Communism is paving the way for chaos are answered, the music's gestures of friendly advice could be said to express the voice of reason [see ex. 14]. In the piece 'Lob des Lernens', in which the question of a seizure of power by the proletariat is linked with the question of learning, the music provides gestures that are heroic, and hence of natural cheerfulness. Thus, too, the final chorus, 'Lob der Dialektik' [In Praise of Dialectic], which could easily have the effect of a purely emotive triumphal hymn, is kept within the confines of the rational by the music [see ex. 15]. (It is a common mistake to assert that this sort of – epic – presentation rejects emotional effect altogether: in point of fact its emotions are simply purified, avoiding the subconscious as their source and eschewing excesses.)[141]

In *Die Massnahme* theories are 'transmitted from the music' in a series of pieces to be used as a medium for struggle by vigorous choirs singing at the top of their voices. The choruses were of 'organizational character'.[142] *Die Mutter* calls on a less massive and more varied use of the medium. Not only Eisler's particular speech melodies but above all the rapid and energetic alternation of chorus and solo singer or speaker made a considerable impression at the time. The principle of dialogue and discussion extended right down to the regular alternations between voices and instruments (as in 'Lob des Lernens').[143]

Ex.14   *Die Mutter*, 'Lob des Kommunismus'

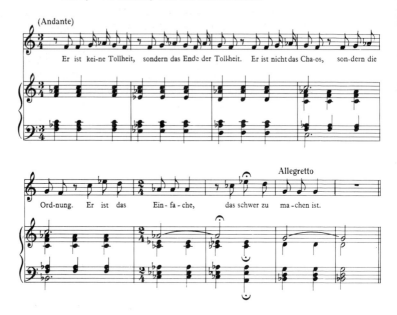

This corresponds to the complex process of assimilation in the play: that of the individual to the revolutionary collective – a way that at first is paved with protests. As in *Die Massnahme*, the choruses represent the Party, understood as the advance guard of the class. In common with those of Greek tragedy, they provide social generalizations and advice which, in Brecht, as 'eulogies', display the formal characteristics of odes and hymns. From the great tradition of European music Eisler uses above all Bach's treatment of continuo and ostinato, as for instance in the 'Grabrede', a 'striding' piece of Passion music.

The music of the 1932 version concludes with the chorus 'Die Partei ist in Gefahr' [The Party is in Danger]. The call to strengthen its ranks is interwoven with the current warning. The *way* in which Eisler combines the oppositions inherent in the text – weakness and doubt of the individual, necessary common militancy – in only two melodic lines, contrasting these rhythmically,

Ex.15   *Die Mutter*, 'Lob der Dialektik'

Ex.15 *continued*

until the appeal becomes irresistible, shows not only his mastery of his craft but also the responsibility of his artistic work (see ex. 16).

In the way that it relates to the text, Eisler's music is a *music of argument*; and herein lies the secret of its power to convince. The compositions in *Die Mutter* display this quality raised to a new level and show up the absurdity of other alternatives, such as that which tries to complement self-sufficient music with declamatory assertiveness. The intention is to bring together artistic and political requirements. Those works in which Eisler and Brecht

Ex.16   *Die Mutter*, 'Steh auf, die Partei ist in Gefahr!'

felt they had succeeded in this they called '*brauchbar*' (*usable*).[144]

With *Die Mutter* they sought to use an exemplary figure to link the pre-revolutionary phase of the Russian industrial proletariat with the current experiences of the German workers who constituted their public. They wanted to help to strengthen both their *collective memory* and their *power of resistance*. This was all the more necessary since fascism, giving itself out as a 'national revolution', was becoming increasingly strong and was beginning to win over the working masses as well as the petty bourgeoisie.

In May 1932, when Brecht and Dudow were present in Moscow at the film première of *Kuhle Wampe*, Eisler travelled to the Soviet Union in order to write the music for Joris Ivens' documentary film *Die Jugend hat das Wort* [Youth has the Floor].[145] He reported on the creation of a federation of steel works in Magnitogorsk (Urals) by young members of Comsomol, and addressed the youth of the world: as an example, he wanted to show the vitality and liberated energy with which the youth brigades built up socialism; and at the same time, how new forms of work created new kinds of people. Eisler picked up 'industrial sounds and folk songs of the local national minorities on the spot' and used them for his score, 'in which original sounds, music and singing are joined seamlessly together'.[146]

The text for the *Ural-Lied* [Song of the Urals] in this film is by Sergei Tretiakov. At that time Eisler was planning to write an opera with him.[147] Tretiakov was the Soviet artist with whom Eisler and also Brecht were in closest agreement. They sought an operational art and an aesthetic devoid of illusion and avoiding 'effects of intoxication'. Precisely because they were sensitive to the mechanisms of emotional integration in bourgeois art and culture (even in their degenerate, trivial form), they stood out for new formal means that could represent the forces capable of changing reality. Previous 'methods are exhausted, their attractions are spent'.[148] The techniques of artistic production should no longer be backward-looking. A new relationship to the (increasingly documentary) material and its construction was now necessary. The most important questions now were who was to

9   With Joris Ivens (centre) and John Ferno in Magnitogorsk (1932)

benefit from the result and in what way. Planned experimentation in search of new methods, the montage of old and new elements better able to define the social nature and tendency of the product, these now became as important to artistic creation as analytical preparatory work was to science.

Eisler's strategical goal was by no means merely a new musical 'style', but a socialistic musical culture.[149] For the period of transition and militancy he demanded that the composer should not be content to trust in his spontaneous ideas and his technical ability. The traditional practice of seeking out a subject through which to impart one's 'message' – hoping for the public to 'understand' it – appeared inappropriate. The new methods of musical technique should firstly do away with whole complexes of ideas and listening habits, and secondly – assuming that the composer joins in the movement of the revolutionary masses – give expression to the new historical processes and contradictions: to help people to recognize what has not yet come about and to announce unknown possibilities which can at first only be sensed.

This goes as far beyond the theory of art reflecting reality and its simplified mechanistic scheme of a foundation and superstructure as it does beyond the 'revolutionary romanticism'[150] that was beginning to mark productions of that time, which – despite claims to the contrary – maintained art's contemplative relation to reality (and to its own recipients).

The radical and *critical* basic intention relates in exactly the same way to the musical heritage. Eisler considered that in a time of struggle it was '*a priori* a vain effort' to win 'for the workers the music of feudalism and . . . of the bourgeoisie' without questioning it:

for in the economic situation of the workers it is impossible ever to adopt the attitude towards art taken up by the bourgeoisie. This is the old classic mistake of the reformist point of view which of necessity leads to compromises, and which also of necessity plays off a more aesthetically worthwhile material against what is politically more worthwhile, and thus, without wishing to, advances the aims of the bourgeoisie.[151]

As a consequence, during this period, Eisler composed neither chamber music nor concert songs and rejected the symphonic manner because it produced predominantly individual psychological effects. Instead he developed methods of composition through which he could, with apparent violence, set about annihilating the charm of identification and the immediacy of beautiful sound: to the end that music and text could once more be experienced *consciously*. Since music reaches the understanding by way of the emotions, it should help to clarify and unify the *passions* without which political revolutions are impossible. The association of music and text should make transparent the new vision of the world, so that it can be accepted rationally, and at the same time prepare for the conflicts which must precede its realization. In addition to organizing his composing, this meant teaching and laying his political and aesthetic strategy open to discussion.

At that time Eisler was, in his own view, a Leninist, and hence an organic intellectual of the working class, as defined by Gramsci. His *association* with it was the source of a common way of thinking. This means he was no longer the sort of specialist from outside who contributed his artistic or theoretical know-

ledge and abilities as a partner in an alliance, but who generally
only exercised his special function in one of the superstructural
sectors and hardly continued to be an independent political thinker. For *class consciousness* can neither be acquired in an abstract
way outside or above the class, nor does it properly already exist
in the form of a party of the Leninist type that is *a priori* deemed
correct. Rather it must constantly be renewed and it is precisely
here that the task of the intellectual lies as a pivot between the
foundation and the superstructure.

The responsibilities of artists go beyond 'what' they produce: a
lasting change of consciousness can only be effected by something
communicating more than formal and technical innovations,
which in turn must be evolved from social aims. This is the *prior*,
and the form the *prius*, and for this reason too a high technical
standard is a prerequisite of artistic work. Tretiakov sums up his
experiences with early revolutionary art as follows:

To move from form to social definition, and not the reverse, proved to be
historically correct. Those who went the opposite way, trying to construct the things that were necessary in our day and in doing so ignoring
their material and its properties, very easily fell back into the old aesthetic
routine, and thereby produced work that was not only meaningless but
even actually harmful . . . Of course, on the other hand, it was necessary
to take into account those groups of people working with material, who
stopped half-way and were not able to apply their knowledge of the
material's properties to the necessary tasks of the day . . .[152]

As far as composers were concerned, this indicated fairly exactly the difference between Eisler and Weill, as was seen by Brecht
too. Weill's surrealistic plunge into brilliant anomalies, Romantic
ambivalence, allowed his alienations to take on their own life: the
alienated reality never returned in recognizable form. Weill's
attitude remained negativistic, self-indulgent, intuitive. The
stance of Eisler's works at this time was both resolutely destructive (of bourgeois values that had become threadbare) and constructive, in that they put into practice and rendered tangible ideas
of collective activity under new circumstances.

Looking back over the political artists of the Republic, Brecht
found Eisler 'the most successful example of popularity' for the
very reason that 'his practitioners were the popular masses'.[153] He

was the pupil of a teacher who had made music so mathematical that his works were accessible only to a few fellow professionals. But the pupil turned to the great masses. Only a few virtuosos could perform Schoenberg's pieces, but millions performed Eisler's ... The pupil worked ... in assembly rooms, sports arenas and large theatres ... Everything political was alien to the work of the teacher; there were not even allusions concerning his preference for monarchy; in the works of his pupil, not a single one of his political ideas is absent.

The coincidence of a revolutionary era with his own talent and training enabled Eisler to write an internationally viable music which might rather have been expected to come from the country of the October Revolution. Instead it was composed by a musician who was deeply indebted to both Viennese Schools – the classical one and that of Schoenberg. The historical change – from the refinement of a dissolving late-bourgeois culture to the aggressive art of the rising class – did not happen of its own accord, as a natural transition: it came from the efforts of an individual. For this reason, Eisler demanded that 'the modern composer . . . *must change from a parasite into a fighter*'.[154]

3
Fifteen years of exile

Bases in Europe

On the invitation of Anton Webern, who wanted to perform some of his works and to rehearse *Die Massnahme*,[1] Eisler travelled to Vienna in January 1933. He could not have foreseen that this was the beginning of a fifteen-year exile for him.

The danger of reverting – from a militant artist into a leftist-bourgeois avant-garde specialist – increased steadily as the difficult circumstances of his emigration persisted. That neither Eisler nor Brecht ultimately yielded to this danger cannot be explained away simply by reference to their political convictions alone. Both were particularly hard-hit by being deprived of their German public, because, since 1930, their combined forces had been devoted to developing a new type of art which was to make direct communication with the masses possible. Their disappointment over the (not inconsiderable) proportion of the working class that were 'falling into the trap' of Nazi demagogy[2], as well as their dissatisfaction with the inconsistent tactics of the KPD, might certainly have given rise to an attitude of patient reticence. The pressure to renounce the political and artistic positions they had reached in *Die Massnahme* and *Die Mutter*, and the increasing Stalinization of the Soviet Union which was also not without its effects on the arts: all this in the long run invited them to retreat on to more traditional ground – to write moderately critical but very distinctly individual works which could attract attention by virtue of their technical standards.

In 1933 (or subsequently) there could be no question for Eisler, or for Brecht, of emigrating to the Soviet Union. That country, in which they both found much to admire and of whose historical pioneering role they were always mindful, remained foreign to them in many respects. Its civilization was still distinctly backward compared with those of European countries. Neither could have expected more than a limited appreciation of their artistic intentions; their links with Tretiakov and a few friends would have given them all too frail a platform from which to infiltrate those artistic movements that were increasingly regressing from the early revolutionary phase. Moreover, neither Eisler nor Brecht (who were not Party members) was invited by the KPD to emigrate to the Soviet Union.

By contrast, the artistic life of those countries in which exile seemed to them possible was dominated by the laws of the market-place. This meant pressure to become a 'star', to have one's name constantly in the public eye, and to procure the commissions and invitations which could guarantee one's material existence. The cultivation of contacts with the bourgeois culture industry, and the need to be prepared for compromises, bordering on the unacceptable, were virtually unavoidable. The need to commercialize one's own originality (sticking to one's formulae whenever possible) could not always even be complied with, if there was no demand.

The circumstances in which Eisler and Brecht went into exile were not altogether unfavourable. At the early age of thirty-five, they had a reputation in both camps: in the international workers' movement, as a result of its extensive cultural organizations; and in bourgeois artistic circles as innovators in fields such as film music, theatre and dramatic theory. Admittedly, this twofold image was by no means uncomplicated; yet not only was it to prove the economic salvation of the two, but it was also to prove extremely fruitful artistically. Both made use of the contradictions of their own situation and introduced scepticism and hope as expansions of their political topics, which now became more complex; for almost everywhere the transition to socialism was being deferred.

The transfer of power to the fascists – which the latter proclaimed as a national uprising – in the Germany of 1933 spelt a 'solution to the crisis' as far as capital interests were concerned and a catastrophic defeat for the German (and later also the European) workers' movement. It was now necessary for them to redirect

their campaign away from its defensive position. From the summer of 1934 the KPD promulgated its strategy of a *united front*,
and from 1935, together with the Comintern, that of a *people's
front* against fascism.

The first wave of emigrants met with not a little sympathy.
Public opinion in the European countries was still reacting
sharply to the announcements from the German Reich. Shock
succeeded shock 'in violent bursts': the Reichstag fire, the burning
of books, the Dimitroff trial, reports of torturing, executions and
anti-semitic crimes. Intervention from abroad still seemed possible since the Nazi leadership was considered by no means consolidated (a view shared by the majority of emigrants too); rather,
the predominant view was that this was a radical right-wing
interlude of limited duration.

One of the centres for counter-propaganda in Paris was the
group centred on Willi Münzenberg, who was continuing the
work of the IAH there. It assisted in founding and directing the
international aid committee for victims of German fascism and
the German Library of Freedom. The Münzenberg Press, to the
extent that it was still operative, joined the anti-fascist campaign.
The same aims were pursued by the Editions du Carrefour, which
he took over in 1933 and quickly made into one of the most
important of the exile publishing firms.

It was this firm that early in 1934 published Bertolt Brecht–
Hanns Eisler: *Lieder, Gedichte, Chöre* [Songs, Poems, Choruses].
This jointly prepared volume contained an extensive musical
supplement and was intended above all for practical use: as an
Alternative Songbook. Its immediate usefulness must have been
seen by its authors in terms of singing and recitation – by either
individuals or groups – at rallies. Its public was envisaged as not
only émigrés but also resistance fighters within Germany to whom
it was possible to forward copies via the Saar region. The book's
'very favourable' reception was evident from early on. To his
friend in Skovbostrand (Denmark), Eisler wrote that orders 'have
already been placed for 700 copies *before* publication'.[3]

The political content of this small, handy collection is characterized by a refusal of idealistic alternatives. Mind versus mindless-
ness and culture versus barbarism could only remain abstract

slogans in the face of the fascist mobilization of the masses. The first priority was not to complain about the official destruction of their own books, music and records, which could now be reproduced in Germany only illegally. The first priority was now much clearer: it was to recognize that the Nazi terror, militarization and a state of apparent war were proceeding apace with increased exploitation of the proletariat. Its situation had deteriorated. Its needs, but also its responsibilities after the largely blinkered attitudes of the crisis, had grown. And, as a result, its delusions threatened to multiply: Nazi propaganda was attempting to cover over and disarm class opposition with the whitewash of the 'people's idealism'.

The aim of the book was to keep alive political solidarity, which was more than ever being punished with violence. Thus, alongside the 'Lied vom Klassenfeind' [Song of the Class Enemy], the satirical Hitler chorales and the bitter critique of the 'cheapening of the world' by complaisant intellectuals, there is a counterbalance of thoroughly positive groups of songs. One such group contains songs and choruses from *Die Mutter* and *Die Massnahme*; another the Wiegenlieder für Arbeitermütter [Lullabies for Proletarian Mothers], which Eisler set as 'calmly flowing' speechsong, exalting kindness and decisiveness[4] (see ex. 17).

The 'Ballade vom SA-Mann' [Ballad of the Storm-trooper],[5] about the starving fellow-traveller, acquires only through Eisler's music that dark inescapability and ponderous menace which make the warning directly palpable. In the 'Ballade vom Baum

Ex. 17   Wiegenlieder, 'Als ich dich gebar'

Ex.17   *continued*

und den Ästen'[6] [Ballad of the Tree and the Branches] the music
contrasts its rendering of the vulgar brutality of the Brownshirts –
as an occupying army in their own land – with the dreadful
ending for which they will be called to account (see ex. 18).

The volume *Lieder, Gedichte, Chöre*, clearsightedly enough
assembled during the first year of his emigration, was also to
provide Eisler with the texts for his largest anti-fascist work: the
Deutsche Sinfonie, whose composition he began a year later.

Leaving Vienna in 1933, Eisler went to Czechoslovakia[7] and
thence to Paris in order to work on a film by Georg Höllering and
Jacques Prévert.

Victor Trivas, for whose pacifist film *Niemandsland* [No-
Man's Land] he had written the music in Berlin in 1931, had made
a new film of Paris street scenes: *Dans les rues*. For this rather
mediocre film Eisler wrote some music which was particularly
applauded by the critics, and from which he shortly afterwards
drew his fifth Suite. His chanson 'Mon oncle a tout repeint' from

Ex.18   'Ballade vom Baum und den Ästen' (Four Ballads op. 41)

this film was to become popular; it was sung by Marianne Oswald
(a friend of Prévert's) and was issued as a gramophone record.[8]

Far more important from both the political and the artistic
points of view was Eisler's second collaboration with Joris Ivens,
which started at that time. This produced what has today become
a classic in the history of documentary cinema: *Nouvelle Terre*
[*New Earth*]. On 10 August 1933 he wrote to Brecht: 'I am at
present synchronizing the fabulous *Zuyder-Zee* of Ivens. This is
going to be of really high quality . . .'[9] He has 'done the whole of
the end of the text as well', he adds.

In its original version the film shows how, by building an
enormous dyke, part of the Dutch Zuyder-Zee has been dried out
and new, fertile land obtained. Eisler proposed a topical last act,
or rather a finale which throws into question the entire film up to
that point and lays it open to discussion. To this, Ivens wrote:

At the climax after the closing of the dyke we see the draining-out, the
new land, the first buildings, the first sowing at the place which used to be
the bottom of the Zuyder-Zee. And then the first harvest is shown . . . full
of joy and happiness that the sea has finally been conquered and the 'New
Earth' has brought forth such wonders. But then the commentator
brutally bursts this bubble of hope:
*But the crops did not serve for nourishment, but for speculation. There
was too much grain and not enough work.*

Suddenly the film's perspectives broaden on to the whole world; the
international stock exchanges are shown and the games which they play
with the needs of people. The harsh voices on the film's soundtrack form
a dialectical counterpoint to the images. Over the pictures of plentiful
cornfields we hear the slogans of the hunger marches in London and
Berlin, and over the newsreel photographs of the hunger marches we hear
the cry of the Bavarians: 'We are drowning in corn!' Over the wan face of
a hungry child on the screen the soundtrack gives the market prices for
corn on the stock exchange. As the perspective broadens to take in more
of the international situation and the contradictions become more obvious, the commentary and images make bigger and bigger jumps. 'In
Manchuria six thousand people are starving to death. Mr. Legg, the
President of the American Farmers' Union, says: A fatting pig eats as
much corn as a family of five consumes. Give the corn to the pigs. Corn is
too cheap!' The following sequence showing the destruction of foodstuffs
is introduced by the grunting of a pig which has been overwhelmed with
corn on Mr. Legg's instructions. And as the tragical absurdity of the

situation becomes increasingly clear, the film closes with a satirical ballad
. . . [of the Grain Dumpers].[10]

It was not least because of Eisler's decisive intervention that
Ivens in *New Earth* hit upon what was later to be his major theme:
that of collective *work* as a double fight: *for* mastery over nature
and *against* the exploitation of man by man. Elements combined
in *New Earth* include positive as well as shocking themes: the urge
towards mastery over nature – as shown in *Die Jugend hat das
Wort* – and that type of crisis that makes every effort vain, as
in *Kuhle Wampe* (from the score of which Eisler re-uses some
passages).

The film also represents a venture into unexplored technical
territory in its method of combining screen montage with sound
montage. Here Ivens and Eisler were in particular developing
experiments made by Dziga Vertov. Space and time are treated as
raw material for a new type of construction; an integral cohesion
of meaning is formed out of what started as widely separated
material. The rhythm of the film-cutting, the use of trick camera-
work and the speeding-up or slowing-down of frame sequences
are applied systematically as compositional elements. The latest
work in acoustics permitted the recording and mixing of music,
synthetic sound effects and original sounds;[11] this in turn allowed
them to be related in an independent and multifaceted way to the
visual events.

It is precisely by means of its complex montages that the film
acquires that *added* reality, that effect on the spectator of being
catapulted into the action, which causes him to look further than
the facts and to translate the political message, the meaning of the
thing, into the terms of his own situation. Obviously integrity and
a sense of responsibility towards the public are essential on the
part of the artists.

In every respect *New Earth* is a film of its times – times of crisis.
There could scarcely have been any other way of exposing so
unambiguously the principal contradiction of bourgeois society
than by using these new formal methods. The collision is at once
pure and devastating: on the one side the triumph of the joint
activities of workers and engineers as a victory over nature; on

the other side their reward of redundancy in a society which behaves as if the interests of realizing capital take natural precedence over those of the workers, who are regarded as a mobile work-force to be employed or dismissed as requirements dictate. Ivens reports that at first the French censors did not pass the film – for the following revealing reason: 'c'est trop de réalité'.[12]

At the same time Eisler was pursuing a more neutral form of didacticism with a series of pedagogic instrumental pieces. Their aim was to train musical thinking and listening and to set tasks in technical performance. In Paris in 1934, Heugel published two volumes of *Petits Morceaux pour les enfants* (op. 31); their freshness of manner is permeated with echoes of keyboard pieces of the eighteenth century. Shot through with the serene transparency of the Enlightenment, the pieces take children thoroughly seriously: as small adults.

Another work with a pedagogical aim is the *Präludium und Fuge über B-A-C-H* for string trio op. 46. Completed in June 1934 and published in 1936 by Hermann Scherchen's journal *Musica Viva* in Brussels, it aims to 'demonstrate to young musicians that it is possible to make simple, easily understood and logical music using the twelve-note technique'. In this 'practical' investigation of the material, what is original is the way in which Eisler here overcomes self-imposed academic obstacles: he treats the B-A-C-H motto in sequence to produce the row, and casts the work in triple counterpoint.[13] Like the rules of any game, these factors create obligatory conditions to which the composer must submit. This involves restrictions. But within these restrictions, any desired combination may be unfolded. Compositional invention is liberated by the fact of being subjected to rules. Necessity and freedom enter into an exciting relationship: in this way, traditional formal knowledge must learn to think in terms of new procedures.

Even so, the largely 'correct' writing of the trio is scarcely typical of the manner in which the exiled Eisler increasingly turned back to twelve-note technique. Since his first essays in serialism (ten years previously in *Palmström* op. 5) he had manipulated dodecaphonic rules somewhat freely. This attitude only became widely established at a later date. In 1938 Ernst Krenek wrote:

However, it is . . . to be expected that twelve-note technique . . . will become freer. Composers will no longer use the whole row incessantly, but will take characteristic groups from it, permit particular variants in specific situations within the chosen row, and so forth . . . In other words, it is to be supposed that after the strict training it has been through in twelve-note technique, atonality is approaching its state of first maturity in which it has no further need of this self-contained apparatus. What it learnt through twelve-note technique, namely its wealth and density of motivic relations . . . will become second nature to it.[14]

The outer movements of the *Kleine Sinfonie* op. 29 may serve as an instance of this. Eisler had already begun work on this *anti-symphony*, which is compressed into a time-span of ten minutes, in Berlin in 1931. When he completed it in London in the winter of 1934, it was no longer simply a work of protest 'against the inflated, turgid, neoclassical style of music';[15] but rather a symphonic montage whose parodistic gestures contain something of the contradictions of the most recent developments in Germany in the form of protest and indictment (see ex. 19).

The two central movements are drawn from works of theatre music of the final years under the Weimar Republic, though their role is considerably changed. While in the *Allegro assai* of the second movement the sounds of militant songs are fused in symphonic writing, the third movement, headed 'Invention', sounds like a satire on, in Brecht's phrase, 'Tui-Intellektuelle'.* In a dialogue between strings and a brass duo (with wa-wa mutes!) Eisler imitates the bla-bla of their melancholy chatter, that repressed narcissistic babbling in an indistinct register. It is an example of that subtle wickedness which cuts to the quick and gives satire its real sting.

First given in April 1935 by Ernest Ansermet in a broadcast from London, Eisler's *Kleine Sinfonie* was to become one of his most frequently performed works. It also rapidly established itself

---

* *Translator's note.* A contemptuous term coined by Brecht from the letters I(n)T(ellekt)U(elle); may be roughly translated as 'intellectual poseurs'.

Ex.19   *Kleine Sinfonie*, fourth movement

in the Soviet Union, as – not without satisfaction – he reported to
Brecht in July 1935:

It is particularly nice that the greatest musical bigwig in the USSR, Mias-
kovsky, on whom everything here hangs, is enthusiastic, above all about
my symphony, which of course is now being played here, and he is going
round telling everyone that it is the most magnificent piece he has ever
heard. This oral propaganda by the official representative of Soviet

music, whom I have always opposed as a reactionary and with whom I
have had the greatest disagreements, is enormously favourable for me.
Now I am not simply viewed as a revolutionary composer but as a great
foreign specialist. This also shows how wrong my tactics here were when
I thought one had to shut up the old bigwig with technical achievements.
Since in addition to my international popularity I am now esteemed as a
symphonic technician, my position has improved vastly . . .[16]

The work which has remained the least known of those which
Brecht and Eisler wrote together, and which contains many of
their most successful marriages of text and music, is *Die Rundköpfe und die Spitzköpfe* [The Round-heads and the Pointed-
heads].

In 1932, before their emigration, they had begun work on an
anti-fascist play – initially in the form of a comedy directed
against reformism.[17] Their model was Shakespeare's *Measure for
Measure*, of which Brecht intended to prepare a new version.
When, in February 1934, Eisler visited him in Denmark, a
thorough rethinking was necessary for two reasons: the course of
events within Germany, which required explanation, and the
changed conditions of theatrical production in exile.

One year after the German workers, the Austrian workers
suffered their heavy defeat; the unfavourable outcome of the
February campaigns meant a further advance of the fascists.
News arrived of growing anti-semitism. Racist ideology was a
further factor that obscured an inadequately developed class
consciousness. Against this gloomy background Brecht and Eisler
resumed work on the play. Furthermore they had to take a different theatre audience into account: the predominantly bourgeois
audience of the major European cities. This audience expected wit
and originality of plot, rapid changes and sharp contrasts, scintil-
lating dialogue, episodes of virtuosity and witty exposures of
impostors.

Nevertheless, in the new version, militant (and didactic) features were not altogether neglected. It had to be made clear *why*
the Nazi movement had apparently succeeded in replacing *class*
struggle with *race* struggle. The play depicts this as a temporary
distraction engineered by a radical ideologue and his followers in
the interests of capital, whose stability is uncertain. (The 'final

solution' of the Jewish question was at that time impossible for the authors to foresee.) Success becomes possible because of delusion and false attitudes on the part of the opposition: its members find that individual alternatives have a boomerang effect. At best one sacrifices one's comrades instead of oneself; and the situation is necessarily worsened by abandoning the common fight.

False consciousness – active and passive, as manipulation and as failure to understand – assumes a complex and contradictory guise in the attitudes of the characters. In order to retain the clear distinction between what is correct and what is false, Brecht made use of *parable* form. This preserves the ability to see things in terms of an overall picture and permits *abstraction*. Only in this way could racism and the phrases of the 'people's community' be kept separate through all the ramifications of events. In order to make it possible to get a better view of the action, it was placed at a distance: the fictional setting is South America, with the proletarians represented by tenants and their adversaries by landowners. The enmity between Round-heads and Pointed-heads, between 'Tschuchen' and 'Tschichen', between Aryans and Jews is shown, on the other hand, as a fiction for which the man-in-the-street has to pay.[18] Whether it is the landlord de Guzman or the tenant Callas: their actions are not motivated by their 'character', but by the fact and 'to the extent that they are *personifications of economic forces*, the representatives of specific class relationships and interests'.[19]

It was in connection with this play that the concept of *alienation* (*Verfremdung*) first appeared in Brecht in a systematic way. By means of acting techniques and visual and acoustical separation, specific phenomena 'are isolated (alienated) as being self-contained scenes outside the domain of the everyday, the natural and the expected'.[20] Alienation derives from the principle of constructional *montage*: it interrupts the existing continuity so as to create a new and open one. Only in this way is it possible to work documentary material into the play and to unleash fresh dynamic forces from the new tensions set up between the individual and his environment. In the age of technology, montage becomes the chief principle of the artistic imagination because 'true reality has subsided into the functional';[21] only by renouncing traditional effects of illusion can it be reproduced.

In Brecht's strategical concept, music acquires an extremely important role in this. Of the music in *Rundköpfe und Spitzköpfe* he writes: 'This music too is in a certain sense philosophical . . . it avoids narcotic effects, chiefly by linking the solution of musical problems with the lucid and clear elaboration of the political and philosophical meaning of the poems.'[22] Since the play was addressed to the 'wider' public and was more attentive to the requirements of pure entertainment, Eisler wrote 'song music'.

The latter is only partly true, as in fact would very quickly become evident if the music were to be understood simply from the theatrical point of view. Eisler's remark that the fourteen numbers he composed went 'far beyond the scope of incidental music', and that this was a 'play with music',[23] suggests that they could belong in a Viennese Singspiel or in a popular opera buffa.

Delight in couplets is brought up to date, and they themselves are satirically honed. Eisler scores for an expanded jazz group and uses a number of elements from the contemporary blues, tap-dance and slow waltz, which lose their dance-like quality in the context of alienation. In his use of sound he helps to make clear the facts of equivocation, venality and ideological fraudulence – but also the grain of truth in falsehood. Thus he writes serious music with the resources of light music.

The deceptive appearance of contradictions leading nowhere is produced in Brecht's songs by an unusual piling-up of restrictive terms such as 'granted, only, perhaps, often, however'. These are reflections of what the characters felt in the early years of the Hitler régime: uncertainty about the possible hardening of existing conditions. The rulers were directing their efforts towards this and the ruled were inclined to come to terms with it. Brecht, who was not at all prone to idealizing the proletariat, laid open to criticism their spontaneous sense of what was right and their healthy common sense: in the face of the new situation such realism was inadequate. For it was the concern of fascism to perpetuate and whitewash over the social results of the collapse of capitalism.

In his 'Lied von der Tünche' [Whitewash Song] Eisler translated the crude aggressiveness of the Huas (SA) as a chorus whose style suggests depraved militant music. In the 'Ballade vom Wasserrad' [Ballad of the Waterwheel] the music displays resistance to the text (see ex. 20). The scope of the image's associations has acquired too much autonomy for the good of the intended (social) meaning. In his manner of composing the preceding verse Eisler moves such a distance away from the metaphor that appears in the refrain that even the hopeless attitude of Nanna (who is singing the ballad) is criticized: for her the waterwheel signifies the return of the same old power system.

In the 'Lied von der belebenden Wirkung des Geldes' [Song of the Invigorating Effect of Money] music and text join in ambivalent clarity and double-edged precision as befits the dialectical

Ex.20 *Die Rundköpfe und die Spitzköpfe*, 'Ballade vom Wasserrad'

eulogizing of that unpleasant but indispensable commodity. The overall shape and internal symmetry of the composition appear to support its affirmative character; the insertion of the ritornello before, between and after the verses creates a convincing means of linking and rounding-off. However, the eulogy enters a twilight world not only by virtue of being performed by a corrupt judge (as a representative of justice he indirectly denounces its corruptibility by defending it as necessary). But much more importantly, the music throws doubt on the text by a series of subtle digressions, as for instance when, at the triumphant gesture of 'Look up: the chimney is smoking!', the comfortable triple time of the slow waltz lays bare the self-satisfied meanness of such enjoyment of life (see ex. 21). Finally, one cannot ignore the self-irony of the writer and the composer: the situation of 'Everyone goes after something and gets it where he can' is one that they themselves as émigrés had been in often enough. The tradition found in the early Singspiel of using traditional forms of solo song to characterize persons of rank is honoured by Eisler in the 'Kavatine der Isabella'. Here, in a discreet *pianissimo*, the landowner's sister expresses her horror of carnal appetites; at the thought of sin, her performance dips to *ppp*. Her aspirations to purity raise questions, and chaste feelings are shown as the exclusive luxury of a rich heiress. Ground rent is the guardian of her subjectivity.

Ex.21   *Die Rundköpfe und die Spitzköpfe*, 'Lied von der belebenden Wirkung des Geldes'

That Eisler by no means disdains violent effects is shown by the duet of Isabella and Nanna. In one of the most comical scenes of the play, the lady of rank instructs the girl of easy virtue in the three chief virtues of abstinence, obedience and poverty. So as to give more satirical point to the scene, Eisler sets the instruction as a parody of Gregorian plainsong. Each of Nanna's mechanical repetitions permits an insolent second-hand imitation; because of the rapidity of the performance – an acceleration resulting from lack of interest – the sacred aura of Gregorian chant dissolves as if of its own accord (see ex. 22).

Ex.22   *Die Rundköpfe und die Spitzköpfe*, Duet of Nanna and Isabella

In the song in which Nanna introduces herself ('Gentlemen, at seventeen/I went on to the love market') and in the 'Kuppellied' [Song of the Procuress] sung by the madame, Mrs Cornamontis, cold-blooded, big-city features appear which distinguish these songs from the other music. In both – the first being a strophic

Ex.23 *Die Rundköpfe und die Spitzköpfe*, 'Lied der Nanna'

song in blues tempo, the second being closer to a popular ballad –
venality appears as the theme much more forcibly than elsewhere
in the play. Nanna's blues song casts only gentle melancholy
shadows over her self-image: in her, the prostitute, merchandise
has acquired human dimensions (see ex. 23).

The madame Cornamontis appears scarcely less depraved. She
gives out her worldly wisdom in the lines of the refrain 'Money
makes us sexy, as experience teaches us': the material cost has
priority, and everything else is incidental. (Conversely both composer and writer opposed materialism without sensuality.) On the

Ex.23   *continued*

Ex.23 *continued*

'Lied der Kupplerin' [Song of the Procuress], the last to be written, Eisler wrote to Brecht:

The effect lies in the fact that the music is terribly common and ordinary. It must be sung by a drunken fat slut with traces of Titian-like beauty. It is musically easy to sing but hard to perform. Very free in tempo . . . It remains to be mentioned that in this song the principal motive from Richard Wagner's Tristan und Isolde is used as an accompaniment, as the master must always be honoured where it is necessary[24] (see ex. 24).

Ex.24   *Die Rundköpfe und die Spitzköpfe*, 'Lied der Kupplerin'

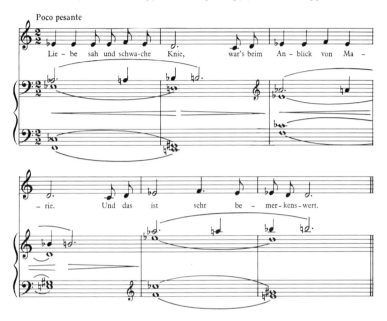

Jokes of this not entirely frivolous sort enrich the writing and
enhance the intellectual enjoyment. However, in order to give his
vocal music its power of immediate sensual attraction Eisler
ensured in particular that *melodic inspiration* was ready in abundance whenever he needed it. It may be supposed that, without his
trained resistance to the inconsequentially pleasurable and without his political awareness, this talent might have caused him to
submit to entirely commercial temptations, especially under the
difficult circumstances of his exile. The music for *Die Spitzköpfe*
shows where he drew the line. By partially referring back to
precedents in musical history, Eisler succeeds in refining the
'popular'; greater accessibility, necessary for the 'wider' public, is
not paid for by lowering one's sights, but by fresh invention.
Even though the revolutionary movement appears here only on
the periphery ('Sichellied' – Song of the Sickle), wit and diverting
musical forms do not exclude far-reaching criticism.

However, right from the start, *Die Rundköpfe und die Spitz-köpfe* ran into difficulties: firstly on account of the seemingly purely local associations of the 'race problem', and subsequently on account of its fresh developments. When at the end of 1936 it was finally given its first performance by a Copenhagen experimental theatre company,[25] the authors had been trying to get the play performed on a European stage for over two years. In fact Eisler and Brecht nursed great hopes for this work in particular, which was their first major contribution in the struggle against fascism and was also of importance in the new parable form that they were evolving.

Of necessity, too, their material interest *in* the play was hardly less than that expressed *by* the play. A letter written by Eisler in Paris in May 1934 makes it clear how the émigrés' tight budget allowed hope to grow in their minds. The very confident tone in his hurriedly written, business-like report later proved to be over-optimistic.

Dear Brecht. I have waited a few days until I had something more concrete to report. 1. Yesterday the Zurich directors (Rieser and his wife, who is Werfel's sister) came to see me and I played through the play to them. They were *very enthusiastic*, but were worried about a few things. The result: I have given them an option on the première until 10 June at the latest. Between now and then Rieser has to give me a contract. He said at once that he needed some passages toned down and softened. Naturally we can only discuss this together. So: If Rieser produces a contract before 10 June it will be necessary for you, Pis[cator] and me to have concrete discussions with the Zurich directors about the performance and also about any alterations that might be necessary for Zurich. So, if Zurich offer a contract, as well as a series of proposals that would make the play acceptable for Zurich, you would have to come either to Paris or to Zurich to organize all that. You would then in fact be travelling because of an existing contract for the first performance!!! The outlook is very good. Let us hope it will come off. If I get the contract I will cable you. 2. About the Danish negotiations: I must stay here until 10 June, until Zurich have made their decision. (Zurich want *only* a first performance. They are planning guest performances, world press, etc. They are snobs.) Perhaps I will go then. But: I still have no new film commissions and so little money that for the moment I could barely afford it. But if I sign up for a film before 10 June then I will come in any case since the slightest possibility must be followed up. 3. The English negotiations remain excellent. I will send definite news within the next few days. 4. I have had another approach from America, this time a different group altogether who are suggesting a concert tour (with travelling expenses paid both ways). 5. It is a nuisance that Karin's [Michaelis] houses have been disposed of. My financial situation is so meagre that the project will come to nothing. For: 8 journeys (there and back) cost 3200 francs. On top of that Ruth's [Fischer] rent will still have to be paid. I simply don't have this money, and I have to budget accordingly. 6. To sum up. First let's wait for Zurich. If we get a contract before 10 June everything will look better. Then we can make fresh arrangements. Meanwhile my other negotiations are still in train. I am very 'set on Zurich'. Write a few lines. Best wishes, your Eisler. (The Isabella–Judith duet has come out very well. Unfortunately Ratz works very slowly. I am making progress with the 3rd volume of the musical education book. *Texts!!*)[26]

Work on films was now easier to come by than theatre performances, which rarely came about because of the difficulties of translation. The big-budget productions were admittedly generally entertainment films, and even when conceived in a progressive spirit they hardly rose above a pitiful standard. One such film, which was meant to ridicule the 'Führer' in the guise of a sultan, was produced in London in 1934 as 'Abdul Hamid' (= Adolf Hitler). In the summer, Eisler, who was prone to temperamental outbursts, wrote to Brecht that the film was

politically 'respectable', but unfortunately still rubbish . . . After fighting for a whole day I had (for decency's sake!) to give in. I have never so much regretted not having money. I would dearly like to throw the whole rubbishy thing in the swines' faces. After a day in the film world the *much-abused* Skovbostrand seems like a marvellous paradise to which I look back regretfully. It is more loathsome than laughable, that's the tricky thing.[27]

(Two years later Eisler and Brecht, for reasons of financial pressure, were collaborative assistants on the extremely questionable film of 'I Pagliacci' with Richard Tauber. Eisler, as supervisor of the musical recording, persuaded Kortner, who was at that time the author of the screenplay, to propose to the film's director that Brecht should be asked to collaborate on the scenario. For the playwright the outcome of the venture was financially successful but morally a 'dreadful defeat' since 'the lowest of the film mob would rather pay Brecht money than listen to a single one of his proposals'.)[28]

In the autumn of 1934 Eisler and Brecht wrote a series of political songs to support the formation of the united front. The first effective alliance between the KPD and socialist groups came about before the Saar elections of winter 1934–5. The 'Saarlied' [Song of the Saar], to be sung simply, calls for the defence of the status quo and resistance against affiliation to the National Socialist Reich.

Whereas the 'Saarlied' did not outlive the occasion for which it was written, the 'Einheitsfrontlied', composed at the same time in London, became internationally famous. Like the 'Solidaritäts-lied' it is one of those great first-person-plural songs whose march-like rallying metres have an immediate uniting effect – militant music which pledges its singers to the text and invites participation. The Front is referred to in a concretely polemical way. Eisler wrote at the time:

A new revolutionary song begins with the words: 'And because a man is a man, he needs something to eat, if you please! Idle talk won't satisfy him, that will make no food.' These revolutionary sentences are contrasted with the constantly recurring utterances of the fascist authorities who acknowledge that they can offer the worker no material reward, but are proud to have spiritually uplifted him. Here the music plays a significant part. This sort of spiritual 'uplift' means for the worker that he must 'raise' himself above the 'humble' facts – that wages are falling and prices rising, that the unemployed are being pressed into domestic service, that the worker is robbed of all his rights and exposed to the whims of the 'works manager' . . .

A cultural improvement, he continues, is unthinkable without general welfare. 'Mozart and Beethoven must have as much to recommend themselves to the proletariat as a healthy home, good food, a meaningful profession, a sound education for its children and an assured old age.' With a direct gibe against the hardened separation of art from life in the outlook of the bourgeois moderns, against the aestheticism which persists in finding the needs of the workers uninteresting, he sums up: 'A great culture begins with the creation of a high standard of living for all. *This too is part of culture.*'[29]

These considerations and postulates form part of the fundamental assumptions behind his social convictions as a composer.
He was confirmed in them by a three-month lecture and concert
tour through the USA early in 1935. Here, having undertaken an
educational trip, attended by much publicity, on the invitation of
Lord Marley's Committee for the Victims of German Fascism, he
found music and politics more widely separated than ever. This
was despite the fact that the America he visited had been in a crisis
and suffered a depression for more than five years, and that the
beginnings of political art were in the making. Socially critical
tendencies in, for example, literature and the theatre were tolerated during Roosevelt's New Deal policies. Whilst the country's
new administration was partly of social-democratic inspiration,
the numerically small Communist Party at that time exerted a
marked influence on progressive artists and intellectuals. Nevertheless, apart from Marc Blitzstein, there were only a few among
eminent musicians who identified closely with it.[30]

To begin with, Eisler was fascinated by the huge dimensions
and stark contrasts of the United States. It also intrigued him that
here capitalism was unconcealedly — one might say unabashedly —
in evidence. Shortly after his arrival he wrote to Brecht:

... this country is really magnificent, because here there is a great lack of
superstructure. Here class opposes class in an extremely naked way and
the struggle takes on the most extreme forms of brutality. That is a
refreshing feature. And further there is this splendid pragmatism even
though theory is not entirely lacking. Despite many worries I feel very
well. In contrast, the Continent appears like a great morass.[31]

Beginning in Boston and New York, his tour took him through
more than fifty towns to Los Angeles and Hollywood. The evenings were generally centred on Eisler's lecture on culture and
fascism and a series of political songs in which he accompanied
the young New York baritone Mordecai Bauman[32] at the piano.
Usually there were also choral performances; they were organized
by the various local committees of the League Against War and
Fascism. His success was generally due to their response. For the
opening concert at the beginning of March (advertised as 'Millions Sing His Songs!') several thousand listeners gathered in the
Mecca Temple in New York; in the Ford city of Detroit, on the

other hand, there were only a few hundred; particularly severely
hit by the depression, the organizations here were also weak.

In nearly every town, apart from the 'Solidarity Song', it was
the 'Moorsoldatenlied' [Peat-Bog Soldiers' Song], arranged by
Eisler, that made the greatest impact: in the ensuing years it
became a popular song of the American Left. At a number of
concerts towards the end of the tour he succeeded in persuading
the public to join in the singing. In New York three recordings
were made with Mordecai Bauman.[33]

The American press (with the exception of the Hearst empire)
responded mainly sympathetically. Professional interest too was
great, because serious music in the USA had hitherto been the
preserve of rich old ladies who made their influence felt by
financing it. Certainly Eisler's political songs were not considered
serious music; but the arguments in his lectures, his questions
about the social aims of music and the connnection between the
musical and the capitalist crisis, together with the concerts,
evoked a considerable response.

The concerts also made an impact in other places. Under the
date 3 April 1935 the German Embassy in Washington DC for-
warded to the Foreign Office in Berlin consular reports from New
York and San Francisco of Eisler's appearances. From there,
copies went to the Ministry of the Interior, the Gestapo and the
Ministry for Propaganda. The report from San Francisco, which
at that very time was the scene of a major dock strike, is extremely
revealing. Its basic tone is sedulous and subordinate, its style
clumsy.

Before an audience of approximately 450 persons, of whom more than
400 were Jews, about 20 negroes and the remainder white socialists and
communists, the composer Hanns Eisler, who has supposedly escaped
from a German concentration camp, gave a musical lecture lasting for
nearly one hour on the evening of 20 March of this year at the local
Scottish Rite Auditorium ... The first song ... was an elegiac lament,
performed in rising and subsiding tones and closing on a note of hopelessness ... The third song was called 'Praise of Learning' (Lob des Lernens)
and in precise form and categorical manner invited the workers to
educate themselves; here the affirmative tone of the recurring rhyme 'You
must be ready to take over' lent to the whole an impact which had a very
marked effect on the audience ...

10   During the first concerts in New York (1935)

The report concludes:

The final item, 'United Front', refers to the demands of the proletariat in clear musical language and calls for the path indicated by the workers to be followed, ending on a note of triumph heightened into fanaticism.[34]

Eisler's first journey to the USA had a twofold result: for one thing he made a name for himself in America as a composer; for another he received an invitation to return that same autumn to teach as a guest lecturer for a term at the New School for Social Research in Manhattan. He had got to know a number of important musicians, and published a great deal in newspapers.[35] His journey was sponsored by, amongst others, George Gershwin, Aaron Copland and Henry Cowell.

Last but not least, he had been able to negotiate in New York over possible performances of *Die Massnahme* and *Die Mutter*, though without being able to foresee the result. It proved extremely difficult to arrive at a common political attitude amongst left-wing artists of different countries.

Solidarity was already fragile among his own countrymen and steadfastness was very variable, particularly since long years of exile had begun to look a distinct probability. On his journey back to London Eisler wrote to Brecht in a mixture of rage and concern about their common acquaintance George Grosz whom he had met in New York. The letter, dated 9 May 1935, for all its delight in malice, is an example of responsible analysis – aimed at saving a previous ally from a 'change of spirit'.

Grosz: this man has become anti-social. He has discovered capitalism for himself as an extremely comfortable way of life. Socialism he knows only in the form of the *Café des Westens* . . . The fact that this . . . for a realist like Grosz . . . is intolerable is easy to understand. But until now he has not yet taken cognizance of the fact that for about 80 years there has been a scientific socialism. He has put on a thin veneer of anarchistic smut. Scratch it off and one sees a quite abominable, insipid, narrow-minded bourgeois. Unfortunately this can be sensed in his output, although technically he has made magnificent progress. Since he is going to be in Denmark in the summer you must try to cure him of his stupid ideas. He has no *real* differences of opinion with us, as with, say, the Trotskyites; it's just a difference of '*general attitude*', the fathead!!! A pity about him; perhaps it can be remedied. Be sarcastic with him, as he is enormously proud of being a 'heretic'. Prove to him that such 'heresy' is no more than ignorance and narrow-minded bourgeoisie, and then you will be able to influence him. This is very necessary. Take all his descriptions of America with a large pinch of salt.

For example, according to him there are no American revolutionary workers. (The general strike in Frisco was just the work of 'ghosts'.) He scorns the 'masses'. His second sentence is always: 'Amongst us educated men we can certainly say', 'the stupid masses need that', etc.

A quite abominable narrow-minded bourgeois who must be changed as quickly as possible, otherwise he will become an enemy, and that would be tragic, since he is a really great painter, as his latest works also prove. So: Beware! Grosz wants to join the dogs!! Very sincerely, Eisler.[36]

In this year of travelling and music festivals Eisler barely got round to composing. At the beginning of June he was in Strasbourg: Piscator had commissioned him[37] to direct the International Olympiad of Workers' Music. Concerned to assist in promoting the formation of the United Front, he accepted, not without a struggle with himself. For as chairman of the jury acting as the artistic selection committee he came face to face with what he had fought against for years in the Weimar Republic: the sentimental pathos of workers' choruses that had fallen prey to petty-bourgeois influence and the crashing uproar of marching bands prevailed. It was precisely the fact that they were well intentioned that made these performances hard for modern ears to bear. On 1 June 1935 Eisler wrote to Brecht:

... Pis[cator] has done something quite horrible to me with this Olympiad . . . from the musical point of view. Politically I am trying to squeeze anything out of it there is to be squeezed . . . After this pleasure I am already beckoned by Reichenberg, where I am to speak on 15 June. Likewise a music festival that no one has supervised. All this thoughtlessness, cultivation of societies and metaphysical notions of good old Pis. make me feel very gloomy. I already very much wish I were sitting working with you . . . Since January I have put about 16,000 miles behind me and have entirely forgotten what manuscript paper looks like. I think there are five lines and you have to draw blobs on them and attach them to stems. Dear old music; I still remember it in its days of real greatness. (All this because of the Olympiad) . . .[38]

The climax was his own contribution: with Ernst Busch, whom

he accompanied at the piano, and 3000 singing workers, he launched the 'Einheitsfrontlied'.

Ten days after the Strasbourg Olympiad, Paris saw the start of the International Congress of Writers 'For the Defence of Culture'. Eisler had to go to the music festival of the North Bohemian Workers in Reichenberg and was unable to take part. Brecht, however, went over from Denmark. His speech, 'A necessary statement in the fight against barbarism', ended with the appeal: 'Comrades, let us speak about the distribution of property!'[39] Brecht made allowances for the fact that in the ears of the predominantly bourgeois writers this must have sounded radical. He sceptically opposed the efforts to win them over at any price as allies of the People's Front. Among his writing colleagues – for the most part well placed – he saw that the majority were 'Tuis' from whom little could be expected against the threatened spread of fascism in Europe. On this point he became embroiled in an argument with Eisler, who considered the strategy of the People's Front the only one possible at that time. The two never wrote a song of the People's Front.

From Reichenberg Eisler went to Moscow. He was elected president of the International Music Bureau (IMB), which he subsequently reorganized. His next stop was Prague, where the Thirteenth Festival of the ISCM was taking place; then he conducted negotiations on behalf of the Popular Front with the social-democratic Internationale der Arbeitersänger [International Association of Singer-Workers] (IDAS). He did not succeed in achieving useful results: the negotiations broke down. As is known, neither in 1935 nor subsequently was a solid German United or Popular Front established among émigrés (not even among the singer-workers, let alone among other musicians). The hope that earlier differences could be forgotten in a common fight against fascism proved deceptive.

In September Eisler took the steamer from Le Havre to New York to begin his term as a guest lecturer at the New School for Social Research. He taught composition and gave a series of lectures on the crisis of modern music.

Brecht's and Eisler's plan to make a decisive impact in New York with a successful play (after their failures on the Continent) seems to have come close to fulfilment in the autumn. *Die Mutter* had good prospects. Brecht came specially from Denmark. Together with Eisler, he tried in October and November to exert influence on the theatrical and musical executive of the Theater Union, the only workers' theatre in USA at that time. After serious disputes between the theatre and the two authors, the outcome was disastrous. The reasons for this were, besides the hopeless translation, the naturalistic production and the inadequate standards of musical performance. *Die Mutter* was psychologized in a vulgar way; it came out 'like something at the Tegernsee peasant festivals'.[40]

It was thoroughly slated in the bourgeois press. One exception was the *Herald Tribune*, though admittedly it was more interested in the authors than in the performance. In its Sunday edition of 1 December 1935 there appeared a major article on the development of both artists since the twenties. Meanwhile the title made a somewhat premature prediction: 'Bert Brecht and Hanns Eisler are Hitler's Gift to Broadway'.[41] The *Herald Tribune* clearly saw them as following in the footsteps of Kurt Weill. The message was: great prospects for the émigrés. But it was not of the kind that the authors of *Die Mutter* wanted for themselves.

Renaissance of the cantata

From 1936 to 1937 Eisler's work began to show signs of stylistic changes in line with its intended functions. Its thematic content and forms became at the same time narrower and broader. The strategy of the Popular Front urged artists to address a broader public extending as far as the central Left. On the other hand the subject matter was restricted by the common factor of anti-fascism. Eisler was confronted by a complex problem: to stray cosily into an art of subjective experience was politically proscribed more than ever; conversely, the aggressively anti-bourgeois vocal music of the pre-exile years required clarification for a public that was in part differently motivated. In the interests of effectiveness he could not entirely abandon echoes of tonal music, yet at the same time this public expected musical novelty.

Eisler replied with a renaissance of the *cantata*. Its potential seemed to him best suited to the practical needs. Using twelve-note technique, he by-passed the classics and Romantics and went back to Bach, transforming these apparently heterogeneous elements into a style of peculiar acidity whose polyphony acquired a patina of great intensity.

The first of these works was *Gegen den Krieg* [Against War] op. 51, to texts by Brecht. The latter's friend Margarete Steffin told Walter Benjamin on 20 July 1936 (two days after the beginning of the Spanish military *putsch*): 'Besides that he has been writing marvellous new things – "Krieg", which Eisler is making into a cantata, is among the finest he has written.'[42] In fact in this cantata (or rather motet for four-part *a cappella* chorus) Eisler achieved a mastery over stylistic concision of a density and *comprehensibility* rare in modern choral music.

Gegen den Krieg is constructed with precise symmetry: a theme and a coda, both in unison, enclose 24 variations which in turn form two halves around a central intermezzo (between XI and XIII). Within these there are subdivisions: using Schoenberg's technique of developing variation, Eisler produces variants which are grouped together as segments. The way in which the segments are balanced against each other seems to correspond exactly to the demands of the text. But in this instance Eisler has subjected them to his requirements as a composer by means of extensive alteration and reordering. He focusses and groups them in such a way that he can give expression to an overriding idea which is not present in Brecht's more extensive, compartmentalized structure.[43]

Eisler's new structure for the text as a whole spans the entire range from the sober assertion of the absolutely evil effect of the last war on the 'lower' class of both sides (in the theme) to its unanimous rejection (in the coda) by those who have been made ready: 'This war is not our war!' The first section of the variations (I–X) quotes the lying propaganda of the 'bosses' and spells out the consequences. The second (XIV–XXIV) shows the concrete form of these consequences in military images. With the short central intermezzo Eisler inserts the complementary subjective aspect. The text 'Again they talk of honour. Marie do not weep' acquires its pathos from being played down; the chorus, at half-strength and singing almost gently, produces more pain in this passage than any wails of horror could. Thus the grief of the individual is made the central point, even though it is immediately withdrawn: otherwise the listener might identify too much and thus lose track of the overall picture.

One of Eisler's borrowings from the pre-classical tradition is his manner of imitative declamation which places textual interpretation in the forefront. Just as the sacred music of the seventeenth and eighteenth centuries was based on textual sayings (in prose), so Eisler treats the substratum obtained from Brecht's texts in the same way. The alternation between sections set for full chorus and for a small number of voices, rhythmic contrasts and, above all, the treatment of the row are organized in such a way that the fullness and assurance of the whole grows with increasing complexity. At the same time the organization of the material becomes denser without performance becoming technically more difficult for the chorus. The illusion of a peculiarly self-contained tonality arises because of a lack of row transpositions – the row generally appears in its prime form – as well as through plagal cadences and triadic structures.

The theme introduces the row three times, the first variation has the row in canon, etc., and tension is built up across increasing contrasts so that the concluding choral fugue (XX–XXIV) produces a feeling of finality whilst the theme is as it were dissolved away and neutralized: the fugue, keeping to the text 'This war is not our war', mounts to a four-part *fortissimo* leading directly into the unison coda: unity is established (see ex. 25).

With this, Eisler's power of compositional invention comes into play, together with the range of possible combinations of material so as to exhaust the spectrum of solutions. The theme is 'developed' and the whole is made convincing. An emotional arena is established which is full of a 'neutral' pathos such as can only be achieved in composition by using the resources of twelve-note technique. The things which appear as understatements, or those that might occasionally, to use a term from the sphere of jazz, be called 'cool', in fact acquire a much greater power of

Ex.25   *Gegen den Krieg*, Variation XXIV

objectivization than the expressive pathos of traditional styles, whilst the factual content of the text is made clear.

This is equally true of the nine solo cantatas, the *Lenin-Requiem* and the *Deutsche Sinfonie* which Eisler composed at that time. After his visit to the International Brigades in Spain (early in 1937), for whom he wrote a number of songs,[44] he spent the spring and summer back with Brecht in Denmark. The nine chamber cantatas for solo voice and four instruments which were written there in May and June mostly use texts by Ignazio Silone[45] and were intended for concert use.

Silone's accusations – related to circumstances in Italy – are generalized in Eisler's version of the text: fascism appears not as a national problem but a class problem, and war as its consequence. His own impressions of the Spanish Civil War, the news of the bombardment of Guernica by Hitler's Condor Legion in April, the fear that fascism was leading to a Second World War, all this was on his mind as he considered which texts to select. Military service and rearmament in Germany, the increasing involvement of political and economic powers: the 'success' of the Nazi régime – and the numbers of its victims – were taking on considerable proportions.

Even in the titles of the cantatas current events are registered. They are *Kriegskantate* [War Cantata], *Nein* [No], *Die den Mund auf hatten* [Those who had their Mouths Open], *Kantate auf den Tod eines Genossen* [Cantata on the Death of a Comrade] etc. But even the classic émigré attitude is rejected. The *Kantate im Exil* [Cantata in Exile] criticizes the outlook which constantly regards the situation as 'temporary' and settles down to enjoy its own masochism instead of seizing the freedom which 'does not come as a present'.

Diction plays a particularly important part in the performance of the cantatas. As in Bach, what is required is linear, instrumental singing. Contour is more important than beauty of sound. It is more appropriate to stress consonants than vowels.

The *Lenin-Requiem* and, more remarkably still, the far more extensive *Deutsche Sinfonie* were composed by Eisler during his exile without any prospect of a performance.[46] Today they seem great works of remembrance, written as if already looking back at the time during which they were composed.

He completed the cantata dedicated to the memory of Lenin, for which Brecht wrote the text, shortly before the twentieth anniversary of the October Revolution. It is in nine sections and is scored for contralto and baritone solo, chorus and orchestra. The job of writing it was a tricky one: he had to find a way of guarding a homage to a great man from the gloom of religious associations, and of giving mourning an active profile, a revolutionary impetus, instead of allowing it to debilitate the mourners.

Brecht found his solution in the attempt to check any tendency to glorification, by reducing Lenin to his function, as it were: to the fight against exploitation. The fact that he fulfilled this function and the manner in which he did so, stubbornly and unyieldingly, make him the embodiment of the revolutionary – a useful model. From his very simple depiction of a meeting between a member of the Red Army and the dead Lenin, Brecht evolves reflections and images which demonstrate this. The last lines read: 'He was our teacher./He has fought with us./He is enshrined/In the great hearts of the working class.'[47] The final image is the only one which unwittingly comes close to the veneration of a saint. Eisler guards against this in the music.

The composer places this image (which is almost like a Russian ikon) exactly at the centre of the closing Passacaglia (No. 9), making it the latter's climax and at the same time conferring on it an effect of alienation: at the words 'Lenin is enshrined . . .' he reverts again to the first four bars of the harshly dissonant introduction and removes the listener so far away from the imagery that he cannot immediately react emotionally to it. These complex bars, 'in which both the row and its retrograde are contained simultaneously',[48] undermine any reminiscences of bygone pieties that might otherwise have been possible (see ex. 26). The exact opposite of a form of worship which would tend to become self-sufficient, the secular Requiem of Eisler and Brecht helps to make Lenin's greatness functional: useful in the continuing fight.

By means of musical forms, Eisler places this in a historical perspective. The forms range from a rudimentary use of the precentor–choir relationship, through recitativo accompagnato

Ex.26   *Lenin-Requiem*, Passacaglia

and choral fantasia to the aggressive rhythms of the song and the ballad of the period of militancy in Berlin. The 'Lob des Revolutionärs' [Praise of the Revolutionary] from *Die Mutter* is used again unchanged, except that it has been rescored for symphony orchestra.

The intention is plain: the listener is meant not simply to trust to the musical (and textual) processes, but to feel questioned by them and answerable to them. The pleasure of the unaccustomed in new music, which demands every effort, does not stop short at fascination; the shadow that accompanies it is the warning to the listener not to push aside too hastily the demands made on him. In conjunction with the text this warning acquires a political dimension: the endeavours to free the world from exploitation have only just begun.

A document of anti-fascist resistance

The barbaric setback which the victory of National Socialism represented in this context, the numberless and often nameless sufferings and sacrifices, but also the resistance and solidarity of the persecuted all went into the work which Eisler was later to think of as his magnum opus: the *Deutsche Sinfonie* op. 50. Its theme is the *anti-fascist resistance* in Germany during the thirties.

The work is in eleven sections, occupying an entire concert programme; it is somewhere between a symphony and an oratorio and requires considerable forces: four vocal soloists, two speakers, large chorus and orchestra. Eisler worked on it for several years. His original concept proved too limited for this work, which was to become his largest in scope. Its central idea came into being during the first lecture and concert tour in the USA when he was trying to explain to the American public what Nazism had done – not only culturally – to Germany. In July 1935 he wrote to Brecht:

By the way, I have a very interesting idea for a composition, in fact I want to write a large symphony which will have the subtitle 'Concentration-camp Symphony'. In some passages a chorus will be used as well, although it is basically an orchestral work. And certainly I want to use your two poems, 'Begräbnis des Hetzers im Zinksarg' [Burial of the Agitator in a Zinc Coffin] (this will become the middle section of a large-scale funeral march) and 'An die Gefangenen in den Konzentrationslagern' [To the Prisoners in the Concentration Camps]. The first sketches I have made for this (in Detroit) are extremely promising.[49]

Already in 1938 the title *Deutsche Sinfonie* seems to have been firmly established,[50] although after the war Eisler again considered another one: 'Die deutsche Misere, Oratorium' [The German Predicament, an Oratorio].[51] The 'predicament' was no longer what had originally been intended – the concentration camps; it was the reason behind their existence: the *association between fascism and capitalism*. In the camps he saw its most logical expression – both symbolic and extremely concrete.

In order to make this association palpable, Eisler assembled texts by Brecht (and his own) in such a way that the entire work could be constructed as a *crescendo* of immense dimensions. Accusation, warning and the call to resistance are brought together, reinforce each other and become increasingly urgent. From the Prelude (Largo) there arises, in denunciatory and bitter tones, the cry: 'O Germany, pale mother. How you are defiled with the blood of your best sons!' From this point on, Eisler unfolds the contradictions of this situation of genuine horror – and those that led to it – in a steady build-up. With increasing distinctness the spirit of rejection grows too. Nowhere does desperation keep the upper hand for long. In the last vocal movement a worker narrates the story of his life, representing the history of the workers' movement since the First World War. The conviction that he arrives at, however late, in this 'Lied vom Klassenfeind' [Song of the Class Enemy] of Brecht serves as the final word of the *Deutsche Sinfonie*, throwing light on the past and future history of the movement in elucidation and prognostication. The manoeuvre to distract the people is now countered and replaced by the insight, affirmed by the whole work, and hitherto lost sight of by many: 'And the enemy is the *class* enemy.'

Eisler develops a very original dual structure in order to loosen the compact and emotionally highly charged nature of the material. Eight vocal sections are interspersed with three orchestral movements which are linked with them either thematically or by the use of a common row.[52] Taken on their own, these three instrumental movements form a symphony within the symphony, in the sequence Allegro – Adagio (with Scherzo) – Allegro. Individually, Eisler places them after those vocal pieces to which he wants to give particular emphasis; thus the first two pieces, in which the theme is the concentration camps, are linked together ('An die Kämpfer in den Konzentrationslagern' [To the Fighters in the Concentration Camps] and 'In Sonnenburg'). The broadly elaborated closing Allegro follows the 'Lied vom Klassenfeind'. The whole work opens up and broadens out towards this ending: the last two pieces (before the Coda) make up almost half of the length of the entire work.

In the second part of the *Deutsche Sinfonie* (Nos. 7–10) a political idea has visibly influenced the musical architecture. The idea of the association of intelligence with working people has caused Eisler to group together, as his last three vocal pieces, three cantatas in which the subject is in turn the intellectuals (as revolutionaries), the peasants and the workers.

Eisler has composed the 'Begräbnis des Hetzers im Zinksarg' in such a way that the cynical triumph over the brutally struck down victim (the text is taken from a fascist speech) is transformed into a eulogy of the revolutionary in perverted form. For the true content of what is denounced in the Nazi pose – the insistence on material interests and militant solidarity – is presented 'in a friendly way' and almost gently by a soprano in the spirit of a march (see ex. 27). Blended into the macabre context, the ominous assertions become those that are put in question by themselves. Only in and through the ear of the listener does the sense of the text acquire its significance: as refuted.

Among the artistic innovations which already anticipate techniques of musical broadcast drama belong the 'conversations' in the 'Bauernkantate' [Peasants' Cantata] (No. 8).[53] Their subversive character is translated into sound. A whispered dialogue to be spoken 'without expression' is given relief and depth by an accompanied humming chorus and static blocks of sound. Danger, muted protest and impatience at having to wait take on a new dimension in space.

Ex.27   *Deutsche Sinfonie*, 'Begräbnis des Hetzers'

The workers' cantata, which dominates the whole work and which Eisler composed to an extremely long text by Brecht, is a centre shifted to the end, and is hard to grasp as a whole. The *Deutsche Sinfonie* turns out, moreover, to be difficult and scarcely reveals itself at a first hearing. If the great synthesis of symphonic, choral and solo sections, of dodecaphonic, pre-bourgeois and militant-music elements is thoroughly unprecedented in its conception, the occasional echoes of Mahler and the recourse to early methods in general give op. 50 as a whole a dark atmosphere. It may be supposed that Eisler's concentrated style, which is geared to concise units, could prove unsuitable for a large-scale form. The variety and density of elaboration which affects even the smallest detail could be felt by listeners unaccustomed to concentrated listening over longish periods as causing the individual sections to cancel each other out. In this way there could arise an impression of greyness or even of monotony, as if the musical material used was too slender.

The real difficulty of listening appropriately consists in the fact that the audience for which the *Deutsche Sinfonie* was intended can scarcely bring to it the necessary musical knowledge and experience; on the other hand, the audience which is better able to offer these requisites feels less concerned with the subject of the work and tries to forget about it. This is why Eisler's op. 50 has remained to this day one of his least-known and least-performed works.

In whatever way it may be judged by the future history of music, there could scarcely be a composition to compare with it from those years, or one possessing the same significance as a document of the most melancholy era in Germany's history so far, and of her resistance to it.

The quarrel with Lukács

One of a series of operatic projects that Eisler planned, started on, but never completed was the opera *Goliath*.[54] This did not get further than the first act, which he wrote with Brecht in Skovbostrand early in 1937. The intention had been to use the biblical story of David and Goliath as the framework for a libretto, adapting it as an anti-fascist parable which would show the people of Gad (the Germans) in conflict with the Philistines (Nazis). The work was interrupted by a journey Eisler made, and was never resumed. In the summer, then, there already existed fifty pages of score and the project was a going concern; it was destined for performances in the popular theatre with new methods of music theatre designed to bring a political message to a broader public.

At that time Eisler was more inclined than Brecht to regard his attitude as linked with the efforts of the Popular Front, which he supported with lectures. In the autumn of 1937, in Prague, he again met Ernst Bloch,[55] and in December the two published a joint essay in the form of a dialogue, 'Avant-garde art and the Popular Front'.[56] This fictitious conversation between a sceptic and an optimist revolves around the point of whether and how 'the most socially progressive awareness today can already be associated with the most aesthetically progressive and vice versa'.

The Sceptic fears that the artistic avant-garde, in its isolation from the masses, might be crushed to nothing between the hostile camps of fascism and the Popular Front; for even in the latter are to be found 'representatives of a vulgar conception of art'. The Optimist draws a distinction between the avant-garde 'of the studio and of constant experimentation', which until recently had predominated, and that which is concerned 'with using the boldest resources to represent the interests of the masses'. The Popular Front needs the progressive artist 'because it is not sufficient to possess the truth, but it is necessary to give it the most timely, precise and colourful expression'. At the mention of the supposed obstacle of 'quality', which the Sceptic is not prepared to sacrifice under any circumstances and which he understands as the 'highest point of our times', the Optimist declares: 'Experience has shown that with new artistic resources one reaches the social consciousness of the masses in such a forceful and compelling way that quality is felt not as an obstacle but as the most effective impulse shown by the work of art. It is precisely the artistic level that gives life to the material, creates a better realization and perspective . . .'

This is the Eisler of *Die Massnahme* and *Die Mutter*: the experience he speaks of is his own. To the Sceptic's main problem, that of the degenerate taste of the proletariat and the petty bourgeoisie and their addiction to *kitsch*, he replies: instead of 'taking up a fatalistic attitude . . . towards the cultural waste produced by capitalism' the artist might become 'aware of the social conditions behind this state of affairs and (make) these themselves the content of his art'. Both Optimist and Sceptic agree on the policy advocated in their concluding thesis: 'Therefore the Popular Front and the artist, both of them jointly affected, must jointly take up and carry through the fight.'[57]

Almost simultaneously the exile organ *Das Wort*, which was edited in Moscow, had put up a thesis for discussion, which came rather to the opposite conclusion. This was the work of an influential cultural politician in the KPD, Alfred Kurella, and maintained that the spirit of Expressionism led to fascism.[58] If in itself it could have been taken as merely fatuous, its consequences appeared dangerous by virtue of the fact that it took a prominent trend of the earlier avant-garde and proscribed it as representative of the avant-garde as a whole. The evolution of Gottfried Benn was held up as a frightening example and as typical of the whole tendency, apparently in order to produce clear points of reference in the discussions that had already been going on for years about the appropriation of the cultural *heritage*, about *popular characteristics* and *formalism*.

In retrospect Kurella's generalization seems doubly irresponsible: coming out under the banner of the Popular Front it was inopportune and could give offence to many of the bourgeois sympathizers who had yet to be won over; at the same time, at a period of growing political mistrust, it could add impetus to a general suspicion of artists as fascists, and poison the atmosphere for dialogue.

Eisler and Bloch were concerned that the systematic application of judgments, were it to become common practice, would lead to an inquisitorial attitude. If it were to come about that particular artistic procedures were canonized and prescribed as obligatory whilst others were *a priori* under threat of excommunication, this was bound to impede current and future production. 'Systematic and productive heritage' was the heading of the comments with which they entered the fray in January 1938 with the intention of identifying and averting possible grave errors.

Once again using the form of a dialogue, Bloch and Eisler – the one as an art-lover, the other as an art manufacturer – pleaded for a 'productive appropriation of the cultural heritage', something that needed to happen 'in a thoroughly *critical* way ', with careful selectivity and freedom from intimidation in the face of big names. This was clearly directed against their opposite number in their own, Marxist camp: Georg Lukács. For it was on the latter's doctrine of the exemplary value of the art works of the rising bourgeoisie – and of the subsequent destructive decadence, the result of a parallel decline – that Kurella had based his judgment of the avant-garde. The scheme is comparable to a double staircase: on one side the steps lead upwards from Lessing to the highest point – the realism of the novels of Goethe and also of Balzac and Tolstoy – and on the other side the steps lead down from Naturalism to Expressionism and finally to Surrealism.

Right at the start Bloch points out 'the danger that views on contemporary art are becoming narrower, and that new artistic tendencies are being undervalued in an abstract way'. 'These theorists in any case admit of too little in the present, and in the past they choose and value the classics almost in a classical way. What ignorance about modern art speaks out from their omissions . . .'[59]

And Eisler spoke even more plainly; ultimately, he and Brecht had practised new art forms successfully not merely in a studio context. 'The schematism they cite leads to a disaster both in artistic and in political terms. Young people came to us because we had greater cultural freshness.' Eisler's violent campaign against the narrow-minded traditionalism of the workers' musical movement and its reformist consequences was still recent history. On top of that, composers were faced with new questions which were already arising from the progress made in acoustical science.

In our day, sound films, gramophone recording, broadcasting and finally the transformation of social forms of entertainment have given rise to new problems of artistic production, and these cannot be solved simply by reference to the greatness of Beethoven and the rottenness of monopolistic capitalism. Even the 'beautiful sound' of nineteenth-century harmony which exercises such attractions is not a static phenomenon but rather a historical one, and one that it is not remotely possible to preserve in a classicistic way. So the theorist who sometimes likes to take on the role of a schoolmaster in his suggestions to modern artists – should be urged to be cautious. Formalism is not to be conquered by academicism but only by new material which strives towards a form appropriate to itself and determined by content.[60]

Eisler founded his charge that Lukács' verdicts bore an idealistic, abstract and ultimately disfunctional relationship to the times on their lack of genuine knowledge about new art and the needs of the public. The reading of novels, with its necessarily individual, passive participation and its interiorization of experience, was too narrow to serve as a basis for generalizations.[61] Bloch, too, criticized this narrowness. For Lukács, reality was extrapolated from a pure 'idea' of historical materialism and found itself confronted with fatal exceptions. 'I need not here point to modern artists of the stature of Picasso, Stravinsky, Schoenberg, Eisler, Bartók, Dos Passos and Brecht ... they radiate from a world that does not yet exist.'[62] Lukács' conception did not admit of anticipatory movements in the superstructure, and it was allied to political Manicheism: 'Almost any opposition to the ruling class which is not a priori communist it considers as part and parcel of the ruling class.'[63]

In the tone in which these polemics are couched we can detect some annoyance that Lukács, known for some time to both Bloch and Eisler as a fine intellect and by no means an ignoble character, had berated deviant conceptions *ex cathedra* and was increasingly arguing mechanically instead of dialectically. The woodenness of the sterile phraseology into which he was slipping gravely undermined his persuasiveness.[64]

Brecht too responded polemically to Lukács' method of reconciling a very humanistic variety of Marxism with the requirements of the Popular Front and Stalinist politics. In a series of essays (not published at the time) and entries in his working journal he gives 'the professor'[65] black marks for having sublimated the class struggle into a transcendental presence; for criticizing formalism in a merely formalistic way; and for concepts of the organically self-contained work and of a comprehensive view of the world which are historically outdated. Instead of seriously looking into the suitability of montage and open form for reproducing the apparently fragmentary and conflict-laden reality of capitalist countries, Lukács offers facsimiles of bourgeois realism and commends them as examples to be imitated.[66]

Certainly the 'aesthetic credo' which Lukács rooted in Goethe and Hegel was 'closely linked with his conception of "revolutionary democracy" as a long-drawn-out transitional phase'.[67] He was less interested in the artist 'who broke radically with his class than in the one who remained within the intellectual arena of "revolutionary democracy"'.[68] The political concept of long duration which had developed in the 1920s was probably reinforced by a concern that bourgeois art might not be sufficiently highly valued by the proletariat.[69] Thirdly, it should not be overlooked that Lukács, who since 1930 had been the most important spokesman for the directives emanating from Moscow, was endeavouring to apply the theory of socialist realism that had evolved there to the German situation. This had been evolved in conjunction with the fulfilment of the first Five-Year Plan (1932) and the 'abolition of class differences' through the collectivization of agriculture. It was considered necessary to show the reality of the harmonious structure in a positive light, with exemplary heroes in the foreground and all conflicts overcome.[70] Empathy with and uplift through realistic ideal figures seemed to Lukács to be the common factor of great bourgeois and socialist art.

For Eisler and Brecht questions of assimilating and reworking the heritage had nothing to do with conservation or doctrinaire discussion, but were specifically creative problems which occupied them in a practical way. Even montage was a form of 'ratifying the old culture: perceived in surprise as one passes by, rather than from the point of view of one's education'.[71]

Escape to America

At just forty years of age, in January 1938, Eisler travelled to the USA for the third time; this time to settle there. It seemed as if nothing remained in Europe of the possibility – already severely restricted in 1933 – of combining music with politics. Not that Eisler can have seen any greater opportunity for this in the USA; but the prospect of being temporarily restricted to just two areas of composition – concertante music for the bottom drawer and film music for bread and butter – made it advisable to choose (from what was now a restricted number) one of the less vulnerable countries for his exile. In New York he could again renew his contacts with the New School for Social Research; and there might also be commissions for film music.[72]

The number of German artists and intellectuals who continued their emigration as far as America during that year was particularly large. Those who sought to move further away from Nazi Germany included Bloch and Adorno, Thomas Mann and Oskar Maria Graf.[73] After five years of preparation, Hitler was beginning to reorganize the higher echelons of government and the army with a view to war. The 'annexation' of Austria in March, the English and French policies of appeasement, the army's invasion of parts of Czechoslovakia and the resignation of President Beneš augured ill. Within the Reich, anti-semitism entered a new phase with the 'Kristallnacht' ['crystal night'] of November.

Eisler did well to emigrate to the USA. At that time in the Soviet Union the cult of personality was reaching new heights, show trials and 'purges' were in full swing.[74] In his flight from fascism,

Eisler could here have easily gone from the frying-pan into the fire, particularly as the victims included writers to whom he was close: Tretiakov and Ernst Ottwalt, who had collaborated on *Kuhle Wampe* and for whose radio short story 'Californian Ballad' Eisler had written the music in 1934.[75]

It was true that in the USA the bureaucratic hurdles Eisler had to clear exceeded anything in his previous experience. He possessed an Austrian passport and a visitor's visa issued by the American consul in Prague. This was valid for six months. At first the prospects of a more extended stay appeared small, above all on account of his left-wing history. In Brecht's milieu in Skovbostrand, where people were beginning to look around them to find the best route out of Denmark, Grete Steffin wrote to Benjamin: 'The Eislers write that their residence permit (they only have a visitor's visa until the middle of June) will probably not be extended and they will then have to leave. The only countries that come into consideration are the Scandinavian ones . . .'[76] He did, however, obtain an extension for six months and in the meantime applied for a 'quota visa';[77] but at the beginning of March 1939 he received an extradition order – leaving him only the option of beginning the whole business over again from abroad. This was despite the fact that since the middle of 1938 he had had the backing of influential names, including the famous columnist Dorothy Thompson, the writer Clifford Odets and, last but not least, the President's wife herself, Eleanor Roosevelt.[78]

The first year in New York was made harder by chronic lack of money. Eisler was initially assisted by a concert of welcome (featuring his works) which the American Music League gave in his honour at the end of February in the New School and whose takings were intended to support him. Marc Blitzstein, who had come to fame as a young composer with his opera *The Cradle will Rock*, lent his assistance; Eisler himself conducted – including two of the cantatas he had written in the previous year, with the baritone Mordecai Bauman as soloist. A few smaller concerts followed in April. A grant helped him over the ticklish summer months – this he received from the American Guild for German Cultural Freedom, following a special plea from Ernst Toller[79] who was on the Council. Eisler had written the music for two plays by Toller in London in 1934–5, *Fire in the Kettle* and *Peace on Earth*. This aid organization had been founded in 1936 by Hubertus Prinz zu Löwenstein and one of its two presidents was Thomas Mann.[80]

When the winter term arrived, Eisler resumed his teaching work at the New School. This had in the meantime – under the directorship of Alvin Johnson – become a 'University in Exile', particularly for German intellectuals.[81] It also catered for adult education and offered both theoretical and popular courses. Politically it was much more moderately progressive than at the start of the 1930s. Nevertheless it presented itself in its journal *Social Research* far more forcibly than other institutes with anti-Nazi articles.[82]

Amongst other things, Eisler gave a series of twelve 'Lectures on the social history of music'. This very lively, if necessarily broadly skeletal outline – stretching from native songs up to Schoenberg and Stravinsky – was addressed to inexperienced listeners; its guiding thread was love: the expression of the subjective relationship in the principal eras of musical history. Obliged to simplify in the extreme, Eisler recommended the method of proceeding with three basic steps, which he summarizes as follows at the beginning of the fifth lecture: 1. Examination of the general economic and political conditions of a period; 2. Investigating musical development from the point of view of the development of materials and 3. Analysing the results: how do economic and political conditions affect music.[83] He was assisted in translation by a counterpoint pupil of Marc Blitzstein, Harry Robin, who shortly afterwards became his assistant.

Since his first appearance in 1935, Eisler had achieved considerable renown with the advanced Left Wing in New York – almost more than can have been welcome to him in his situation. Because of his imperilled position he was obliged to avoid being openly associated with it. He wrote the music for a dramatic performance of Hofmann Hays' *A Song about America*, staged by Jules Dassin, under the pseudonym of John Garden; the subject-matter of the play was the struggle for social justice in the United States since the Declaration of Independence, the first sentences of which were set to music by Eisler. The occasion was a large-scale festival to the memory of Lenin in Madison Square Garden. The opening song 'Sweet Liberty Land', which Eisler set in the style of a Negro Spiritual, became famous. As Hays recalled, '*Sweet Liberty Land* was a hit with the left-liberal movement and for some time was practically the national anthem of the American Communist Party in those happier days of the United Front. The Party was never able to do anything comparable again.'[84]

In the thirties, the American 'Red Decade', the later political confrontation did not present itself so unequivocally: 'on the one hand there was big business and anti-Communism, and on the other hand liberals and admirers of the Soviet Union . . . Especially with the crisis in the world economy and the advance of fascism in Europe, the feeling became more widespread that the only ray of hope that remained was the Soviet Union.'[85] The more conservative among the émigrés objected to the Americans' lack of prejudice; they invariably failed to understand the ideological challenge but were lost in admiration for the constructive achievements. Thus Rosenstock-Huessy: 'In 1933 America's intelligentsia were exclusively interested in Russia, and it is difficult to imagine today the extent to which America's young intellectuals would regard as old-fashioned anyone who did not profess communism.'[86]

Even so, from this point on, Eisler exercised the greatest discretion. After the Anschluss in March, his Austrian passport was worth less than before. It took almost three years of dispiriting filling out of application forms before he could receive his papers for a permanent residential permit.

After 1938 concurrent work on chamber music and film scores became his main occupation. Firstly he completed in New York the 'Reisesonate' [Travel Sonata] for violin and piano which he had already begun in Prague. There followed a string quartet in two movements, Variations and Finale, which despite an original plan for the treatment of twelve-note technique, sounds more academic than the witty and more accessible Violin Sonata. Common to both is Eisler's penchant for strong contrasts and opposing characteristics. Sprightly energico and feroce passages are juxtaposed with others of discreetly distant lyrical tenderness – not infrequently marked *grazioso* and at all events to be played without sentimentality.

Practice and theory: the project for film music

Only at the first glance does it appear an almost macabre irony that Eisler, who since his years in Berlin had castigated and fought against the separate growth of serious and light music under market conditions, was just the one person who appeared to embody this division in the USA.

Film music, and particularly that coming from America, is generally identified with commercial *kitsch* – of a quality as low as its standards of technological reproduction are high. That this need not be so, and that there could be a genuine rapport between the most progressive compositional technique and the most recent technological advances was what Eisler set out to prove in the ensuing years in New York and Hollywood. As a pioneer in this field he had ten years' experience behind him – from the time when in 1927 he and Hindemith had been commissioned by the Triergon Society to compose a small film score each for the Baden-Baden Music Festival.

At the time the Berlin music critic Hanns Gutmann had tried in an essay to predict the future development of sound films. He was not, he noted, so naïve as to imagine that 'aesthetic considerations could always . . . carry some influence with the moguls of the art industry'. However, in the future, the profitability even of an original film score would be assured, since the authentic music was now recorded on the sound track and could be reproduced at will. These new circumstances have to be taken into account through an appropriate style and an altered way of composing. Technical progress in the context of the arts has always arisen from the urge to give art 'increased effectiveness'. Conversely, it still remained true that *new techniques call for new art*.

However, the initial function of the sound film – corresponding to the misconceptions previously practised in the silent film and then in broadcasting – was to be that of a surrogate for existing art: it was to begin as a cheap substitute for opera and operetta, ballet, revue and theatrical spectacle. Like its predecessors, the new medium was to split up existing works of art into their component parts and reproduce only those which it could handle. After this early phase it necessarily became a matter of making use of every available resource and technical facility without applying them to an existing art as a sort of substitute, but rather to integrate visual and acoustical resources into a completely new style for sound films. If, Gutmann concludes, it is 'the most important task of present-day music to transform utility music once more into an artistic music, and art music into a useful music, then the sound film has the best prospects in this respect too'.[87]

These prospects, which were hoped for on account of the medium's impact on the masses, were soon to be squandered by the world of commercialism. For the sound film was not the offspring of artists, but of capitalist groups who had quite different hopes in producing it. Even so, concessions were made for areas unconnected with the immediate market, which took on the role of a kind of alibi. Consequently, the brute fact that films are expensive placed those directors and composers who were not willing constantly to sacrifice their artistic demands or their political convictions in the following dilemma. They could only maintain and develop their technical level with advanced works. These were a dispensable luxury for the big film industry. Thus, except for grants, what remained was the obligation to put up one's prestige for a lucrative offer and make allowances for what it entailed in terms of subject-matter and sponsor. Then it would be possible to resume one's own work on the strength of the money thus earned. As it happened this dilemma was fairly well illustrated by the first two films for which Eisler wrote the music in New York in 1938–9.

The second of them, *Pete Roleum and his Cousins*, as the title suggests, was financed by the American oil industry. This was a film using puppets and animation, and, shown in magnificent technicolour, it was the major attraction in the hall of Combined Petroleum Exhibits at the New York World Fair of the summer of 1939. It was a public relations exercise for this branch of industry.

11   With Helen van Dongen in New York (1939) at the shooting of
Joseph Losey's cartoon film *Pete Roleum and his Cousins*

Joseph Losey, whose film career it launched, directed the film together with Helen van Dongen, the niece of the Dutch painter, who was at that time living with Ivens.[88]

The technical innovations of 'Pete Roleum', including those on the soundtrack, attracted attention. For the animated film Eisler wrote a number of brief, mercurial pieces, which for the first time were recorded using a process similar to stereophonic sound. His assistant, Harry Robin, whom he made 'supervisor for sound', produced outstanding work to earn a Rockefeller Fellowship for training as a sound engineer.[89]

In contrast, Joris Ivens' documentary film about the fight of the 'Four Hundred Million' Chinese against the Japanese invasion represented, for the artists who contributed to it, an exercise in political solidarity on a non-commercial basis.[90] Financed on a tight budget, the film, which under normal circumstances could not have been made, was produced with Ivens doing the filming under unusual conditions and finally with Dudley Nichols providing the commentary, Frederic March speaking it and Eisler composing the music all for no fee. Hardly any industrial sponsors could be found to expose East Asian fascism; it was difficult, too, to provide funds for the new kind of music which so significantly enhanced the film.

Ivens' chronicle of the Chinese struggle for liberation and national independence was obliged to make do with inferior visual material and relied heavily on Eisler's music. Collaboration on it was particularly close: a number of sequences (bombardment and sandstorm) were put together on the basis of the music. Not the least of its virtues was that without imitating Chinese timbres and rhythms it captured the atmosphere of the Far East. In particular it avoided flag-waving heroics. A good example of Eisler's specifically realistic approach is in the way he composed the bombing raid on Canton: as variations on a theme which uses the air-raid warning signal.

Ivens tells us that Eisler first examined the function of a film sequence in its context and then sought out the dimension it lacked, but which needed to be present; on this basis he imagined a new quality for the whole, and this he tried to achieve in his composition, and later by mixing.[91] Naturally the typical short,

12   Eisler with Joris Ivens (lying), studying a map of China in Valley Cottage, New York (1938). Ivens' first film on China, *400 Millionen*, dates from this time.

self-contained sequences appropriate to a documentary film were ideally suited to the succinct style of his writing. As a critic wrote, Eisler's score demonstrates that film music can be of the same standard as that found in the concert hall. This was a reflection on the impressionistic film scores of Hollywood, which were 'a mishmash of Tchaikovsky, Debussy and Victor Herbert'.

In point of fact the film score for *400 Millionen* was so concentrated that Eisler was immediately able to compile two works of chamber music from it: *Variationen über ein marschartiges Thema* [Variations on a March-like Theme] ('The Long March' is that of Mao Tse-Tung's Red Army) and Five Pieces for Orchestra, a brilliant set with a one-and-a-half-minute passacaglia as its central section, a masterpiece of contrapuntal invention and concision. It was not in every subsequent film score that Eisler could maintain the standard that permitted him to extract concert versions. His chamber music of the ensuing years, taking the place of the suites he had been writing since 1930, was largely derived from film scores. It is living proof that *applied music*, if it is sufficiently elaborate in itself, can have several functions and is perfectly able to stand on its own feet.

In March 1939 Eisler's residence permit had expired and the extradition order reached him. This meant he was in danger of being deported. A Mexican visa might mean (temporary) salvation with the hope of re-entering the USA as soon as possible with a re-entry visa. Under the progressive President Cardenas, Mexico was then a political sanctuary which had also received many of the Germans who had fought in Spain with the International Brigade. In a letter addressed to the trade-union leader Toledano which he roughed out on 9 March 1939, Eisler wrote:

A visa for Mexico is a matter of life and death to us. We know that Mexico is the only country that guarantees asylum to political refugees and for this reason I venture to turn to you with a request for help. I am a composer (my name is one of the five best known in modern music), a pupil of Arnold Schoenberg. I am myself also a teacher of composition and harmony. My compositions are performed in all the major cities of Europe and also of America, and I have composed the music for fourteen films and plays. I am certain that I can also be of service to the musical movement in Mexico. In any case I would in no way be a burden on your country. I would be very grateful to you . . . if it were possible for you to give me speedy assistance . . .[92]

Eisler was successful. Through the intervention of the Mexican composer Silvestre Revueltas he was given a job teaching harmony and orchestration at the National Conservatory in Mexico City. The circumstances which went with the job were very mixed. In April he was able to move into a luxurious house, formerly the residence of the Brazilian ambassador, where he could accommodate numerous guests. But his pecuniary needs persisted and salary payments could hardly be expected amidst the red tape of Mexican bureaucracy. In addition there were endless negotiations at the American Consulate about the re-entry papers, which he finally obtained by making a detour to Vera Cruz.

Among the guests during that summer were Joris Ivens and Helen van Dongen, and also the baritone Mordecai Bauman

who introduced Eisler to Clifford Odets. At the time Odets was
already a successful writer for the theatre and films. Eisler was all
the more keen to make contact with him because he was missing
his theatrical work with Brecht. Already within the next year he
composed the score for Odets' *Night Music* in New York. During
these months Brecht sent him *Mutter Courage* [Mother Courage]
and *Das Verhör des Lukullus* [The Trial of Lucullus]. Eisler wrote
to Brecht recommending Hofmann Hays – who was then also in
Mexico City – as a translator. The two plays came out in 1941 as
Brecht's first American publications.[93]

To a letter from Piscator announcing that he was to be a
colleague at the New School in New York as from the winter term
when he would be starting his dramatic workshop there, Eisler
replied in August that he was willing to undertake a course on
theatre music. He added: 'Here I have written a play with a very
talented young American, Hofmann Hays, *The Life of Daniel
Drew* – who was a big speculator of the last century . . . Naturally
there are a lot of songs and music in it.'[94] (In fact he did not get
round to composing this, but six months later wrote the music for
Hays' *Medicine Show* – a satirical plea for more government
assistance in matters of health. Jules Dassin staged it on Broadway
early in 1940.)

On many of his evenings in Mexico Eisler entertained Spanish
campaigners at his home; they would sing songs and ballads
from the Civil War and he would accompany them at the piano.
The mood was nostalgic and often bitter. The victory of Franco's
Phalangists would scarcely have been possible without the aid of
the German army. That the latter was moreover preparing for a
far bigger war was becoming increasingly apparent. It was in this
atmosphere that news arrived of the Hitler–Stalin pact. Whilst
the left-wing émigrés had already been divided about the rights
and wrongs of the Moscow trials, the Jews among them in particular reacted indignantly against this pact with the régime of
concentration camps, which they considered that no amount of
tactical advantage could excuse. Eisler too rejected this pact.
For nearly two years, in fact until the entry of the German army
into the Soviet Union cleared the lines once more, Eisler was
shunned by members of the Communist Party, who even avoided

greeting him.[95] They even went so far as to suspect him of Trot-skyism – which in his case was quite absurd. However, at that time the term 'Trotskyite' had lost its earlier more precise mean-ing through excessive use. It was simply applied to any Marxist who criticized the line of the Communist Party of the Soviet Union. Hitler's declaration of war made it easier for positions to be clarified.

Immediately after his return to New York, Eisler put in motion a new plan which was intended to guarantee his financial indepen-dence for a while. Armed with a commission from Oxford Uni-versity Press for a book on film music, he asked the director of the New School, Alvin Johnson, to intercede with the Rockefeller Foundation for an appropriate research project. John Marshall, the Foundation's director, requested particulars. On 1 November Johnson wrote to him in a letter accompanying the outline for the project:

The Rockefeller Foundation has done a wonderful work in making it possible for scores of refugee scholars to live through the period of adjustment. When the history of American culture is written fifty years from now the historian will point to many new impulses given to the sciences by this work of the Foundation. The arts, particularly in their creative aspects, are more difficult to deal with. It would be hard to hold a man like Eisler within the framework of an ordinary educational institu-tion. Necessarily he will develop relations with [the film] industry. But it is an industry which plays or ought to play a tremendously important part in our culture; and any contribution that tends to raise its level of merit deserves support.[96]

Previous recipients of grants included Joris Ivens, who had already started on a project for an educational film for the Rockefeller Foundation in 1936,[97] and T. W. Adorno, whose Princeton Radio Research Project received its support. Eisler met with a surprising amount of helpfulness. Once he had succeeded in obtaining the co-operation of the Museum of Modern Art Film Library to work with the New School and the Rockefeller Foun-dation and was able to present a very positive opinion from the sociologist Paul F. Lazarsfeld, his project was rapidly approved. It was to begin on 1 February 1940, was to run for two years and was allocated the considerable sum of 20 000 dollars, of which 6000 were to be Eisler's honorarium.

The object was to investigate the relationship between the moving picture, music, original sound and synthetic sound with a view to finding new possibilities. It started out from the hypothesis that radically new music, and in particular twelve-note music, could fulfil a much more effective function in films than traditional music, which had descended to the level of mechanical clichés. In order to give a practical demonstration of how advanced musical material was to be introduced into a film score, four experimental productions were planned, to take place at half-yearly intervals. Here Eisler was to show, by means of sequences from feature films and documentaries, *why* their music was so bad, and to write his own alternatives so as to permit concrete comparisons. What was initially envisaged was a small public of cinema people from New York and Hollywood; later it was decided that groups of interested amateurs and students would be able to borrow the material. The productions were centred on four contributory problems: 1. the use of new musical material, in other words harmonies, rhythms and forms, in films; 2. scoring and its relation to the recording microphone; 3. problems of mixing, including the combining of dialogue with music, and 4. the relationship between musical dramaturgy and the plot of a film. Basic questions of aesthetics were also to be included in the discussion.[98]

As a whole, Eisler's film music project was directed more towards a new artistic practice than to empirically provable theoretical findings. The heart of the entire undertaking, and at the same time the starting point for the results later formulated in the book *Composing for the Films*, was a detailed analysis of and subsequent composition for an early silent film by Ivens: *Rain*. He documented its visual effects. Made in Amsterdam in 1929, it had been remade as a sound film three years later by Helen van Dongen, using impressionistic music by Lou Lichtveld which was ill-suited to it. Eisler went through every take and examined the rhythms of the images and the specific emotionality of the manifold effects of the rain which Ivens had already filmed as a symbol of sorrow.

The various expressive possibilities within this emotional field were cast in the form of variations for quintet. The *Vierzehn Arten, den Regen zu beschreiben* [Fourteen Ways of Describing Rain], which he himself considered his finest piece of chamber music, was at the same time a homage to Schoenberg: Eisler adopted the instrumentation of *Pierrot lunaire* and placed an anagram using Schoenberg's initials at the beginning and at the end. 'I do not want to say', he declared later, 'that the crucial theme of the twentieth century is, shall we say, the anatomy of sorrow – or the anatomy of melancholy. But that too may present itself in a work of music.'[99] Not only the (distant) horror of the war, but also the loneliness of the big city and longing for peace are combined in what Eisler called these 'Fourteen Ways in which one can be acceptably sorrowful'.

Eisler chose the instruments of *Pierrot* not just in honour of Schoenberg. He wanted to prove that a chamber instrumentation for film music was not only adequate but a good deal more appropriate than the use of the customary film orchestra with its bloated string section. For above all it is a question of finding an *instrumentation suited to the microphone*. From the start, Eisler's own turned towards not only Schoenberg but also to early Stravinsky and jazz. The shift of emphasis to wind instruments for the sake of a harder and more neutral sound with precise audibility of the polyphony was in the first place something of a consequence of his reaction against the symphonic tradition. He was at the time one of the first composers to try out new methods of acoustical transmission – the 'wireless' ones of broadcasting and those incorporated in film soundtracks. His latest film music and the chamber-music versions of it confirmed to Eisler in America that his scoring, which had meanwhile become more refined, was well suited to the new technical requirements. In fact, the diminution of the dynamic range and of intensity of timbre as well as the loss of firm outlines and spatial depth through the use of the microphone could not be made good simply by calling on larger orchestral forces. What had to be considered was much rather the complementary use of new electrical instruments (such as the electric piano, organ and guitar).

In Eisler's view, psychologizing was one of the deadly sins of film music; it was typified by expressions peculiar to the industry, such as 'to get atmosphere, to establish a mood'. The use of new musical material to correspond to the dramaturgical task in hand was intended specifically to guard against such false, mechanical associations.

The important thing here is not the greater availability of dissonances but the dissolution of the pre-established conventional musical language. Everything derives directly from the concrete demands of the image. A piece full of dissonances can be perfectly conventional in its processes and one which uses relatively simpler material can be thoroughly advanced and fresh because of the constructive use of its resources. Even a sequence of triads can sound strange if they are taken away from their usual run of associations and simply derived from the suggestions of the particular image in question.[100]

Thus, just as the old timbres were unsuited to film music which took its job seriously, it was all the more true that the conventional symphonic *forms* were too: the inferior recourse to chromatic tensions in the manner of Wagner which still firmly held sway were matched by a leitmotiv technique which had already become mechanical. How terribly out of place it was could be demonstrated by comparing it with those possibilities which had more recently become available. In *Composing for the Films* Eisler wrote of this:

The special aptitude of new music for constructing consistent, precise small forms in which there is nothing superfluous, which come straight to the point, and which require no extension on architectonic grounds, is quite obvious ... The emancipation of the individual motivic shapes from symmetry and repeatability allows even the individual musical ideas to be formulated much more incisively and dramatically and the relationships between the various characters to be free from all embroidery. In new music there is no room for padding.[101]

It can meet the demand to increase the dramatic 'presence' of the film by its ability to construct its forms using the sharpest contrasts – in a similar way to the technical principle of abrupt changes of image. The composer is then compelled to think in fragments rather than in developments, and must use the relationship between these fragments to produce what would otherwise be effected by the form resulting from thematic development.

In place of traditional musical architecture there was now organization on the basis of the form of the images.

The sensitive responses of which new music was capable, largely due to its concise miniature forms, at last permitted a genuine dramaturgical function. Instead of, as previously, providing a romantically descriptive imitation or an illustrative accompaniment to the plot or its mood, it could form a dramaturgical counterpoint to the sequence of images, in other words, relate to them in a complementary way. What was to be sought after was not an identity of image and music but rather a relationship of question and answer, affirmation and negation. There was indeed a unifying motive in the gestures, but at the deepest level the relationship to the unifying motive should be an antithetical one. By presenting the musical events, alongside the visual events, the music thus placing itself in contradiction to the surface happenings, the *meaning* of the scene, or of the document, could be brought out. This precisely calculated state of tension could generate its own internal drive giving an extra dimension to that of the cinematic plot.[102]

This can be demonstrated in a purer form with the more marked objectivity of a documentary film than in a feature film. For this reason, in addition to Ivens' *Rain*, Eisler chose firstly scenes of children which Joseph Losey had filmed in a camp, and then scenes of nature, mainly taken from the film *White Flood* [*Eis*]; this depicted the cold and the forces of nature in the Arctic, ranging from a snowstorm to crashing icebergs.[103]

From the Arctic scenes Eisler produced the splendid Chamber Symphony op. 69 for 15 solo instruments, and from his music for the camp scenes came the Septet No. 1 op. 92a. This consists of variations on American children's songs.

When Silvestre Revueltas died in Mexico late in 1940, John Steinbeck and Herbert Kline asked Eisler to go from New York to Mexico City to take his place and write the music for *The Forgotten Village*. Steinbeck's novel, on which the screenplay was based, deals with ignorance and superstition in an Indian village which, though overrun with an epidemic, resists modern medicine. Eisler had six weeks in which to write an eighty-minute score which had to be precisely synchronized with the film. The work was nerve-racking, but he was to be repaid by the impact it made.[104] Although the film came up against censorship problems, Eisler's collaboration with Steinbeck was a factor that helped to smooth the way for his move to Hollywood. While he was still in New York he put together from this sizable score a Suite in nine movements, the Nonet No. 2. In April 1942 he moved from the East coast to the West.

In the concluding report of his film project, which Eisler completed after a six-month extension in October 1942, he recalls that he had set out to show how the gap between the highly developed photographic and scenic techniques of film and the notably more underdeveloped state of film music could be closed. In his later book, which embraces a much more ramified association of ideas, he mentions as one of the causes an all-too-neglected discrepancy: the opposition between seeing and hearing has grown historically.

People adapt to the rational and ultimately highly industrial bourgeois order of things through the use of their eyes, since these are accustomed to understand reality right from the start as a reality of things, in fact basically of consumer goods; this adaptation was not provided in the same degree by the use of the ears. Compared with seeing, hearing is 'archaic' and has not kept up with technology. It could be said that to respond basically with the unselfish ear rather than with the alert, appraising eye is in some way contrary to the late industrial epoch. For this reason there resides in aural perception as such, to an incomparably greater extent than in the optical, an element of the collective. At least two of the most important factors in occidental music, harmonic and contrapuntal polyphony and its rhythmic articulation, directly indicate a multiplicity after the model of the ecclesiastical community of former times. This direct relationship to the collective which adheres to the phenomenon appears to be associated with the spatial depth, the feeling of something all-embracing and drawing individuals into itself, which characterizes all music.[105]

The book is also a pointed critique of the cynical abuse by the culture industry of this element of collectivity in the standard film music of Hollywood. This encourages the perpetuation of modes of feeling which have long been out of date, supplies acoustical reinforcement to the visual illusion and melodiously mixes nebulous yearning with slick jollity; this is done by means of set pieces derived from late-bourgeois music. This makes such music politically dangerous, even if only in a very indirect way. Whilst reinforcing the vague feelings the audience have brought along with them, it confirms individual relationships, and beyond these the social structure, just as they are. Such music makes for lack of awareness, and hinders change. It aids the constant rehashing of the threadbare scheme of 'through-darkness-into-light' as the 'tense' feature film with a happy end. Any possible objections are silenced by the impressive level of technical perfection – always the highest possible – with which the whole show is produced: this gives it the appearance of something interesting, something which obeys its own logic, and hence that is in some way reasonable.

The change in this practice for which Eisler hoped has still not come about today. At the time he hoped to create a fresh basis for the genre, which serious composers had treated in a perfunctory way, though his film-music project together with his own compositions and his elucidations of them in a book. But directors and producers continued to cling to the unshakable prejudice that film music on the one hand should be easy on the ear and on the other hand should not be disturbing. This again frightened off composers, who preferred to write for the ballet. Eisler's demands have been as little met today as at the time when he formulated them.

The claims of his undertaking are further reflected in the list of consultants he appended to his concluding report. They range from Brecht, Charlie Chaplin and Clifford Odets through Fritz Lang and William Dieterle to musicians like Schoenberg, Steuermann and Kolisch, as well as the conductors Jascha Horenstein and Fritz Stiedry.[106]

This list also includes his most important collaborator: T. W. Adorno. As his researches into radio music were closely related to Eisler's and he too moved from New York to Hollywood at almost exactly the same time, it seemed logical for the two to collaborate, particularly on the book for the Oxford University Press. When *Composing for the Films* was about to come out there in 1947 under both their names, Adorno withdrew his for political reasons.[107] The fact that Adorno was responsible for much of the final text can easily be seen from its style.

Hollywood – a temporary refuge

Eisler arrived during the *late* phase of Hollywood's 'greatness' when early in 1942 he made it the final stopping-place of his exile. It was still the 'glamorous' Hollywood of the star cult, the glittering revues with big bands in the background and the pretentious extravaganzas that provided millions of anonymous filmgoers with models for the dreams of their waking hours. Show business and musicals were in full swing. Television had barely begun to reveal itself as a possible rival.

At the same time, however, the war was again making it possible to produce films with a political content: this was the time of anti-Nazi films and strongly pro-Soviet feeling amongst many artists; they admired the resistance and the victories over fascism as deeds of collective heroism, declared their solidarity with missions to supply aid and provisions and demanded the establishment of the second front.

During the war, Hollywood became a new centre for German émigrés, or more precisely those among them who were eminent in literature, music and the theatre. Heinrich and Thomas Mann, Feuchtwanger and Döblin, Werfel, Frank and Zuckmayer lived there, as did Schoenberg, Ernst Toch and Bruno Walter, directors like Max Reinhardt and Berthold Viertel, and actors such as Kortner, Lorre and Homolka.[108]

However, this concentration of great names in a single place did not by any means result in any extensive communication amongst themselves. Cliques, personal resentments, reciprocal demarcations that had often been brought with them from Europe were again cultivated. Moreover the majority felt out of place. In the face of the film industry whose overwhelming interest in profitability they regarded with scorn and thought of as cynical, many émigrés nevertheless entertained hopes of material success. The virtually continual frustration and the feeling of rivalry with one another created a tense atmosphere. The contrast between the not unrespectable standards of living of some and the humiliating circumstances of the majority rarely corresponded with the varying respect which they had enjoyed as artists in Germany and Austria. Segregation was frequently the outcome.

Hardly any of them came into contact with progressive American or English artists staying in Hollywood at the time: Steinbeck and Dreiser, Odets and Isherwood, Chaplin and Laughton. Eisler was one of the few who represented points of contact between the various circles (and arts): music and film, theatre and literature.

Immediately after his arrival Eisler met Brecht, who had been living in Santa Monica since July 1941. For five years their only contact with each other had been by post. Initially Eisler had hoped in New York that Brecht would settle on the East coast for some time so that they could there resume their joint productions. Thus in August 1941 he wrote to Piscator:

Brecht has already written to me. I am glad that he is at last out of that miserable predicament. With his family, things will not be easy for him; the best thing would be if he could make some money in Hollywood before coming over here. Obviously for this he will have to make use of his contacts, as this is the only way in which he could get a job. To make use of Weill too in this way is perfectly correct. Just think what a *financial* position the poor chap *must* be in after all that. And two *children* are no joke. It makes things very expensive: schools, clothes, living expenses, etc. Let us hope that he gets a job and will then be in a position to stay with us for some time in New York and work with us. But in any proposals we put to him now we must at all events think first of his financial situation. If we could offer him financial guarantees then the whole thing would be different. But where could we find any?[109]

Brecht found life particularly difficult in the 'centre of the international narcotics trade',[110] as he called Hollywood. In his journal he recorded his displeasure even with the spontaneous, unreflective behaviour of those Germans in his milieu who sought contacts in the film industry.

Here it is difficult for émigrés to avoid either falling into furious abuse of 'the Americans' or else 'talking with their weekly cheque in their mouths', as Kortner reproachfully says of those who earn good money and speak well of their employers. Criticism is in general directed at certain phenomena of rampant capitalism, the far advanced commercialization of art, the complacency of the middle class, the emergence of training as something to be bartered rather than utilized, the formalistic nature of democracy (which has lost its economic foundation, namely the independent rivalry of independent producers of market goods). Thus Homolka throws Bruno Frank out because he stands up and thunders: 'I will not permit the President to be criticized here', Kortner reveals Lang as the perpetrator of an anti-semitic remark, Nürnberg hates Lorre etc.[111]

Six months later he noted: 'When I see Eisler it is a bit as if I am stumbling around muddle-headedly in some crowd and suddenly hear my old name called.'[112] The memory of their work together – and the prospect of more like it – seemed to him his only security against losing his footing in an environment he felt to be hostile.

All the same, during the years which followed, the work they did together amounted to comparatively little in concrete terms. The main reason was that Eisler was now spending a lot of time on his chamber and orchestral music and was in every respect moving closer to his teacher Schoenberg again. A further reason was the driving need to earn his living: Eisler wrote eight film scores in Hollywood.[113] Ultimately there came about a temporary estrangement, to which a further contributory factor was Eisler's contact with Adorno and Thomas Mann, whom Brecht disliked. Their only work together in films was on Fritz Lang's anti-Nazi film *Hangmen also Die*;[114] the only substantial theatre music he wrote for Brecht was that for *Galilei*.[115]

This kind of thing was certainly eclipsed by a production in which the spirit of exile is incomparably captured: Eisler's 'Hollywood Song Book', for which he chiefly used texts by Brecht. 'This collection . . . represents a landmark in the history of song, just as had previously the great cycles of Schubert, Schumann, Brahms and Hugo Wolf. The originality of the musical invention and richness of characteristic types are perhaps its most impressive features . . . Everything is incredibly vital.'[116] The rich variety which creates this vitality is that of the contradictions that the work deals with. In the midst of war it requires some justification to be working on songs which have as their theme one's own existence, one's hopes and one's memories. 'To work lyrically here', Brecht noted in his working journal, 'even if relating to the present, means retreating into one's ivory tower. It is as if one were working in gold filigree. There is something whimsical, eccentric, blinkered about it. Such lyricism is a message in a bottle: the battle for Smolensk is about lyricism too.'[117]

As signals of what seems to have disappeared from sight, as observations made from a great distance, both text and music are characterized by a peculiar sense of *remoteness*. This isolation – from the present, from the environment, from one's self – is written into them. This is especially true of the seven *Hollywood-Elegien*, but also of many of the settings of poems Brecht had written in the preceding years in Scandinavia. The songs to words by Anacreon and Hölderlin constitute special groups.

In terms of compositional technique, Eisler achieves this re- moteness by means of a new kind of synthesis. He makes use of elements from his early Viennese songs, in motivically developed passages, as well as from the militant songs with their accompani- ment of supporting chords. Numerous stylistic references (rang- ing from the great Lieder tradition from Schubert on to classical jazz) are pasted together as in collages. However these brief, extremely concentrated structures sound perfectly homogeneous. In fact the music is dominated by the structural principles of twelve-note technique; but the originality of the songs lies rather in their fusion of features of different types of song into a new whole. It is as if an interchange of experiences was taking place between them. Thus the familiar appears in an unfamiliar con- text. In the relationship between words and notes Eisler's ex- periences with the dramaturgical counterpoint of film music have left their mark. Dialectically deployed discrepancies and allusions have to be worked out by the listener. Deviations, parodies and omissions deceive the listener's expectation by being associated with what is already known: moreover, in their sensual and intellectual fascination, they represent an invitation to the listener to increase his enjoyment and understanding[118] (see ex. 28).

It may be supposed that only with these barbs did it seem to Eisler justifiable to take up once more such a bourgeois and subjective genre as the song with piano accompaniment. He saw in it the possibility of rescuing political ideas and images from the

Ex.28   *Die Hollywood-Elegien*, 'Über die vier Städte'

da - mit der Ge - stank der   Gier   und des   E - - lends

nicht zu   ih - nen hin - auf dringt.

process of historical submersion, of bringing them up to date and
giving them a new kind of impact. This attitude to the Lied is quite
distinct from that of the Romantics. In their day music could give
the literary subjectivity of songs an atmosphere which elevated
them, and emphatic melancholy could become a theme which in
the salon represented the 'community'.[119] Eisler was not writing
for a small circle. He sought, by means of the concert song,
to impart social understanding, enlightenment – using, as an

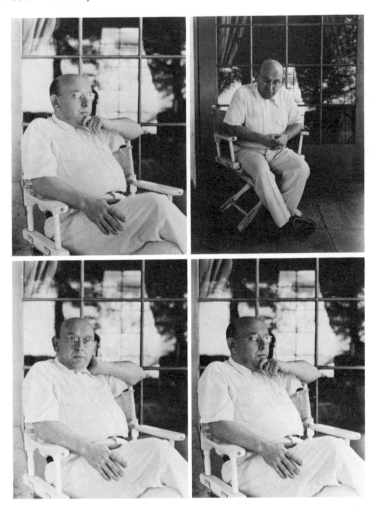

13   Composer in Hollywood (1946). In his house at Pacific Palisades, Malibu

exception, the theme of his own subjectivity which in Hollywood was exposed to special experiences.

In that gloomy eternal spring of Hollywood I said to Brecht, shortly after we had come together again . . .: 'This is the classic place in which one should write elegies . . . We are not absolved in Hollywood. We must simply go along with describing it . . .' 'It' was the dreadful idyll of that landscape which of itself had arisen more from the ideas of land speculators. . . If the water there was shut off for three days, the jackals would be back and so would the desert sands . . . So in that strange, whitewashed idyll it was necessary to express oneself concisely.[120]

Of the *remoteness* of the *Hollywood-Elegien* Brecht noted that it was 'produced by that town: nearly all of its inhabitants possess it. Those houses do not become personal property by being lived in, only by chequebooks; their owners do not so much live in them as make use of them. The houses are appendages to garages.'[121]

The remoteness which permeates text and music appears in various aspects. More important than that produced by the town and the landscape is the repellence of the false fascination of the film industry. Not least the work describes the need to keep one's distance from oneself at this time when the obligation on artists to prostitute themselves left few unaffected.

'Under the green pepper trees/Musicians walk the streets in pairs/With writers. Bach/Has a string quartet in his pocket. Dante wiggles/His skinny bottom.' These are macabre miniatures, which with laconic clarity and concision 'burst open an entire topic'[122] (see ex. 29).

'Every morning, to earn my keep/I go to the market where lies are sold./Full of hope/I line up amongst the sellers.' Most of Eisler's elegies do not extend beyond a single page of score. Carefree, elegant performance is asked for. An exception is the second, which almost overstrains its sarcasm ('To be performed with morose sentimentality'): 'The city is named after the angels/ And one meets angels everywhere./They smell of oil and wear golden pessaries/And with blue rings round their eyes/They feed writers in their swampy pools every morning.'[123]

Many of Brecht's poems took on their final form only after discussion with Eisler. Of his own artistic gains from the

Ex.29   *Die Hollywood-Elegien*, 'Unter den grünen Pfefferbäumen'

Ex.29 *continued*

Dan - te schwenkt den dür - ren Hin - - - tern.

composition of them Brecht noted: 'For me his setting was what performance would be for a play: the test. He reads with enormous exactitude.'[124]

The latter remark is relevant above all to the historical texts – Pascal and Shakespeare as well as Anacreon and Hölderlin – which Eisler selected and elaborated. If the *Hollywood-Elegien* were already descriptions of paradise as hell and an expression of non-identification with his own situation, in the *Fragmente* for which he put together lines from the above authors as texts to be set, Eisler frequently expressed sorrow and bitterness. Discreetly, and without a trace of sentimentality, the émigré acknowledges his homesickness, and laments the 'indignity of the age' (see ex. 30). These songs are to be performed nimbly and brightly, and were intended to give later hearers pause for thought; at all costs they are intended to steer clear of emotive expression of the 'self-satisfaction in one's own despair and one's own defeat'.[125] The flexibility and variety of the musical technique allow the singer no sentimentality and no indulgences of the artistic temperament (see ex. 31).

When Eisler reflects the image of his homeland through

Ex.30   *Anakreon-Fragmente*, 'Dir auch wurde Sehnsucht nach der Heimat tödlich'

Ex.31   *Hölderlin-Fragmente*, 'An die Hoffnung'

Hölderlin (the Jacobin), his intention is to bring out the contradictions of his own situation by 'objectivizing' it and observing it from a distance: at the same time he is *citing* the unhappy history of the relationship of great German artists to their fatherland. For him, as a political artist during the war and in exile, this meant alienation from the workers' movement, impotence in the face of a situation in which young Germans on the Eastern front were 'sacrificing themselves in a false cause'.[126] Depression about the victories of the German army, the absence of any effective internal resistance, and then the ravages of the later stages of the war; all this overlaid the memory of Germany and of the beauty of the 'sacred heart of the people' and her culture, '. . . learning, where your sun/Gently lights the artist to seriousness . . .'[127]

These songs that he wrote at the hour of his deepest depression are also extolling Germany. This indeed was the contradiction which Eisler worked out at a compositional level which is all the more astonishing for the fact that at the same time he was obliged to come to terms with the monopolistically organized Hollywood film industry in order to earn his living. Whilst, with increasing thoroughness, the film companies were organizing the sell-out of individualistic culture, he wrote songs – already for the time after his return – as documents of individual artistic resistance. 'If dialectics exists at all, it exists here',[128] he later remarked about his attitude during these complicated and by no means unproductive years.

The 'Hollywood Song Book', comprising a total of fifty pieces, provides important information about Eisler's handling of composition in his songs. He generally proceeded in four stages: choice of the text, his arrangement of it, its composition and its placement in the cycle.

In the first place he did not believe in uncritically adopting texts even by great writers; rather he sought out what would still be relevant in a contemporary context, and this was not much. But even what little there was would generally be too long to be usable as a song text. Often it would have become difficult to understand (as, say, with Hölderlin's mythological allusions), or else would conjure up absurd associations. To condense such poems and extract topically relevant ideas from them, and then to form them into a new text, was an artistic technique on which Eisler laid great stress.

Eisler's great virtue is that in composing his music he then resists the text he has produced: he does not allow himself to be led into adding a musical 'double', illustrating it, or simply identifying with it. His task is interpretation, elucidation – as with the art of portraiture, which does not start until after the copy of the model has been made. The multiple aspects of the textual meaning, its 'polysemy', have to be liberated.

Finally, the groupings and linkages making up cyclical entities are of importance. In terms of coherence and perspective, individual songs will be too weak to stand alone; only in the cycle can they make their point; and in addition the individual unit can be given further significance by the context of the passage into which it is incorporated. Since by virtue of its Romantic tradition the art song can tempt the performer to take mere mood as a basis and to present intimate material with pathos, and customary practices of solo performance increase this attitude still further, Eisler sought to guard against this not only in his compositional writing but also by means of precise performance directions. Expressivity and the affectation of expression appear almost only in parodistic form. His ideal interpretation was one of elegant and amicable singing, of intelligent informing or reporting, not without discreet emotion. It may be remembered that, according to Sonnleithner, Schubert's view was much the same: 'Moreover, he never permitted violent expression in a performance. The Lieder singer generally is relating only alien experiences and feelings, and he himself does not represent the person whose emotions he is portraying.'[129]

A victim of the witch-hunt

It appears as a bitter irony of history that it was in fact Hanns Eisler – who had acted apolitically since the beginning of the war – who was the first artist in the USA to become a victim of the Cold War.

This fateful development began to loom just when, for the first time, things were going well for him financially. He was living in a house at Malibu (Pacific Palisades), where a number of friends would meet on Sunday afternoons, many of them famous names. Among the closer friends were Clifford Odets and Charlie Chaplin as well as theatrical people such as Harold Clurman and Stella Adler. Here Schoenberg and Adorno met, and there were encounters between people from the film world and the jazz scene too, as when the clarinettist Artie Shaw met Ava Gardner, or Salka Viertel her friend Greta Garbo. Most of them knew about Eisler's serious music only from hearsay; for them he was a social attraction as a brilliant and witty conversationalist and a man of wide culture which also embraced the esoteric.[130]

This milieu was reflected in letters to Odets, who sometimes had to go to New York to work. In December 1945 Eisler wrote to him:

We saw the Chaplins a number of times and had the pleasure of having him here to dinner with Thomas Mann . . . They got on very well. The rigid Dr Mann was delighted with Chaplin, laughed like a schoolboy and lost a little of his German dignity. Chaplin admitted to not having read a single line of Mann's, but was very pleased with him as an audience and put on a Big Show.[131]

In February 1946 he reported that USC (University of Southern California) had just offered him its professorship of counterpoint and composition, so that he would become Ernst Toch's successor.[132] In April 1946 he told of the start on Chaplin's new film *Monsieur Verdoux*, for which he was to act as musical adviser.

In the meantime Charlie has begun work here; he made a number of extended rushes and I watched him directing – his mastery is truly fantastic. Not only does he demonstrate to his actors what he wants but also what he does not want. He writes very good scenes, but naturally he is no author and often certain weaknesses and naïve pseudophilosophical observations are unquestionably bad. If you were here you could convince him and help him – I tried a number of times to speak to him about quite specific matters, but you know Charlie – he is very amiable and pig-headed. But these are only small faults, and taken as a whole what he is making is really a masterpiece. He has very rudimentary notions about music and composes vocal numbers and songs himself which do not please me at all. I don't see how I could work with him. But he is a marvellous chap and it is always a pleasure to spend an evening with him.
    Something very sad: Thomas Mann has lung cancer, and will have an operation in two days; the left lung has to be removed. It is a terrible and hopeless affair, and he has one chance in a hundred. Please speak to no one about this, as it must not get into the newspapers. His brother Heinrich is in complete despair, and his wife is with him in Chicago.
    Schoenberg's health is now better than in the last four or five months when he was having very dangerous attacks; I wish and hope for ten more years for him.
    . . . As you have perhaps heard, Charles Laughton is planning to do Brecht's *Galilei* with Orson Welles directing, but all this is still only at the discussion stage.
    What is Harold (Clurman) doing? How did 'Deadline at Dawn' go in New York? About myself I can only tell you that I find university teaching

14   Playing chess in Malibu (1946)

good fun. Unfortunately my students are not very talented, but they are charming young people and very enthusiastic . . .[133]

At around the same time, in March 1946, Churchill ushered in the Cold War in his Fulton speech; he coined the concept of the 'Iron Curtain' which had gone down over Europe from Stettin to Trieste. In America the transition from anti-fascism to anti-communism had already become apparent since the death of Roosevelt and the end of the war. The reason was the radical shift in direction of the US economic and foreign policy.[134] As a measure against the imminent post-war recession it seemed vital to secure those former markets for the export of American goods and capital that had been hit by the war. In the American view, the first essential was to forestall any programmes of socialization in Europe by applying the brakes to the advance of the planned economy.[135] To campaign against this as 'unfree' was part and parcel of a far more comprehensive anti-communist 'crusade'; this was at the same time conducted internally against supposedly subversive forces which had infiltrated public life and 'served a foreign power'.

One of the publicists for whom the change to a massive anti-communist thrust was very opportune was Eisler's sister Ruth Fischer. Since 1941 she had lived in the USA as an émigrée, and since 1944 had published *The Network*, an 'Information Bulletin of European Stalinism'. Here, but also in the *American Mercury* and subsequently in the Hearst press, she practised a form of investigative journalism which evidently did not stop short of public denunciation.[136]

Since her expulsion from the German Communist Party in 1926, which had brought her career in politics to an end, she had felt herself a victim of Stalinist politics, which above all she accused of abusing the Comintern. It now seemed as if the moment for revenge had come. Close to a state of paranoia, she tirelessly published articles full of accusations and aspersions; later she appeared as a prosecution witness in political trials. Artists in Hollywood saw Ruth Fischer as a 'monster' with psychopathic traits.[137] For her denuciations did not stop short of her own brothers. Charlie Chaplin, aware of the theatrical aspect of the forthcoming scandal, consoled his friend Hanns Eisler with the appreciative remark: 'In your family things happen as in Shakespeare.'[138]

The scandal began in the autumn of 1946 with a press campaign against Eisler's brother Gerhart, who since the thirties had worked in America as an agent for the – since disbanded – Comintern, and since 1941 had chiefly lived as a journalist in New York. When in October the former editor of the workers' newspaper the *Daily Worker*, Louis Budenz, identified him as the real head of the American Communist Party, and in the next month Ruth Fischer published a series of articles in the Hearst press, concluding with the nonsensical assertion that Gerhart and Hanns Eisler had brought communism to Hollywood,[139] the case rapidly gained publicity. The 'Eisler family' became an object of public interest.

Gerhart Eisler and Ruth Fischer were summoned to Washington for 6 February 1947. They were interrogated by the House Committee on Un-American Activities (HUAC), of which

Richard M. Nixon was a member. Ruth Fischer laid heavy accusations against Gerhart and identified him as a Comintern agent. She claimed his brother Hanns was 'a communist in the philosophical sense'.[140] To Nixon's express question whether he was close to Gerhart, she answered in the affirmative.

For the Committee, whose public interrogations were subsequently to be the most important weapon for intimidating the American public and facilitated the Truman administration's swing to the Right, there could be little to interest them in a composer in Hollywood. Nevertheless it was a policy of the new hard line to oust from office the adherents of Roosevelt's New Deal policies – enlightened liberals who still held important government posts.[141] To this end it was necessary to discredit the era of the New Deal in retrospect. The most effective way of doing so seemed to charge high officials with a lack of suspicion towards communists at home and abroad, which was represented as damaging to the national interest. The Hollywood film industry, or more precisely its colony of artists with its Party members and sympathizers, must have provided an ideal target: a major link in the subversive chain leading from Moscow to Washington.[142] In order to make this notion convincing what was needed was an occasion to spark it off which would attract attention. The case of the Eisler brothers suited the Committee ideally because it allowed the connection between the cinema and politics to be made to seem plausible without the necessity for cumbersome manoeuvring. If they could successfully be portrayed as sinister émigré figures and high officials in the State Department could be prosecuted over their supposedly defective entry permits, this would sufficiently suggest grounds for suspicion to make the notion of a dangerous threat credible; in this way it would be possible to generate a climate of widespread mistrust of communism which would at the same time permit the investigators to increase their popularity as hard-line crusaders and to accumulate points for their political careers.

At the end of April 1947 Richard Nixon, a Californian delegate of one year, announced that the Committee suspected communist propaganda in American films. It would therefore send a sub-committee to Hollywood 'to conduct an investigation into Hanns

Eisler and collect facts'. In Nixons's actual words: 'The case of Hanns Eisler is perhaps the most important ever to have come before the Committee.'[143]

The results of the first interrogation which took place at the beginning of May in Hollywood were evidently not sufficiently productive for the Committee chairman. Parnell Thomas – who in fact was sentenced to imprisonment a year later for embezzlement of government funds[144] – informed the press that Eisler had, amongst other things, replied evasively to the question of whether he believed in capitalism.[145] He announced a public interrogation in Washington.

Eisler, who for half a year had been subjected to a storm of attacks and slanders in the press, was justifiably indignant. He suspected that a convenient example was to be made of him in order to limit artistic freedom of opinion in Hollywood and to silence critical voices. In a statement, he attempted to make clear the single cause of the newspaper campaign against him: he was the brother of Gerhart Eisler. 'Is the Committee of the opinion that brotherly love is un-American?', he asked, and concluded sceptically: 'I have no illusions. The struggle is one-sided. I feel like a native who is trying to defend himself against an atom bomb with a bow and arrow.'[146]

On 24 September there followed the three-day interrogation in Washington, which was transmitted by numerous radio stations, and was again conducted by Parnell Thomas. The pivot of the inquisition was the question which was later to acquire a macabre celebrity in the USA: 'Are you now or have you ever been a member of the Communist Party?'[147] Since Eisler could not unequivocally be demonstrated as having belonged to the German Communist Party – his application of 1926 had *de jure* remained without sequel – the Committee tried to establish that he had collaborated with Party organizations in the Soviet Union and in America. An extensive dossier with transcripts of interviews, essays and song texts which Eisler had set to music was brought as substantial evidence against him. Sometimes the exchanges were sardonic. When the chairman asked the leading witness Robert Stripling why he was reading out so much material, Stripling, who had risen from petty officialdom, replied, with all the aggression of the parvenu: 'My purpose is to show that Mr. Eisler is the Karl Marx of communism in the musical field and he is well aware of it.' To which Eisler drily commented: 'I would be flattered.'[148]

The intention of convicting him of a passport offence allowed the Committee to summon leading officials of the State Department during Roosevelt's term of office: Sumner Welles, George S. Messersmith, Joseph Savoretti. The Committee was anxious to prove that they had disregarded immigration regulations; at that time these required that no one should be permitted entry who had campaigned for the violent overthrow of the American government. Communists had not then been specifically mentioned; in the meantime, however, they had come to be included in that potential group – a shift of attitude which was played out in full by the Committee members during the interrogation. They were keeping up their sleeves, as a sensation for the press, the letters exchanged between Eleanor Roosevelt and the acting Secretary of State of the time, Sumner Welles. As with many other émigrés, the president's wife had also tried to help the Eislers in obtaining a residence permit. This perfectly proper exchange of letters was now to be used in an attempt to render communist infiltration of the State Department credible.[149] After the interrogation, Eisler's case was referred to the Justice Department who, however, shelved it. Since on the one hand there was not sufficient evidence of a punishable offence and on the other hand an acquittal would cause loss of face, a compromise was finally reached with the defence. This consisted of 'technical deportation'. This meant a 'voluntary' exit visa to any country issuing a passport with the exception of countries bordering on the USA (Mexico and Canada). Before this solution was found, strong public pressure had to be brought to bear on the authorities. Eisler's friends founded a committee for his defence, published resolutions and urged native and foreign artists to protest on a massive scale. The most effective aid proved to be that of Thomas Mann and Charlie Chaplin.

Thomas Mann, who at the beginning of the year had completed his *Doktor Faustus*, had just returned from a five-month journey to Europe when Eisler's interrogation in Washington began. Two letters make his reaction clear. They should be read in the light of Eisler's later statement that Mann's 'hesitant, irresolute behav-

iour' had often 'irritated Brecht to distraction', against which
Eisler himself objected 'that Brecht overlooked a quality of real
humanity in Thomas Mann'.[150]

On 10 October 1947 Mann wrote to Agnes Meyer:

I myself am not signing *any* more of the appeals with which the desperate
Left Wing is making a nuisance of itself, as I have little appetite for
playing the martyr again. The thesis that it is a case of a certain moral
relaxation in the country after the exertions of the period of Rooseveltian
genius is still the one that appeals to me most strongly . . . For personal
reasons I am concerned about the case of Hanns Eisler. I know the man
very well and he is cultured, witty, very amusing in conversation, and I
have often been brilliantly entertained by him, especially on the subject of
Wagner. As a musician he is, in the opinion of all his colleagues, of the
highest rank. Since the inquisition recommended to the 'secular arm' that
he be deported he has been in danger of ending up in a German camp. I
hear that Stravinsky (a white Russian!) intends to initiate a demonstration in support of him. But I have a wife and children and am enquiring no
further about it.[151]

Already four days later he was enlisting the help of the one
émigré from whose prestige he counted on creating the greatest
effect: Albert Einstein.

. . . I am writing to you today about a matter that is close to my heart for
reasons both personal and of principle. You are already familiar with the
broad outlines of the affair of the composer Hanns Eisler, a man well
known to me, one who in the opinion of all his colleagues is an outstanding musician, and a highly cultivated, witty man. Since the inquisition has
handed him over to the secular arm for deportation he has been in danger
of ending up in a German camp, and his friends here would like to try to
be of assistance to him in obviating such a fate. He hopes – and I do not
know how right he is in this – that by declaring his wish to leave the
country voluntarily he will be able to avoid deportation. For this he needs
entry papers for another country, and for this he is thinking of Czechoslovakia where he has friends and adherents as an artist. A telegram has now
been drafted, the text of which I am enclosing, which will be sent via the
Czech consul-general in San Francisco through diplomatic channels to
reach President Beneš. It would of course help things tremendously if you
were to add your name to those expected to appear on this telegram.
Besides yourself the signatories are to be my brother Heinrich and myself
and also, I hope, the American writer William L. Shirer whose agreement
I am requesting by the same post. As the matter is urgent, please cable
your instructions.

3505/47

REFER TO ABOVE NO.

October 22, 1947

<u>Via Air Mail</u>

Mr. Hanns Eisler
23868 West Pacific Coast Highway
Pacific Palisades, California

Dear Mr. Eisler:

Thank you for your letter of October 20. I wish to assure you that even without the intervention of Mr. Thomas Mann, whom I am glad to call my friend, and the other very prominent friends of yours who sponsor and back the appeal to the Czechoslovak Government, I would not have hesitated to help you, had I known that I could be of any assistance to you and Mrs. Eisler.

As it is, I have immediately informed the Czechoslovak Government of the appeal signed by Dr. Einstein, Mr. Thomas Mann, and his brother Heinrich Mann, Mr. Shirer, and now even by Mr. Charles Chaplin. Needless to say, I have asked in my report about you and Mrs. Eisler for authorization to issue you a Czechoslovak passport whenever it will be necessary and helpful for you and your wife. Unfortunately, I have not the slightest idea how far, under the given circumstances, my intervention will help you, and whether I or my colleague in New York will be authorized to give you the Czechoslovak passport. However, I have informed Minister Jan Masaryk of my report, I have sent a copy to the Czechoslovak Embassy in Washington, D. C., and I have written to two people who, each in his particular capacity, may help in this case.

First, I have written to my uncle, Dr. Edvard Benes, asking him to insist on a just investigation into this matter; and secondly, I have written to the man you have met, Mr. Lubomir Linhart, the Director of the Czechoslovak Film Industry, asking him to approach on your behalf Mr. Nosek, the Minister of the Interior, whose office, you may know, is responsible for issuing such passports as can be delivered to you and Mrs. Eisler.

May I assure you that any kind of help I could extend to you and Mrs. Eisler would come to my mind and heart quite naturally. Please tell Mrs. Eisler of the heartfelt sympathy of my wife and myself. We do believe sincerely that you will get out of the present trouble in the shortest possible time.

Sincerely yours,

Bohus Benes
Consul

15   The relief action of friends in autumn 1947

At around the same time Chaplin sent a cable to Picasso in Paris: 'Can you organize a committee of French artists to protest to the American Embassy in Paris against the shameful deportation proceedings against Hanns Eisler that have taken place here and at the same time forward to me a copy of the protest for us here?'[152]

On 27 November, together with the telegram, *Lettres Françaises* published the protest resolution signed by over twenty French artists including – besides Picasso – Matisse and Cocteau, Aragon and Eluard.

(Thomas Mann and Chaplin, both of them supposedly unimpeachable, were to feel the after-effects of their supportive action when in about 1950 the political climate in the USA once again rapidly deteriorated. Shortly afterwards, in 1952, both got away from the annoyances by settling in Switzerland.)

Eisler was the first of a series of artists and intellectuals who from that time on found themselves blacklisted in the USA. This device allowed inconvenient figures to be ruined by removing the basis of their economic existence: they were no longer able to find work. In fact the case of Eisler – and that of the 'Hollywood Ten'[153] was merely the prelude to worse things. For after a breathing-space of just two years, Joseph McCarthy organized witch-hunting – tracking down everyone not belonging to the political Right – on a grand scale.

Many who had at first stood their ground – including Eisler's friend Clifford Odets – were unable to resist this second wave. The fact that successful Hollywood artists were accustomed to a luxurious life-style made them particularly vulnerable economically. But for some time it had been not only the film industry but also universities and schools, administrative bodies and trade unions which had been the targets of McCarthy's 'thought police' and political informants. Nowadays those years of denunciation, of fear and of hysteria are considered in the USA to have been 'one of the blackest pages in the history of American democracy'.[154]

Four weeks before Eisler's departure, American composers – including Copland, Bernstein and Sessions – organized a farewell concert in Eisler's honour. This was a spirited protest on the part of the musical world which had followed the Eisler case with

16   With his wife Lou in New York (1948), shortly before their return to Europe

sympathy. A surprised public at the Town Hall heard chamber music and songs by the composer whom the right-wing press had belittled as a 'Hollywood composer'. Admiring reviews a column long appeared in the *New York Times* and the *Herald Tribune*.[155] The greatest success was a virtuosic performance of the Violin Sonata by Tossy Spivakovski. The 'Rain' Quintet and Eisler's newly completed Second Septet made all the more impression because they had started life as film music.[156] The subtlety and gracefulness of these works, and above all their rhythmic spontaneity, belied the hardened prejudice of critics that music of German origin was heavy and tiresome.

The success and impact of the concert and his recognition by the professional world which had hitherto only known him by his film music came too late for Eisler. The report in the *Herald Tribune* concluded: 'We hope that his case will be reconsidered and he will be permitted to return, and also that until then his works will reach us regularly from Europe.'[157]

LEONARD BERNSTEIN
AARON COPLAND   DAVID DIAMOND
ROY HARRIS   WALTER PISTON
ROGER SESSIONS   RANDALL THOMPSON

sponsor
a Concert of

HANNS EISLER MUSIC

Suite No. 1 for Septet ("In the Kindergarten") . . . . CHAMBER ENSEMBLE
(Based on American nursery tunes) FRANK BRIEFF, *conductor*

JAC GORODETZKY, *violin*	LUCIEN LAPORTE, *cello*
EUGENE BERGEN, *violin*	JULIUS BAKER, *flute*
RICHARD DICKLER, *viola*	CLARK BRODY, *clarinet*

HAROLD GOLTZER, *bassoon*

Six Songs by Bertolt Brecht and Hanns Eisler . . . . CHLOE OWEN, *soprano*
JOHN RANCK, *piano*

Sonata for Violin and Piano . . . . TOSSY SPIVAKOVSKY, *violin*
Allegretto — Andante — Presto JAN BEHR, *piano*

INTERMISSION

Presenting the Motion Picture: "Fourteen Ways to Describe Rain"
(Film music composed under the auspices of the Rockefeller Foundation)

Seven Piano Pieces for Children . . . . LEO SMIT, *piano*

Suite No. 2 for Septet—In Six Movements . . . . . CHAMBER ENSEMBLE
(Six excerpts from the score of Charles Chaplin's "Circus")

The Alien Cantata for Soprano and Septet . . . . . CHLOE OWEN, *soprano*
(Especially composed for this concert) CHAMBER ENSEMBLE

TOWN HALL

43rd Street between 6th and 7th Avenues

SATURDAY, FEBRUARY 28th, 1948, 8:30 P.M.

Tickets now at box-office

| $3.60 | $3.00 | $2.40 | $1.80 | $1.20 |

(All prices include federal tax)

17   Programme of the farewell concert in New York, 1948

18   Before the flight from New York: saying goodbye to Gerhart and Hilde Eisler

On 26 March 1948, when Eisler and his wife were about to fly from New York to Prague, he read out a statement at LaGuardia Airport. This began: 'I leave this country not without bitterness and infuriation. I could well understand it when in 1933 the Hitler bandits put a price on my head and drove me out. They were the evil of the period; I was proud at being driven out. But I feel heart-broken over being driven out of this beautiful country in this ridiculous way.' On his experience with the HUAC he said: 'I listened to . . . the questions of this [sic] men and I saw their faces. As an old anti-Fascist it became plain to me that these men represent fascism in its most direct form.' The last sentence went: 'But I take with me the image of the real American people whom I love.'[158]

4

The final decade

Eisler's non-voluntary early return to a Europe that was still severely devastated released fresh energies within him. After ten years in the USA his first impressions were mixed: post-war shortages and backwardness on the one hand, and on the other the beginnings of reconstruction and the will towards rebirth were the decisive factors.

On 27 April he wrote to Lion Feuchtwanger from Vienna:

After a marvellous stop in Prague, it is now the city of Vienna, whose loveliness two wars could not destroy, which is getting on my nerves. There is real post-war misery here which is very acute for the average man. Art here is very provincial, as I find most particularly in my rehearsals with over-worked and underfed musicians with whom it would be sheer effrontery to be annoyed when they make mistakes. I have two concerts and a lecture, then on 8 May we go to Prague where I have another lecture and will be writing the score for a Czech film . . . Despite all the difficulties and the provincialism, Europe – even Vienna – has given me very strong impressions, I might even say inspiration . . . I have a greater desire to work and more plans than ever. And troublesome material circumstances, which incidentally have so far been perfectly agreeable, if one excludes the meat – strengthen the spirit.[1]

He celebrated his musical 'come-back' with the incidental music for Nestroy's *Fear of Hell* with which the Scala in Vienna reopened. The invitation to compose it came from Karl Paryla as soon as he had heard of Eisler's return from emigration. For this production, which has gone down in the annals of the post-war theatre in Vienna, Eisler composed some twenty pieces, 'simple, cool, elegant and in no way crudely farcical'.[2] He transformed the Viennese popular element in his music in such a way that, behind the amusing bitterness of Nestroy's satirical travesty, a critique of the restoration with its tragic elements can be clearly perceived.

Eisler, whose chamber music from the years of exile was now being broadcast by Austrian Radio, intended to settle in Vienna.[3] He had hopes of a professorship in composition at the Academy.

However, these were soon shattered by conservative opposition. The city turned down the opportunity of acquiring a musician of his stature to train its rising generation of composers. If during the period before and after the First World War the Schoenberg school was barely tolerated, the musical life of the city thereafter remained relentlessly traditional, even though this meant falling further behind the times. Here it was impossible to break through the inertia of the established.

In May 1948, at the International Composers' Congress in Prague, Eisler gave a talk which attracted widespread attention. Under the title of 'Fundamental social questions of modern music' he discussed the current state of composition. With Schoenberg and Stravinsky, the two dominant figures of Western music, bourgeois musical culture had found itself stuck in a blind alley; it could only find a new function 'in a higher form of society'; there it might be possible for 'music perhaps to take on once again a more friendly and joyful character'.[4]

His talk, which began with an analysis of the American music industry, fitted in well with the Prague agenda – apart from his positive remarks about Schoenberg. The conference manifesto had been formulated with his help. For it he had put down as the most important sentence: 'What should be striven for is a style capable of combining the highest artistry, originality and quality with the greatest popularity.'[5] Thus he took up again his own stance of before 1933. At the time he would hardly have been able to estimate how dangerously near he was coming to comparable formulations that were then being propagated by official Soviet aesthetics under Zhdanov. The discussion was conducted under broad headings; as was to be the case, moreover, at the World Peace Conference of intellectuals which took place in Wroclaw (Breslau) in August and at the Peace Rally of Cultural Creative Workers in Berlin in October, in which he participated, together with Brecht and Arnold Zweig.

On his first revisiting Berlin – after fifteen years – he wrote a poem as a 'Survivor'. His mind was less on the destroyed houses than on destroyed friends.[6] It was not only the city that lay in rubble, but also the workers' movement. That, second only to the Jews, was the biggest victim of fascism. Liberation from it, as brought by the Allied Forces, was felt by the masses as an additional punishment; the occupying forces dismantled the means of production. The hope that the workers would fall about the necks of the returning socialists and communists proved to be an illusory one: the deforming scars inflicted by National Socialism were deep.

Eisler's particular concern as a musician was that listening habits might have been spoilt by fascism, and this was thoroughly well-founded. Late in 1948 Brecht wrote in his working journal of Eisler's 'aversion to the vulgarity and primitiveness of marching songs' and asked him, without success, to compose a 'Song of the Future'. Eisler 'has given me, however, an ode by Mao Tse-Tung, written upon his first flight over the Great Wall, a splendid poem which I am making a version of now'.[7]

When at the beginning of 1950 Eisler settled in Berlin for the second time – Brecht having preceded him by a few months – two German states had already been founded. Eisler elected unequivocally for the German Democratic Republic (DDR), despite all the foreseeable and unforeseeable difficulties a pupil of Schoenberg would experience there. For once it seemed to him that it offered a guarantee that the stamping out of fascism was to be taken seriously. In the second place he hoped that the establishment of socialism would be associated with a new musical culture.

At the time it was not possible to foresee that the Cold War would bring to nothing any hopes of a subsequent reunited Germany. Among the *consequences* of the Nazi dictatorship, the division of the nation and its subsequent trauma was the worst. The victorious powers who were now confronting each other as opposing blocks shaped the two constituent states in accordance with the most extreme stances of each. An atmosphere of mutual distrust, hysteria and aggression built up. The Federal Republic of Germany (BRD) and the DDR each fell into the role of favourite pupil of the respective super-power – the USA or the USSR – which patronized them, taking over their prevailing social structures, administrations and ideologies. More precisely, they were permeated – with varying degrees of resistance – by the respective governments in question. In West Germany, under the chancellorship of Adenauer, capitalism was restored on a massive scale.

In East Germany, where the special conditions for making a start were far more difficult, the 'authentic German Road to Socialism' that was propounded by the SBZ [Soviet-occupied zone] was quickly dropped in favour of the adoption of the Soviet model. However what this meant was not an alignment with the revolutionary Soviet Union of its first decade (which would have been historically impossible), but with a kind of socialism that was represented by the leadership of the Communist Party of the Soviet Union at this precise juncture.

Brecht had constantly reflected on the effects of this historical dilemma – a socialism which did not come from the grass roots but was administrated from above. The position of the arts did not remain unaffected by this inversion.

It is a great misfortune of our history that we have to engineer the erection of the new without having engineered the demolition of the old.

Germany was not granted the purifying process of a revolution. The major transformation which would otherwise come in the wake of a revolution came without it. In a situation where many minds remain in the dark about the relationship of classes to each other, where there is a new way of life that is changing almost daily and for which there are still whole classes of society who lack the appropriate ways of thinking and feeling, art cannot immediately appeal to the instincts and emotions of a multifarious public . . . It has to struggle against old feelings and ideas, exposing and rejecting them, and it must search out and provide new ideas and feelings.

Brecht feared that 'no adequate expression' was being given to 'the day-to-day struggle against the old which we still have to carry out'. 'We are constantly trying to fashion the "harmonious" and the "beautiful in- and for-itself" instead of the struggle for harmony and beauty.'[8] For that new forms were needed.

This was diametrically opposed to the officially propounded cultural policy which at that time was based on Zhdanov. According to the latter, the first essential was to forge links with the 'cultural heritage of the past'. The idea was put abroad that a new culture could only be built up by reverting to the forms of the national, classical heritage and to the art of the people; in this way it could be given a secure foundation to fortify it against what was an already foreseeable swamping of Europe under the American culture industry. It was necessary to foster the cultural past and 'the popular' in new works. What had to be guarded against was Western decadence, and above all the 'formalism' and 'cosmopolitanism' which plagued Western Europe as a consequence of the Marshall Plan.

This *looking backwards right from the start* was to prove a heavy mortgage for cultural activity in East Germany. A conservatism set in which resisted its opponents with incredible tenacity and drew strength from new guidelines such as the following:

> . . . In order to progress beyond the classics it is first necessary to catch up with them . . . and so it would be not at all bad if we had new works being written which emulated the classics in content and form, in brilliance, in beauty and in musicality. If this is 'epigonalism' – well, then, it might not be all that dishonourable to be such an epigon![9]

Behind such *ex cathedra* pronouncements lurked the ideal of a music which would as it were compound Beethoven with Tchaikovsky, using new notes. A double risk arose for the creative arts. Firstly, cosy epigonalism was given the go-ahead, if not positively encouraged with prospects of reward. And secondly, the ideological relics that had been forced out – bourgeois psychology and value judgments – were in this way readmitted, as if through a side entrance. For the classics (and especially the German classics) by no means provided politically neutral values 'in themselves'. As Eisler later put it, they 'in fact wrote for the educated classes . . . and indeed those educated in a special way . . . Our classics have a horrible after-taste of exclusivity'.[10]

Contrary to its own claims, Zhdanov's concept is un-Marxian. It refuses to extend precise differences between nations and classes to the realm of culture. Consequently, undialectical notions survive, such as the one which holds that the works of the bourgeois heritage can be broken up into form and content and provided with a fresh filling. Its judgment of new forms as formalistic, alien and foreign to the people is the equally undialectical corollary. In his working journal Brecht criticized 'the mistaken opinion . . . that it is harder to replace new content *and* new form than either one of them alone'. For him 'formalism is what squanders revolutionary content'.[11] On the petty-bourgeois and philistine application of such maxims, very German in its mixture of respectability and patronization, he noted: 'Opponents of formalism often bluster against new and attractive forms like certain unattractive housewives who automatically denounce beauty and the striving for beauty as harlotry (and a symptom of syphilis).'[12]

Early in 1949, in his lecture 'Listener and composer' – given in Berlin and in Vienna – Eisler attempted to draw a distinction between abstract and realistic *popularity*. The abstract sense proceeds from mere ease of comprehension and leads directly to the commercial hit-song. And just as little is to be gained from the merely traditional concept: 'Yet, in general, popularity is understood as meaning a certain naïvety, a certain emotional intoxication, a quite unjustifiable pleasure in recreation, hence customs and usages which are not easy to bring into line with our modern life.' However, if one looks beyond this to the fact that the most advanced class of the people are the workers, then popularity will mean 'that which addresses itself above all to the workers . . . For the workers are not naïve, and they learn quickly . . . they are eager for innovation; they have learnt how necessary are change, transformation, multiplicity of methods and mobility. And they have large-scale plans and broad perspectives.' The question of a new popularity of this kind in music can 'only be answered on music paper'.[13]

With the question 'popular with whom?' Eisler put his finger on the crux of the matter. For even in East Germany it proved impossible to forge links with a working class of the pre-1933 sort; the expression 'the people' had suffered through misuse – Brecht proposed that it should for a while be replaced by 'populace'. The question of what new public was presenting itself, what were the means by which it could be reached and what level of awareness new work would meet with could hardly be given any precise answer during this early phase of the establishment of a new social order. 'The fact that the listener and listening itself have been subjected to a historical change' was incontestable; the difficulty of evolving a musical practice for a society undergoing such radical change was equally incontestable.

The two years in which Eisler strove directly towards this end

(1949 and 1950) were marked by his collaboration with Johannes R. Becher. This began during the Polish Goethe Festival in Warsaw, in which the two were taking part as guests. Becher requested Eisler to set some of his most recent poems and songs to music. One of them, 'Auferstanden aus Ruinen' [Resurrected from Ruins], was shortly afterwards nominated by the council of the East German cabinet as a new national anthem; Eisler and Becher were awarded the National Prize. With the Cold War bringing propaganda warfare between the two German states, this fact alone was at the time sufficient to inflict a political taboo on Eisler in West Germany for two decades – a phenomenon without parallel in the history of German music.[14]

The *Neue deutsche Volkslieder* [New German Folk Songs] which Eisler wrote to texts by Becher were in musical terms his attempt to provide songs for young people which would be easy to understand and to sing, at the same time avoiding worn-out clichés. They are not lacking in colourful variety, though the evident syncretism of their stylistic elements is now found irritating by sensitive ears. His recourse to Schubert and Mendelssohn, allied to a synthesis of (simplified) features from his own marching, choral and solo songs, produces melodious structures of the kind that may very well appeal to young ears.

The texts are another matter. The weakness of Becher's later poetry is its abstract pathos. The tendency towards a hymnic tone which he retained from his Expressionist period, and towards enthusiastic portentousness, was bound to fall flat in the youth poems, where the subjects are the homeland, nature and the joy of constructive work. Whilst the metaphysical overtones of many words in the German language simply betray him into flowery, abstract and imprecise language, Becher's *Volkslieder* are also spoilt by the theatricality of their plainness. His simplicity feels contrived, fictitious. Becher, one of the most complex and egocentric figures of his generation, suggested – apparently with the best of intentions – a relationship to the landscape and to work, and asked for a singing and 'humming' which belonged to an earlier century.

The unhistorical allusion to pre-capitalist circumstances that is found in the imagery used and the rhymes chosen was the result of

19   Shostakovitch and Eisler in Berlin-DDR (Bach Festival, 1950)

the poet's uncritical view of himself and of his relation to the public (which one?). Becher saw himself as the bringer of culture from above who imparted education and doctrine to others. The conception of the chosen individual bestowing art on the public was of a piece with the inviolate ideal of the bourgeois concept of genius. This did not prevent him from quite sincerely playing off popularity against supposed or actual formalism.

In the Foreword to the *Volkslieder*, Becher wrote: '. . . what is new in our literature (consists) also in the fact that it gives the people that which is of the people in literature, namely new songs which correspond to the new feelings and new ideas which move our people and above all the young . . .'[15] Brecht noted, from his opposite position and in a different context:

What arouses irritation is the attitude of certain opponents of formalism who make a clear or vague distinction between the people and them-selves. They never speak of the effect of a work of art on themselves, but always about its effect on the people. They themselves seem not to belong to the people. Rather, they know precisely what the people want, and identify the people by the latter's wanting what they themselves want.[16]

The relationship between Becher and Eisler, which remained a friendly one in private, soon broke off artistically on account of their different conceptions. In Becher's diary we find entries such as the following in October 1950: 'Also now as before I have the feeling that Eisler has written the genuinely popular tunes with at least a tinge of musical bad conscience, and invariably, in order to suppress any sentimentality, he delights in inserting unexpected note-clashes . . . Conversation with Eisler this evening, rather unproductive, talking around the subject, half-hearted about further mutual collaboration . . .'[17]

The popularity achieved by the *Neue deutsche Volkslieder* soon after their first performances (with Ernst Busch) was confirmed by their inclusion in the repertories of schools and musical youth groups. However, it was illusory right from the start to imagine that they might be able to fend off the influences of Western light music.

When Becher began to write Christmas songs too, Eisler had lost all enthusiasm for this genre. During this period, only one further work came from the two of them – an occasional work, the cantata *Mitte des Jahrhunderts* [Middle of the Century]. This is one of Eisler's weakest compositions and contains passages of appalling vacuity. Its position in his output as a whole is something like that of *Wellington's Victory* in Beethoven's. It is justifiably forgotten.

Opera without music: *Johann Faustus*

At that time Eisler was aware of the danger of aesthetic (and political) regression. Simple recourse to adoptive material, possibly technically simplified, produces at best academic craftsmanship, as for example in the 'Goethe' Rhapsody he wrote for the Weimar festivities (1949). He probably only yielded to these tendencies in a spirit of experimentation and somewhat reluctantly. When the official trends towards the reinstatement of a normative aesthetic became increasingly conspicuous – bringing about a bureaucratic variety of neo-classicism – he endeavoured to counteract this development; for, based on Lukács' theses – in simplified form at that – it was bound to lead to a dead end.

This was the situation from which the project of Eisler's opera *Johann Faustus* evolved. He was aiming high. His intention was to lay the foundation stone of the 'musical theatre' of a new epoch whilst the subject, with its specifically German connotations, was to be treated in an up-to-date way from a Marxist viewpoint. He was not interested in the historical conflict, but in a contemporary one which had a historical dimension. He envisaged introducing the musical and literary traditions, 'elevating' them with new techniques, so that comprehension would be assured whilst a major problem of the present time – presented through historical 'alienation' – would become clear. Entertainment, wit and enjoyment would be important factors.

'In present times opera, as opposed to concert music, is the most democratic of major musical forms since it is more readily accessible than concerts to listeners of widely differing degrees of musical education', Eisler wrote in his notes on Wagner.[18] The attempt to invest opera with fresh meaning was conditional on revaluing the libretto as poetry, as genuine argumentation. At the same time the text needed to meet the composer's requirements. Eisler realized that he had to decide to write the text of his opera himself, following the examples of Wagner and Schoenberg. Both had taken the major step to express content of great significance – though admittedly the content was not such that Eisler considered still of relevance to his time. For him Wagner's use of *national* myths and sagas – together with his desired effects of intoxication and hypnosis – was of no further use, nor was a *religious* conception, such as that found in *Moses and Aaron*, with its moralistic dualism of the ideal and the real, spirituality and sensuality as irreconcilable principles. Eisler's subject was *social* and political.

In his 'Notes to Dr. Faustus' he defined his position in relation to Schoenberg and Thomas Mann.[19] With these two figures, late bourgeois art had run its course. Mann had provided the 'Doktor Faustus' of his novel, the composer Adrian Leverkühn, with certain of Schoenberg's characteristics, and above all with his twelve-note technique. Using this, Leverkühn composed the oratorio *Lamentation of Dr. Faustus* – the final work resulting from his pact with the devil, at once overheated and icy, the antihumanist 'redemption' of Beethoven's Ninth Symphony. Nevertheless, Thomas Mann shows Leverkühn dreaming of a new age in which music will once again to some extent be 'on familiar terms' with the people. Mann draws a parallel between the path of his Faustus (to art without love) and that of the German people up to 1945. Leverkühn can neither embark on the path to a new art, nor can he think of it as a possibility.

By-passing Goethe, Eisler, like Thomas Mann, refers back in his *Johann Faustus* to the puppet-play and the popular romance. However, their conceptions are fundamentally different. That of Thomas Mann, the Wagnerian, is bound up with *national* psychology. Eisler's highlights the *class* conflict of the artist and the scientist.

This new conception of the Faust figure arose from discussions with Brecht. After the two had settled in Berlin, Brecht had made his central concern a theme from the years of emigration: the syndrome of the 'Tuis', or opportunist intellectuals.[20] It seemed as if the time had come for a dialectical survey of the history of the

20   With Ernst Busch in Berlin (c. 1950)

'German predicament', which had reached its nadir a few years previously in the nation's collapse: he directed his critical attention to the history, responsibilities and predicament of the German intellectuals. Brecht feared a repetition of the disastrous development in West Germany. For him the stock from which fascism grew was 'still fertile'. The American influence in West Germany made the warning of the scientists and artists appear urgent to him: the first atom bomb was fresh in the memory. It was in this context that the libretto for *Johann Faustus* was written.

Eisler wanted to show the beginning of the misguided social development. For this reason he combined the Faust subject with the *Peasants' Revolt* and its suppression. One of the root causes of this 'original sin' in German history and of the subsequent disasters was the political behaviour of the German intelligentsia.

Eisler saw the predicament as originating in an extremely unpleasant dilemma for intellectuals: in following the example of Luther they became spokesmen for the ruling classes; and in following Münzer they found themselves firmly on the wrong side of the law. In both cases the consequence of their adopted stances was violence. Their vacillation between the two alternatives gave rise to the hope that they could avoid committing themselves. Did they not simply exist *on a higher plane* than the classes? This was precisely the illusion that Eisler wanted to shatter. He showed that without a genuine militant commitment there could be no possibility of *avoiding* being abused by those in power. Whether against his will or not, Faustus, who would like innocently to wash his hands of it, finds himself in the conservative camp; politically he behaves almost like a miniature Luther.

This is not a matter of sublime Quixoticism of the conscience but of self-deception on a very big scale; it leads to betrayal. Faustus, repelled by the use of arms and hoping to be able to 'hold out' without taking up any stand, opposes the movement of his class (he is the son of a peasant), his people and the revolution, even though he is a pupil of Luther *and* Münzer, and therefore knows the truth; it is for this that the devil takes him.

The libretto portrays Faustus not during but immediately *after* the Peasants' Revolt. The plot centres not on his treacherous behaviour, but on his reaction to it. He fails to provide his own self-justification. For this it would be necessary to banish the class conflict from his mind. At this point he concludes his pact with the devil.

And now there ensues a series of attempts to make use of the pact in order to develop his personality. All of them fail, since Faustus' bad conscience prevents him from freely pursuing these attempts. Their failure, however, causes this same conscience to grow very powerfully in Faustus, and he arrives at the major admission . . . that for a betrayer of the people there can be no true evolution. As in every genuine tragedy this realization does not save him from his downfall . . . In Faustus the truth brought home to him by the Peasants' Revolt lives on until the end, inescapable and ultimately bringing about his death.[21]

The danger of political corruptibility precisely for those who 'do not want to have anything to do with it' was an additional reason for Eisler wanting to introduce contemporary America into the action of this (black) drama. The second act is set in Atlanta. His own Hollywood experiences, including his expulsion, are worked into the plot. The warning about 'false enchantment' refers to the temptation to allow his intellect to be put to misuse by alien interests and to become entangled once again: the whitewash put out for consumption and 'easy-going' attitudes drew attention away from the reality of the military–industrial complex and its political implications.

The Mephisto of Eisler's *Faustus* is an agent of the same Pluto, Lord of the Underworld, who appears in the Prelude in scarcely antique garb as the boss of an enterprise which deals in the slave-trade as big business. This lord no longer needs to bet in order to obtain Faustus (as in Goethe's *Urfaust*), but simply gives the order. Mephisto carries it out.

Faustus' flight to Atlanta is brought about by his need for oblivion and stupefaction. At the same time, after the defeat of the peasants, he tries to rise to a position of esteem and power by offering his services to the great overlords; he tells himself that recognition from above is more important than recognition from below. However, he cannot elicit the approval of the powerful by demonstrations of his arts: his repressed sympathies with the oppressed repeatedly break through. When it finally becomes known that he once sympathized with the revolutionaries, he is played out with the overlords too. He saves himself by – fleeing.

Once again it is a flight from himself, and not the last. Back in Wittenberg (Act III), his life becomes progressively emptier. He is caught in a spiral: with increasing official esteem his behaviour becomes more and more charlatan-like. He promises his own masters, by carrying on with the tricks he learnt abroad, to make gold for them from Atlanta: it turns to dust. With his students in Auerbach's cellar he lectures earnestly on the ancients (in whom he has taken refuge) and is laughed to scorn: would-be pathos ends in a burlesque ballet.

The conflict reaches its climax when Faustus – in fulfilment of the pact with the devil, but a reversal of this fulfilment – is distinguished by the detestable representatives of the nobility with their highest honours – including a further doctorate. They honour Faustus' ideological aid during the suppression of the peasants. The final twist contained in this – 'that ruin takes the form of worldly recognition and being set up as an example for others to follow',[22] Faust knows that at the moment of his highest prestige he is destroyed – reveals the rottenness of the system with which he has been dealing. Faust: 'I thought they would persecute me. Worse has happened: They came to honour me.'

Faustus pays for the intellectual's self-betrayal with his life. From political cowardice he has allowed himself to be politically abused; his abilities were stolen from him and turned against him. Worse, not only did he himself become a victim, but so did others through him. Hence his confession concludes: 'Now I go in wretchedness to my ruin,/As too will everyone/Who has not the courage/To remain true to his cause.'

The principal thesis of the libretto is unequivocal: the artist who turns away from the people at a decisive moment in history and chooses the wrong side forfeits the *effectiveness* of his art. Eisler's tragic representation (by no means lacking in comic elements) has nothing to do with provocative satire; it sustains its unremitting critique solely for the sake of the positive challenge it implicitly contains: to seize the historical opportunity of the post-war period to help to establish a true socialism in *all* Germany.

Precisely in the interests of this necessary effectiveness, Eisler's objective was that his opera should 'be on familiar terms with the people' – in other words,

it must be grasped by unpractised ears as well as by the most practised, and the text must be understood by both the most untutored and the most educated . . . The musical task is no less difficult than the construction of the text. I have at least twenty-one separate numbers to compose, to which will be added a number of smaller and less important musical sections. In this score there must be six or seven essential pieces which will have to be composed with the utmost care, but need to be immediate in their effect. I do not know how long I shall be working at this task. One has feelings in which are compounded eager curiosity and faint-heartedness . . .[23]

There can be no doubt that, at the time, Eisler was intent on embarking on his most important work, and was encouraged by the favourable opinions which his libretto received after it was published at the end of 1952 by the Aufbau-Verlag. Thomas Mann and Lion Feuchtwanger congratulated him, and Brecht had in any case contributed to the idea and to a number of details. There seemed to be good prospects for venturing on the 'major gamble'. In the meantime his project met with extreme resistance.

As it turned out, Eisler published his libretto at the most unfavourable possible time. The difficult transition of the DDR from the anti-fascist democratic period of the immediate post-war years to the 'establishment of the power of the workers and peasants' brought with it an increasing tendency to channel the arts into prescribed classical lines which now appear absurd. This attitude, amounting to one of 'no experiments in culture', was cemented with the policy of alliance between the working class and the bourgeois intelligentsia which was necessary at that point in history. Both were to be united by the cultural heritage. And the key figure of that heritage was Goethe.

Brecht and Eisler considered this conception illusionary and damaging, from the political point of view as well. Under such circumstances, dialectical art, which they thought of as being critical and revolutionary, appeared out of place. Eisler came out of it worst: he was suspected of having irresponsibly perpetrated an affront to German history, to 'humanistic' intelligence, and above all to Goethe. Goethe's 'Faust' – the 'positive hero' *par excellence* – he had transformed into a negative, destructive figure. The misunderstanding led to a debate on basic principles which echoed far and wide. The immediate point of attack was increasingly a thesis *about Faustus* rather than that of the work itself. This originated with Ernst Fischer, who wanted to come to Eisler's assistance with an essay. According to Fischer, Eisler's hero is a *renegade*.[24] For the conservative champions of the heritage this – summarized – view was grist to the mill.

In fact, during the course of the debate, the true adversary of Eisler and Brecht, Georg Lukács, once again made a contribution, though an indirect one. In a simplified form, the controversy underlying the debate about Expressionism was revived, with Wilhelm Girnus and Alexander Abusch in particular acting as chief advocates of Lukács' aesthetic concept. The exchanges in the press of May and June 1953 were followed by several discussions at the Academy of Arts. Eisler defended himself:

I fail to understand how my critics can describe the conception of such a figure as anti-national, anti-patriotic or even deleterious. Wilhelm Girnus goes so far as to say: In this figure Eisler pours scorn on the whole intellectual history of Germany. That's a bit much! Girnus goes on to say: '. . . that the Third Reich fell precisely because it was a betrayal of humanism, so that only in this very fall did the German humanist spirit gain victory.' It would probably be better to say: It has survived it! Can we speak of 1945 as a victory for the spirit of humanism? . . . People should not rudely polemicize against me with such arguments.[25]

We see here clearly what at the time Brecht lamented as the 'decline of dialectics'. The uncritical adoption of the 'great' (because classical) ideas and forms, the separation of intellectual from political history, the sacrificing of class analysis to the inherited arts and the confident expectation that the ideas would have sufficient strength on their own to appeal to the working class – all of this is based on petty-bourgeois rather than Marxist ideals.

In the discussions at the Academy, during which the setting sometimes became that of a courtroom with Eisler in the role of the defendant,[26] only a few friends stood up for him. These included Brecht and Felsenstein, as well as a great figure in the

21   Brecht and Eisler at the Akademie der Künste (Berlin, c. 1953)

German workers' movement who was able to speak sincerely for them: Hermann Duncker. But the consensus against them was, under the prevailing circumstances, too strong; it held fast to a universal ban on *Faustus*.

The fact that a leading functionary permitted himself to speak openly of this work as 'the so-called Faust of Eisler'[27] – as a horrifying example of formalist disfigurement – was bound to be seen by Eisler as a symptom of precisely the predicament he had sought to fight.

Eisler then returned to Vienna for a longish time. A 'state of deepest depression' robbed him of all incentive to compose. Brecht went to Buckow and wrote *Turandot or The Congress of the Whitewashers*. The 'Tuis' who whitewash authority and identify with those in power seemed to him not exclusively a Western problem.

Eisler's hope that with the opera he would be able to be productive in a new form was dashed. His intention to counteract the sterile alternatives of a return to the trivial or the esotericism of dodecaphony was doomed to frustration from the beginning. With the damnation of Faust (and virtually of himself), furthermore, he had come face to face with the narrow-mindedness and petty-bourgeois lack of imagination which always starts by demanding something 'positive' and ends by having to draw the political teeth of criticism in order to abate its vehemence. What was particularly disturbing was that such reactions were couched in Marxist vocabulary.

At this time Eisler and Brecht recognized the danger of misusing Marxist theory for apologetic ends, for the glorification of the past and the existing: in art this could lead to a purely verbal, conformist and oppressive 'humanism'. Wherever living, breathing theory was subordinated to a system of positive dogmas, then hoary scholastics would inevitably set in. This gave rise to the temptation for Party officials little versed in artistic questions to lay down their own conceptions as 'ideologically' binding: equipped with a handy array of theses, they could prescribe matters of form and content according to their own ideas; they became the administrators who provided the sketches, and it remained for the artists to colour them in.

In 1954 Brecht contrasted 'popular and functionary-like', mordantly noting:

Art is not capable of translating official conceptions of art into works of art. Only boots can be made to measure. Besides, the taste of many politically well-educated people is poor, and hence no criterion. Socialist Realism should not be treated as a style, and anyone lacking the aesthetic education to appreciate this stands in need of such training, and should undergo it, before taking up administrative work. It is particularly regressive to oppose Socialist Realism to critical realism and thereby brand it as an *uncritical realism*.[28]

It is obvious that Brecht is fighting the *authoritarian* aspect of the superior, pontifical attitude with which many functionaries compensated for their lack of knowledge in questions of art. Since they controlled what passed between the artist and the public, the emancipation of the latter became more difficult. The official persistence in conventional ideas of form, which not infrequently ingratiated themselves with the petty bourgeoisie, was certain to arouse distaste and lack of interest in precisely the public which

Brecht and Eisler wanted to reach above all: the workers and the young.

In Vienna, where Eisler composed music for the theatre and for films, he longed to be back in East Germany, though admittedly in an atmosphere less hostile to him. In October 1953 he wrote a letter to the central committee of the SED [German United Socialist Party] in which he took pains to explain the strained relationship.

Many of my works lay in my desk drawer, including more than 500 songs, cantatas, orchestral and chamber music. I felt that nobody was at all prepared to accept these works, which have been written over three decades of what has been, after all, a life of constant militancy. Musicians who performed or reviewed works of mine were treated as representatives of a bygone artistic movement. You must understand, comrades, that the entire output of an artist is many-sided and that every composer, in addition to works which are immediately understood, must also produce more complicated music in order to achieve progress in the art . . . I have been extremely closely associated with the German workers' movement ever since my youth. My music always was and still is nourished by it, and not just the music which is immediately accepted by the masses, but also that which is more difficult to understand and which addresses itself to a smaller audience, one that is familiar with the heritage of German music. I can only visualize my place as an artist as being in that part of Germany in which the foundations of socialism are being laid.[29]

In fact the ice was not broken until 1955, and it needed a definitive intervention from Brecht. The situation of being *persona non grata* in the country to which he felt himself most drawn was certainly a blow to Eisler's spirit for a while; even so at the end of 1954 he risked a fresh provocation when at the Berlin Academy of Arts, of which he was a member, he gave a major lecture on Schoenberg. At the time Schoenberg's music was considered in Eastern Europe to be the embodiment of formalism and anti-populist decadence. For Eisler this was one of those prejudices which restricted the development of music and consequently were to be done away with.

I have no need of the Chinese saying: 'He who does not honour his teacher is worse than a dog' in order to assert here that Schoenberg was one of the greatest composers, and not only of the twentieth century. His mastery and originality are astonishing, his influence was and is vast. His weaknesses are more dear to me than the strengths of many another. The history of music is unthinkable without him. The decline and fall of the bourgeoisie, certainly. But what a sunset!

Eisler spoke spiritedly of Schoenberg's achievements in composition, but at the same time criticized the choice of texts in his vocal compositions. As a teacher in charge of a master class in composition at that same Berlin Academy, Eisler saw to it that young musicians did not lose sight of technical standards, though he, like Schoenberg before him, based his instruction on the analysis of the great precursors up to Brahms. His intention was to spark off a discussion, a confrontation with developments in the West, even if it was still not possible to envisage widespread appreciation. The lecture ended:

A thousand million workers and peasants living in the countries liberated from capitalism will at first be able to make nothing or very little of Schoenberg. They have other, more pressing tasks. In music itself there is the fight against musical illiteracy. Only once this has been conquered and the most complicated works of the classics have become truly popular can Schoenberg once again enter into the question. I am not without optimism about the outcome of such a discussion. How many of his works will remain alive, that I do not know; but at least he is bound to gain fame as one who scorned clichés. He neither glorified nor glossed over the social order into which he was born. He disguised nothing. He held up a mirror to his time, to his class. What it showed was not at all pleasant. But it was the truth.[30]

In the year of his final return to Berlin, 1955, Breitkopf and Härtel of Leipzig published the first of ten volumes of Eisler's songs and cantatas. As a 'Foreword', Brecht wrote: 'What is important here is to steep oneself in a great work of vocal music, to look around it, find one's way about and familiarize oneself with it. Here one may educate oneself in many different ways which contradict each other.' To render contradictions productive instead of suppressing them is a prerequisite of dialectical art. 'Realistic artists represent the *contradictions* in people and their relationships to each other and show the conditions needed for their development.'[31]

One of the contradictions in the musical life of East Germany, in which Eisler at that time intervened, was the official rejection of jazz. He considered it a waste of time to try to exclude its influence by means of a prohibition, simply because it was of American origin and – as was asserted – acted as a Trojan Horse to introduce American ideology. Eisler, who for ten years in the United States had been familiar with good and bad jazz, and was using the idiom himself as early as about 1930, pleaded for critical discrimination, open discussion and good recordings. This seemed to him more responsible than making jazz fans illegal. In 1956 he concluded a debate in the Academy with the words: 'We cannot abandon our young people to the West's places of amusement . . . Otherwise they would go there and hear swing music and we would be sitting here holding great discussions on Socialist Realism.'[32]

Eisler was against 'petty headmastership' not only for reasons of taste, but because its blind faith in instruction gets nowhere near the fundamental issues and generally produces only boredom. If art is practised in such a perspective, then there must arise

an abundance of works which are pitched more or less at the same level, just as they introduce the same themes and topics . . . Thus there would be an abundance of works of a pathetic kind, an art of the homeland, songs of praise and celebration of every kind which stupefy the listener while they are going on and will induce him to seek out entertainment of a lower order. The need for entertainment . . . cannot be valued highly enough. However it is no longer good enough to say that alongside the various kinds of art there must also be entertainment. That would be a crude misrepresentation of the relationship between entertainment and art.

Instead it was necessary to affirm at all costs 'that the great masterpieces . . . [owe] their fame not only to the great ideas that they fashion, but above all to their power of entertainment and stimulation. This is what they have to teach us.'[33]

Eisler now made a fresh start in his attempts to eradicate the opposition between entertainment and art, education and enjoyment, to tune in to the current state of listening and at the same time take it further. What he was prevented from doing in *Faustus*, he hoped to achieve, at least in part, with the music to Brecht's *Schweyk im Zweiten Weltkrieg* [Schweyk in the Second World War]. It had a threefold function in this resistance play which Brecht completed in 1943 in Hollywood. Eisler described these functions as follows:

The first: in the scenes of the 'Higher Regions' it permits the representation of German barbarism without parody, caricature, or well-loved cabaret jokes. Criminals are shown as criminals. What is comical is comical in itself. The music remains serious, devoid of good humour, after the victory has been won.

The second: The interludes – polka, march, Beseda etc. – facilitate transitions, also helping out with scene changes. Here there is good humour, joking and amusement, which Brecht always needed and demanded for his plays.

The third: The songs sung on stage and accompanied by the electric piano – as with beer and schnapps these are only available for cash. As distinct from superior music, this admits to being a lowly means of enjoyment . . . to be taken up and whistled, it is the meagre consolation of the oppressed who dream of 'times changing' [see ex. 32].[34]

Many of Eisler's Schweyk songs were later to become popular: above all 'Lied von der Moldau' [The Song of the Moldau], 'Das Lied vom Weib des Nazisoldaten' [Song of the Nazi Soldier's Wife], as well as 'Deutsches Miserere' [The German Predicament] and 'Das Lied vom Kleinen Wind' [Song of the Little Breeze].

The music was not yet completed when in August 1956 Brecht died unexpectedly, in the middle of the preparations for the London performance of *Galilei* by the Berliner Ensemble. For Eisler, Brecht's premature death was not only a personal blow but a setback for the artistic point of view they had both stood for. Only a short time previously he had roughed out an entreating letter; the bad news arrived before it was posted:

Dear Friend, I do not want to speak of our old friendship and my sincere admiration if I now say to you as a communist: Please stop working now. In September Galileo will go on just the same. Don't forget you are irreplaceable! You know that someone who is irreplaceable must take good care of himself until such time as he is replaceable. For the present there is no prospect of that. I beg you, even when you have got over the

Ex.32　*Schweyk im zweiten Weltkrieg*, 'Schwarzer Rettich'

influenza – which will be in a few days – stop working and recuperate. We will all help you to drive away your boredom. As a very . . .

Here the draft breaks off. Eisler must have remembered the lines from the Lenin Cantata they had written together, lines whose seriousness he had set with a particularly light touch: 'When a good man wants to go away/How can we stop him?/Tell him: why he is needed./That will stop him.'[35]

In his works the following year, 1957, Eisler rendered homage both to his friend and to the October Revolution, and once again developed the two principal themes of the emancipation of the proletariat and of anti-fascism. The 'Teppichweber von Kujan-Bulak' [Carpet-Weavers of Kujan-Bulak], who honour Lenin whilst serving their own advantage, was used by Eisler as the basis of a cantata for soprano and orchestra, with baritone and chorus added for the tableaux from the 'Kriegsfibel' [War Primer].

As incidental music for Bill-Bjelozerkowski's *Sturm* [The Storm] he composed three marches to texts by Mayakovsky, very much with Ernst Busch in mind: to be sung with a metallic voice and with aggressive humour. Admittedly these are already historical documents in the context of present-day East Germany, and are now of genuine usefulness more in those countries which are in the process of liberating themselves from colonialism and foreign rule. (Joris Ivens took the first recordings of these marches with him to Cuba when he was making his film about the Cuban Revolution in 1960.) The inspiration for the 'Linker Marsch' [Left-wing March] – and this too comes down to the dialectics of artistic production – came to Eisler during the Salzburg Festival in the summer of 1957.

The following years brought him a number of commissions for films and plays outside Germany, while performances of his music within East Germany continued to be only isolated events. It is not without irony that in April 1959, at precisely the moment when the 'Bitterfelder Weg'* – by which the working class of East Germany were to storm the 'heights of culture' – was published, Eisler's difficult *Deutsche Sinfonie* received its first performance at the Berlin State Opera. At this time Eisler became a respected 'cultural producer', an important figure in cultural politics. He published opinions, gave lectures, not least in factories, and was asked for interviews. He discovered young talents, including such very different ones as Gisela May and Wolf Biermann.

His fame grew, but still without concrete results. Still only a small proportion of his works were printed, and even those by no means found favour with performers, who thought the technical demands too high and the name of Hanns Eisler too political. In conversations with young intellectuals he complained of the back-

---

* *Translator's note.* The 'Bitterfelder Weg' was a State-promoted campaign, initiated at the First Bitterfeld Conference on 24 April 1959, to raise the cultural level of the workers and peasants of the DDR. The workers' own artistic achievements were to be encouraged and established artists were to be sent into the factories. Eisler was sceptical about the whole undertaking.

22   Berlin, c. 1957

wardness and the 'stupidity' of the music industry. 'Why should one not play Rachmaninov, who was always an opponent of the Soviet Union – and have to play Eisler, an old communist, isn't that it? Rachmaninov is played, but not Eisler.'[36] The fact that his music needed five rehearsals rather than two and that its gestures were inimical to the vanity and self-images of soloists made it seem 'ungrateful' to them. In the figure of the conductor in full evening dress, parading his passions before the public in the attitude of a General, Eisler felt that musical idiocy attained its most graphic expression. That choosing conservative programmes entailed naïvely copying the personality cult of the West was a further idiocy. Such tendencies were bound to counteract the enormous exertions that had gone into building up a new East German culture. To treat a new public in the same way as an old one meant making it deaf to new art.

Ernste Gesänge

Shortly before his death Eisler completed his *Ernste Gesänge* [Serious Songs]. Their character is that of a final testament.

This is a late work in every sense, including the way in which it refers to Brahms; here Eisler draws up an account of his own life and weighs up the balance. He dedicated the cycle to his last wife, Stephanie.

The period during which the songs were composed, 1961–2, gave no grounds for writing optimistic songs. The tensions within Germany resulting from the nation's partition reached a climax with the building of the Wall and the announcement of a state of emergency. As in 1930, but in a completely different way, the workers' movement in Germany was also divided.

Eisler had rather to look elsewhere for the gleams of hope pointing to the future. The self-emancipation of the peoples of the Third World was gathering momentum. The first manned spaceflight,[37] the beginning of a new industrial revolution, automation and cybernetics and their future effects on art were major preoccupations of his final months.

The prospect before him – of a future which he himself would

not now know – was dialectically complemented by a review of
his own past, together with a view of *history*: for the first time that
of socialism no longer consisted only of opposition, but it was
now self-created and responsible to itself. 'Perhaps the artist's
task . . . is to see the past correctly and clearly and to . . . link it up
to the future. Anyone who does not do this will supply an untram-
melled unctuous optimism which doesn't sound right and makes
no sense. The future cannot be conveyed in an undialectical
way . . .'[38]

The past which socialism had to overcome was Stalinism. As an
inheritance it was a perversion. In order for it to be overcome it
had to be understood. It had to be branded as still alive, despite
the eradication of its abuses – this was a necessary warning. The
honesty of an artist of Eisler's standards is shown by the fact that
he reminded the movement of that of which he and all his hopes
were a part: its deformities. He was not afraid to give one of the
Ernste Gesänge the unpoetic title 'Twentieth Party Conference'.
The title reveals that the point of the poem lies in its final lines: 'To
live without fear.'

It was not only out of love for Hölderlin's poetic language and
its intensity that Eisler selected half of his texts from that poet. He
saw in him a comparable situation: that of the artist who in his
work responds to a revolution and questions its reversals.

The balance between hope and regret in Eisler's cycle – which is
written for baritone and string orchestra – also characterizes its
original autobiographical ideas. The artist, here looking back in
his old age, was soon to withdraw – not in his work, but as a man
submitting to physical death. This departure, which is sorrowful,
must not be lamented but rather understood, like the autumn, as
natural and necessary. For this, no metaphysical consolations are
needed. The *Ernste Gesänge* culminate in a sentence of earthly
promise: 'What flourishes without him, he praises/Assured of
future happiness.'[39]

In the cycle Eisler has mirrored the course of an emotional
experience or a human pattern of behaviour: reflection–delibera-
tion–depression–aspiration and again reflection. The awareness
of sorrows, one of the dimensions of art, thus does not take on the
guise of resignation. The third song, 'Verzweiflung' [Despair], is a

23   With his wife Stephanie in London (1959)

fragment from Leopardi's famous poem 'A se stesso'; Eisler has condensed it and freed it of all its features of Romantic discontent. Sorrow, as well as occasional underlying anger, is sublimated in the composition: Eisler speaks at a distance, both to and of himself.

The cycle was written for future listeners and pays no heed to immediate comprehension. It is accompanied by the confidence that a work which sounds well in itself and contains a good deal of social truth will gain recognition and establish itself.

The compositional techniques developed by the second Viennese School and by Eisler alike seem particularly appropriate for setting Hölderlin's irregular rhythms. In his essay 'Brahms the progressive', Schoenberg showed that 'developing variation is associated with the contraction of periods, the criterion of *musical prose*'.[40] Hölderlin's conception of the fundamental note in the doctrine of the 'changing of notes' is faintly reminiscent of the way in which the twelve-note row is constantly present as the starting-point in developing variation.

The fundamental note of the *Ernste Gesänge* is – in a transferred sense – a dialectical epigram by Hölderlin to which the seven following texts relate in a literary way as developing variations:

'Many tried in vain to say joyfully the most joyful thing,/Here at last it is spoken by me, here in my sorrow.'[41] Eisler uses it to illuminate just those contradictions which would otherwise be veiled by a facile platitude such as the label of a fulfilled life's work. In fulfilment itself are concealed the dual meanings of creative abundance and a life moving towards its close, time that has been used up. Both life and work alike contain strong and weak periods and moments, and consequently joy and sadness.

The interweaving of autobiographical and social elements is concentrated notably in one section of the cycle; the complexity of the whole can here be observed in detail.

The prologue and epilogue frame six songs, the last of which has the title: 'Komm! ins Offene, Freund!' [Come! Into the open, Friend!]. The elegy 'Der Gang aufs Land' [The Way to the Country], which Hölderlin wrote in the autumn of 1800, is abridged by Eisler to a text of nine lines:

Come! Into the open, friend! True that it's only shining a little today/Here below, and the sky hems us closely in./Today it is dull, the paths and streets are slumbering./It seems as if it were the age of lead./For our singing is nothing powerful, but it belongs to life./The swallows are coming too/Always a few, before the summer in the country./May the carpenter pass sentence from the rooftop:/We, as far as we could, have done our part.

Eisler has taken these lines, which were full of meaning for him, from the original, once more for the dual purpose of suitability for setting and for integrating into the context of the cycle. The technique of montage allows him to place the chief contradiction symmetrically exactly in the centre of the text. He explained these lines in 1961 in conversation with Hans Bunge:

It seems to me marvellous, particularly for us, who not only believe in the social function of art but have practised it, now to be singing of the antagonism: 'For our singing is nothing powerful. But it belongs to life, what we want.' . . . This contains both the positive and the negative aspects. Naturally every artist (and musician too) believes that what he does is of decisive importance for society as a whole. But Hölderlin says 'For our singing is nothing powerful, but it belongs to life', which is much more concrete, more joyous and better than a somewhat stupid naïvety which thinks that it can solve the world's problems with a song. Although . . . songs have played an enormous role in the history of the world (such as the 'Marseillaise' or the 'Internationale'). So both sides must be shown; I show the other side of singing.[42]

Anyone reading Eisler naïvely might well here arrive at the worldly wisdom of a necessarily realistic view of the role of music. But what is in question is more contradictory. This becomes evident from the positioning of the one-line sentence within the structure of the text. It is concentrically bracketed within an outer, positive sense and a closer negative one. The challenge 'Come! Into the open, friend!', making up the first part, is matched by the last – the fifth – which is the closing judgment: 'We, as far as we could, have done our part.' Parts two and four, the inner bracket, correspond to each other as negative: close and dull, the age of lead, and on the other hand the melancholy of arriving too early. The contradiction between the outer and inner brackets, however, is not compressed into the third part – the middle section itself – but is added conjointly to it, illuminating it.

The contrast in the centre is that between the claim of the work ('singing'), namely to be powerful, of great effect, and its real significance in 'life', in its time; for Hölderlin already the relationship is inverse to the extent that, against all expectation, the high claim is negated, but the necessity to life is affirmed. The contradiction between the brackets is that the work over which sentence is passed (here by the composer) is positively affirmed, whereas 'time' – life – still seems narrow, leaden, still awaiting 'the summer'. It is in fact in this way – though in a more complex manner than explained by Eisler himself – that the relationship between art and society is shown 'from both sides' and judged; subjectively, from the viewpoint of the artist who identifies himself with the work, and objectively from the side of 'life', society, which also claims possession of his work, as one enhancement amongst others. If we take the melancholy of a too-early arrival seriously as a historical discrepancy, then the grouping of contradictions yields the following conclusion: the 'singing', the artistic work, is only a phenomenon of its time – still 'nothing – powerful', and the claim which the central section implies despite everything is negated only for as long as it takes for swallows and the summer to appear at the same time, in other words until the artist's leap of awareness is attained by the public at least to the extent that it is capable of listening to his work in a suitable way.

For it is true that in genuine art the experiences of contemporary society are absorbed, and conversely the artist inhabits that society; but at a time when most individuals are reduced to a lower level of awareness by the compulsion to engage in alienating activity (partly because conditions do not yet allow anything else), great art is also unable to develop fully that effectiveness which resides within it. The conviction that the necessary conditions for it would finally be obtained entailed for Eisler the further conviction that in the future art would once more regain its immediate effectiveness.

In the style of the cycle, whose elegiac character is indicated by the title, what is striking, besides the predominantly declamatory writing for the voice, is that the extraordinary intensity of the vocal line owes something to an economy in the accompaniment that recalls late Schubert (of 'Die Winterreise' or 'Der Doppelgänger').

Ex.33   *Ernste Gesänge*, 'Komm! ins Offene, Freund!'

At the same time anything that might have tragic associations is avoided. On the contrary a discreet emotionality, markedly refined by rationality, is expressed, in which there is no lack of withdrawn tenderness. The transparency of the writing holds all sentimentality in check, even in the epilogue, in which elements of affirmative pathos appear.

For 'Komm! ins Offene, Freund!' Eisler prescribes a performance of calm certainty; in view of the contradictions of the text this emerges as a dramaturgical counterpoint. The *alla breve* metre imbues the polyphonic writing with a gently swinging motion – probably to compensate for the dull and the leaden (see ex. 33). The music is characterized by the interval of a minor third, which 'not only introduces the "fugue theme", but also appears in the vocal part . . . above all at the beginnings of phrases. The accompaniment begins by developing as a fugal exposition with four entries of the theme at the interval of a fifth. Afterwards the theme appears three more times in varied form', the last time in the postlude.[43]

Ex.34   *Ernste Gesänge*, 'Komm! ins Offene, Freund!'

als   sei   es   in   der   blei - er - nen   Zeit. Denn nicht— Mäch-ti - ges   ist un-ser Sin-gen,

The central significance of 'For our singing is nothing powerful' is spelt out musically by the sole appearance in the vocal part here of the accompaniment's 'fugue theme'. The immediate link of this phrase with 'the age of lead' – established by the causal 'For' – emphasizes the connection between this still unripe time and the lack of effectiveness in the singing. It remains open whether the 'nothing', certainly the weightiest word in the text, is thrown into doubt by being split over the interval of a seventh – a unique instance in the whole cycle (see ex. 34).

5

Eisler's modernity

One of the great composers of the present century, Hanns Eisler is distinguished from others in that he took the *social function of music seriously*. From it he drew artistic *and* political consequences: in order to lead modern music out of its isolation. It had manoeuvred itself into that position as its techniques became autonomous and since then it had ostensibly ignored current social circumstances.

'The reluctance of the musician to think outside of his art is an exact description of the special feature of music', he noted as the most important reason why the activity of many young composers did not get beyond an esoteric 'abstract protest' against commercial music in the mass media. The 'abomination of the sleekness, the oily filth . . . that flows from every channel in the West and the East' had to be fought against just as much as technical experiments without perspective. However this was still more useful than the continuation of the 'psychological noise-music' of the beginning of the century with its hysterical excesses. Not to speak of provincial subjectivity: 'The social forces of mental production, of the brain, are becoming more refined – and the laborious Adagio movement to heat the emotions will have less and less of a part to play . . . a society which can itself organize thinking by means of machines can see less and less in the naïve spontaneity of a poet or a composer.'[1]

Eisler understood his time as one of *transition* to socialism. With the exception of his final decade he had spent his entire life in opposition. This left its mark on his music – which is the music of an aggressive artistic temperament. In his historical thinking, the 1917 Revolution was certainly the most important turning-point of the century; yet for him and many of his generation the revolution was not an accomplished fact; much more something that had to be fought for patiently.

The attempt to communicate music and politics together during a time of transition led him logically to *angewandte Musik*. Its innovatory association with precise texts – the best of which Brecht wrote for him over a period of thirty years of collaborative work – was successful because he did not consider that the learning of the most modern techniques of composition and the understanding of the classical tradition he had acquired through Schoenberg were sufficient for writing music that had a function he thought worthy of it. His second talent, that for literature, was useful to him here, as were also his early political interests. Of his vocal music and that which was new in it in the twentieth century it could be said, paradoxically, that *the text is primary and the music is not secondary*. Admittedly during his lifetime – and this is one of the tragic aspects of his artistic career – this meant that the praise he received generally came from those who had extramusical reasons to proclaim it. Tendentious praise is far worse than tendentious criticism.[2]

Eisler would have been unthinkable without Schoenberg. The influences of the latter's early and middle atonal periods are stronger than those of his twelve-note period. The development of the second Viennese School after Schoenberg's death, with the serialization of every possible parameter, was rejected by Eisler. In the evolution of music during the 1950s he probably saw a variant of 'L'art pour l'art' in the form of 'la série pour la série'.

Above all the later Eisler constantly drew attention to the – contradictory – fact that the transformation of musical material should not be carried out independently of the function of music, nor of the distinctive evolution of the genre and above all of listening, which changed with society. His own bold use of montage techniques, his new methods of achieving development through juxtaposition constitute an attempt to take into account in his compositions a process that was similarly multi-layered. For him as a musician, dialectics as 'the great method' meant perpetually approaching afresh the constant reshaping of the contradictions in a reality that was becoming increasingly complex; only in the last ten years did he allow the emphasis to shift.

Only now is Eisler's importance as a theoretician beginning to emerge – as admittedly is the scope of his music, which after his emigration was only sporadically published, and then with dubious priorities. The hermetic exclusion of his works from West Germany now appears absurd, but is by no means yet overcome nationwide. It is true that, conversely, Eisler's music, like his theories, resist rapid acceptance in musical circles. A comparison with the attitude of Adorno, Eisler's friend in Hollywood and subsequently the most influential musical theorist of West Germany, makes it clear why. Here it is plain that Eisler had to reject Adorno's post-war positions; 'It is one of the peculiarities of that Institute in Frankfurt that it sees all tendencies towards dissolution as progressive, with a sort of half-baked Marxism . . .' Eisler reduced this attitude to the superb, intentionally very summary formulation: 'They only want to be more clever than the bourgeois theorists, but they do not want to take issue with them.'[3] The principal theme of late Adorno, the salvaging of subjectivity, the insistence on 'unregimented experience', on spontaneity and imagination, meant salvaging in the name of aesthetics. Under the trauma of the experience of fascism, Adorno, after 1945, arrived at a far-reaching equation of capitalism and socialism as being systems of total manipulation. Subjectivity (basically the Romantic bourgeois subjectivity), threatened with 'socialization', looks to art for consolation and the chance of immortality. The concentration of his analyses on partial phenomena, whose rights as against the 'whole' are ultimately so overvalued as to turn his priorities upside down, obviously replaced his view of the political confrontation of concrete social subjects: the great confrontations of classes and levels of society are hidden out of sight. The observer adopted the perspective of the suffering subject and the dividing line separating it from suffering in itself was merely blurred. Such subjectivism was only able to exercise very limited force as a dialectical weapon.

But also, it had never occurred to Eisler – who, besides his teacher, owed as much both to Webern and to early Stravinsky – to link himself puristically to a musical lineage such as, say, that of Mahler–Schoenberg–Berg. Moreover, this was not solely on account of practical needs in composing. Eisler's suspicions about such a regression to subjective inwardness, to a premature return to private art, must have been directed elsewhere: at the disappearance of the great subjects from art, the abandonment of themes which concern not the few but the many.

If we wanted to compare Eisler with Brecht, who agreed with his own artistic conceptions as wholly as was at all possible between friends of the same standing, both Marxists, the first thing to mention would be Eisler's more diversified position. The difference was above all noticeable during the years of exile. Isolated from his creative environment (the theatre) and not in much demand as a playwright, Brecht in emigration needed a self-image as a classicist in order to survive. This was apparent in his reversion to more conventional techniques, in his cementing of positions that were in many respects less exposed than those he represented in around 1930.

In Hollywood Eisler felt the compulsion, as a 'freelancer' in the highly specialized film business, to take on at the same time the role of an artistic industrial worker; this meant having to function precisely – and to some extent on the spot – in top gear. Despite the perversity of studio work, the advance of rationalization, which provoked reaction daily, concealed within itself those tendencies which dictated the general development to the arts.

Cinema, depending on the interplay of various kinds of media and hence the synthetic genre *par excellence*, required in a particular degree simultaneous imagination, thought and production. The public's grasp of time became faster, and perception was dulled more rapidly. For a musician in this field to work rationally to the extent that, like it, he had his own modern techniques at his disposal, meant composing small units which, though interchangeable, would initially be so compact in themselves that they could be juxtaposed in new combinations, in a different context and with quite another objective.

Conversely, for the precision of such advanced work to be made good use of, situations are required in which the public is no longer under the influence of out-of-date working conditions or narrow productivity. This may account for some proportion of the difficulties which Eisler's music met with after his return from emigration.

As an artistic type, Eisler was the metropolitan intellectual, of extreme sensitivity and nervosity, who could happily do without

the 'idiocy of country life'. As a native of Vienna, seen by intellectual friends in New York and London too as 'very sophisticated',
he was by no means devoid of those exceptionally susceptible and
even gentle traits of character, occasionally shaded with melancholy, which distinguished him from the less sensual and in many
respects more ascetic Brecht. Eisler's irresistible penchant for the
daring turn of phrase as well as his liking for gambling as –
following Novalis – experimenting with chance, gave his personality facets and a variety which do not readily fit into the usual
categories.

Impatience in mastering contradictions often made him a
feared polemicist. The later Eisler was somewhat milder in his
judgments, after many experiences of the difficulties which each
change must entail and the reverses which follow it. A century
earlier, Heine, with a similarly precise eye for such lapses of
synchronicity, had summed them up in a dramatic image: 'The
world is a great cowshed which is not so easy to clear out as the
Augean stable because, while it is being swept, the oxen stay
inside and continually pile up more dung.'4

Eisler thought that in mere pointless throwing around of new
acoustic resources the relationship of the composer to his material
became alienated. Yet even the social revolution remained sterile,
as one only of principles and of conditions of production. Subjectivity and intelligence themselves, ways of feeling and thinking,
these needed to be transformed. The one *without* the other must
always produce that divided situation which misleads the individual into a regression into the past, often nostalgically glorified.

In his art Eisler insisted on the totality of the challenge which
music above all things can keep alive in the conscious mind; even
if he was obliged to concede that the process would take a little
longer than he had expected.

His *Ernste Gesänge*, and with them his work as a whole,
conclude in an open manner: with a unison pizzicato on the
strings – vibrations into the future.

Notes

Overture

1 Eisler, *Musik und Politik*, p. 394.
2 Marx–Engels, *Werke*, Berlin-DDR 1964, vol. 23, pp. 27f.
3 Brecht, 'Zum Geleit' in Eisler, *Lieder und Kantaten*, vol. I.
4 Bunge, *Gespräche*, p. 30.
5 Eisler, *Musik und Politik*, p. 394.

1. Early years in Vienna

1 Tuition of private pupils took place at Schoenberg's home in Mödling, near Vienna, where he lived from 1918 until 1925.
2 Alban Berg, *Briefe an seine Frau*, Munich and Vienna 1965, p. 391.
3 Universal Edition, founded in 1901, was at that time one of the most important publishers of new music.
4 The friction between Schoenberg and his publisher arose not only from arguments over payment but also from Hertzka's house policies.
5 In 1919 Schoenberg obtained for Eisler, who was totally penurious at the time, a position as third proofreader at UE. The second reader was then Alois Hába, who was studying composition with Schreker in Vienna.
6 Quoted from carbon copy in the Schoenberg Collection at the Library of Congress, Washington.
7 *ibid.*
8 cf. Adorno, 'Nach Steuermanns Tod' in *Impromptus*, Frankfurt am Main 1968, pp. 150ff. Eisler was very close to Steuermann both in Vienna and, later, when they were fellow émigrés in America, and was also friendly with his sister, Salka Viertel. Salka Viertel, starting out as an actress, became a writer of screenplays in Hollywood, and was married to the film director Berthold Viertel, with whom Eisler was also friendly.
9 Bunge, *Gespräche*, p. 168.
10 In the autumn of 1920 Schoenberg went to Holland for six months;

he had been invited by the conductor of the Amsterdam Concert-
gebouw, Willem Mengelberg, to appear there as a guest conductor
and to give courses in composition. As assistants, Schoenberg took
with him his two pupils Max Deutsch and Hanns Eisler. cf. Hans
Heinz Stuckenschmidt, *Schönberg – Leben, Umwelt, Werk*,
Zurich 1974, p. 245.

11 Schoenberg accepted. The Sonata bears the dedication: 'To Arnold
Schoenberg, with the greatest respect'. The Six Songs op. 2 that
Eisler mentions (three of which he sent to Schoenberg in 1922 as a
Christmas present) are 'dedicated to Dr Anton Webern'.

12 Original letter in the Schoenberg Collection, Washington.

13 Oral communication from R. Kolisch in Boston, 10 October 1973
(transcribed from a tape recording).

14 Oral communication from Max Deutsch, 10 January 1973.
Deutsch, who began his career as a conductor, has for some years
taught composition in Paris. Besides Deutsch, Eisler was also
friendly with Karl Rankl, Erwin Ratz and Josef Trauneck. Ratz
eventually became President of the Mahler Society. He died in
December 1973.

15 Bunge, *Gespräche*, p. 168.

16 At around the beginning of 1926, shortly after Eisler, Schoenberg
moved from Vienna to Berlin.

17 Eisler, *Musik und Politik*, p. 15.

18 *ibid.*

19 On 21 December 1950, shortly before his death, Schoenberg
made this observation about the new technique: 'I have in fact
constantly said why I felt impelled to introduce a method of composition with twelve notes. In the first place: not as a method of
composition, but as a method – *my* method – of *composition with
twelve notes.* Its aim is to *replace* the structural effects of functional
harmony by a different germinal force: a series of unchanging
relationships between notes. Secondly it was designed to regulate
the appearance of dissonant harmonies in *non-tonal music.* (In
tonal harmony, however, it would be superfluous). Thirdly, I have
repeatedly stressed that it would also be possible to use *other*
methods. I have guarded against its being termed a "system" . . .
Mine is no system but a method, in other words a *manner* in which a
preconceived formula may be used with consistency.' See Jan
Maegaard, 'Schönberg hat Adorno nie leiden können' in *Melos*,
September/October 1974, p. 262. See also Erwin Stein, 'Neue
Formprinzipien' in *Musikblätter des Anbruch* (Special Schoenberg

Number), Vienna 1924, pp. 286ff., and Eberhard Freitag, *Arnold Schönberg*, Hamburg 1974, pp. 97ff.

20 cf. H. F. Redlich, 'Die kompositorische Situation von 1930' in *Anbruch*, June 1930, pp. 187ff.
21 In *Österreichische Musikzeitschrift*, 5/6, 1969, p. 286.
22 Stein, *op. cit.*, p. 287.
23 Eisler, *Materialien*, p. 239.
24 *ibid.*, p. 237.
25 Freitag, *op. cit.*, p. 24.
26 *ibid.*, p. 54.
27 Arnold Schoenberg, *Harmonielehre*, Vienna 1922, p. 16. (Trans. Roy E. Carter, *Theory of Harmony*, London 1978.)
28 Arnold Schoenberg, *Style and Idea*, New York 1950, p. 98.
29 Bloch, *Das Prinzip Hoffnung*, vol. III, Frankfurt am Main 1968, p. 1282.
30 Hába, in *Sinn und Form: Sonderheft Hanns Eisler*, p. 351.
31 Notowicz, *Gespräche*, p. 27.
32 Rudolf Eisler (1873–1926) was a pupil of Wilhelm Wundt in Leipzig. He became known above all for his *Wörterbuch der philosophischen Begriffe* [Dictionary of Philosophical Concepts] (1899).
33 Notowicz, *Gespräche*, p. 29.
34 *ibid.*, p. 215.
35 *ibid.*, p. 30.
36 Rudolf Eisler, *Kritische Einführung in die Philosophie*, Berlin 1905, p. 365.
37 Notowicz, *Gespräche*, pp. 220f.
38 *ibid.*, pp. 30f.
39 *ibid.*, p. 214.
40 *Sinn und Form: Sonderheft*, p. 352.
41 Li-Tai-Pe, *Gedichte. Nachdichtungen von Klabund*, Leipzig 1915.
42 Notowicz, *Gespräche*, p. 218.
43 Oral communication. See note 14.
44 Hanns Hautmann, *Die Anfänge der linksradikalen Bewegung und der KPÖ 1916–1919*, Vienna 1970, pp. xiif., also pp. 32f.
45 *Sinn und Form: Sonderheft*, p. 348.
46 Oral communication from Irma ('Muschi') Friedmann in New York, 16 August 1973.
47 Notowicz, *Gespräche*, p. 49.
48 *ibid.*, p. 47.
49 *ibid.*, p. 38.
50 *ibid.*, p. 35.

51 It was not until 1960 that the Second Sonata appeared in print (published by Breitkopf und Härtel, Leipzig).
52 T. Wiesengrund-Adorno, 'Hanns Eisler. Duo für Violine und Violoncello op. 7, Nr. 1' in *Musikblätter des Anbruch* 1925, p. 423. What was probably Eisler's most concentrated work of the 1920s – the Piano Pieces op. 3 – was also the subject of a rapturous review by Adorno (in *Die Musik*, July 1927, p. 749).
53 *Sinn und Form: Sonderheft*, p. 353.
54 Eisler's diary did not come to light until 1975, when it was found among the papers of Erwin Ratz. It is to be published in vol. II of his collected writings (*Musik und Politik*).
55 cf. Eisler, *Musik und Politik*, p. 380.
56 *Palmström* op. 5, p. 12. Dedicated to Karl Rankl. (Universal Edition 1926 and 1971.)
57 Hans G. Helms, 'Schönberg: Sprache und Ideologie' in Ulrich Dibelius, *Herausforderung Schönberg. Was die Musik des Jahrhunderts veränderte*, Munich 1974, p. 89.
58 Notowicz, *Gespräche*, p. 35.
59 Eisler, *Materialien*, p. 187.
60 H.-H. Stuckenschmidt, *Schönberg*, Zurich 1974, p. 224.
61 Notowicz, *Gespräche*, p. 42.
62 Eisler, *Materialien*, p. 236.

2. Berlin – music and politics

1 *Schönberg – Katalog der Gedenkausstellung*, Berlin 1974, p. 34.
2 *Berliner Zeitung*, 4.11.1924. See also Else C. Kraus, 'Schönbergs Klavierwerk steht lebendig vor mir' in *Melos*, May/June 1974, pp. 134ff.
3 *Neue Preussische Kreuzzeitung*, 5.11.1924; also *Börsenzeitung*, 2.11.1924, *Morgenpost*, 1.11.1924, *Deutsche Zeitung*, 9.11.1924, *Deutsche Allgemeine Zeitung*, 14.11.1924, *Berliner Tageblatt*, 15.11.1924, *Börsencourier*, 5.11.1924, *Allgemeine Musikzeitung*, 7.11.1924, *Lokalanzeiger*, 16.11.1924, *Signale*, 5.11.1924, etc. These press cuttings were kindly placed at my disposal by Frau Else C. Kraus (Ascona).
4 Rolf Lindner, '50 Jahre deutscher Rundfunk' in *Ästhetik und Kommunikation*, 14, 1974, pp. 13ff. (Special Media Number.)
5 Maria-Antonietta Macchiocchi, *Pour Gramsci*, Paris 1974, pp. 215ff.

6 Arthur Rosenberg, *Geschichte der Weimarer Republik*, Frankfurt am Main 1961, pp. 57, 63.
7 Ossip K. Flechtheim, *Die KPD in der Weimarer Republik*, Frankfurt am Main 1969, p. 198; also *Chronik zur Geschichte der deutschen Arbeiterbewegung*, vol. II, Berlin 1967, p. 163.
8 *Chronik zur Geschichte der deutschen Arbeiterbewegung: Biographisches Lexikon*, Berlin-DDR 1970, p. 131.
9 *Chronik zur Geschichte der deutschen Arbeiterbewegung*, vol. II, p. 178.
10 Hannes Heer, *Thälmann*, Hamburg 1975, p. 88.
11 Asja Lacis, *Revolutionär im Beruf*, ed. H. Brenner, Munich 1971, p. 82.
12 *ibid.*, p. 85.
13 Erwin Piscator, *Schriften*, vol. I (*Das Politische Theater*), Berlin 1968, p. 67.
14 For Franz Jung's play *Heimweh*; cf. Piscator, *op. cit.*, p. 218.
15 Johannes R. Becher, 'Über die proletarisch-revolutionäre Literatur in Deutschland' in *Zur Tradition der sozialistischen Literatur in Deutschland. Eine Auswahl von Dokumenten*, Berlin 1967, p. 29.
16 Benjamin was already using this term in 1926.
17 Letter of 10 March 1926 in *Sinn und Form: Sonderheft*, p. 96.
18 Eberhard Freitag, *Arnold Schönberg*, Hamburg 1974, p. 119.
19 *ibid.*, p. 118.
20 Letter of 3 March 1926 in *Sinn und Form: Sonderheft*, p. 95.
21 Printed in *Sinn und Form* (Berlin-DDR), xvii/1–2, 1965, pp. 259f.
22 *Sinn und Form: Sonderheft*, p. 97.
23 Letter of 11 March 1926; original in the Schoenberg Collection, Washington.
24 Letter of 12 March 1926 in *Sinn und Form: Sonderheft*, pp. 97f.
25 Bunge, *Gespräche*, p. 43.
26 Note from the 1950s, single sheet in the Hanns Eisler Archive, Berlin.
27 H.-H. Stuckenschmidt, *Schönberg*, Zurich 1974, p. 281.
28 Schoenberg, letter to J. Rufer of 23 May 1948.
29 Letter to Rufer of 18 December 1947 in Arnold Schoenberg, *Briefe*, ed. E. Stein, Mainz 1958, pp. 262ff.
30 Stuckenschmidt, *op. cit.*, p. 252.
31 cf. Notowicz, *Gespräche*, p. 51.
32 See K. Riha, '"Heiraten" in der *Fackel*. Zu einem Zeitungs-Zitat-Typus bei Karl Kraus' in *Karl Kraus Sonderheft*, Munich 1975, pp. 116ff.

33 Notowicz, *Gespräche*, pp. 5of.
34 Letter of 19 April 1929 in *Sinn und Form: Sonderheft*, p. 109.
35 *Anbruch*, 1929, p. 220.
36 Heinrich Kralik in *Die Musik*, July 1928, p. 779.
37 *Musikblätter des Anbruch*, 1927, p. 271.
38 *Sinn und Form: Sonderheft*, p. 369.
39 'Die neue Religiosität in der Musik', *Musik und Politik*, pp. 61ff. The following quotation: oral communication from S. Priacel in Paris, 28 May 1973.
40 Heinrich Heine, *Sämtliche Werke*, ed. E. Elster, Leipzig, Berlin and Vienna 1887–90, vol. IV, p. 560.
41 'Der "tote Punkt". Ein Beitrag zur deutschen Literatur der Gegenwart' in *Zur Tradition der sozialistischen Literatur in Deutschland. Eine Auswahl von Dokumenten*, Berlin 1967, pp. 17ff.
42 cf. 'Vom bürgerlichen Chorgesang zur revolutionären "Kampfgemeinschaft der Arbeitersänger" (Zur Entwicklung der Arbeitersängerbewegung)' in *Kunst und Gesellschaft: Hanns Eisler*, pp. 29ff.
43 Heine, *Sämtliche Werke*, vol. I, pp. 31of., pp. 312f., and vol. II, pp. 201f.
44 On 26 April 1925. cf. *Chronik zur Geschichte der deutschen Arbeiterbewegung*, vol. II, p. 178.
45 *Chronik zur Geschichte der deutschen Arbeiterbewegung*, vol. II, p. 192 and Ossip K. Flechtheim, *Die KPD in der Weimarer Republik*, p. 235.
46 *Musik und Politik*, pp. 436ff.
47 Quoted from Martin Esslin, *Brecht. Das Paradox des politischen Dichters*, Munich 1970, p. 55.
48 Cf. H.-H. Stuckenschmidt, 'Musik und Musiker in der November-gruppe' in *Musikblätter des Anbruch*, October 1928, p. 294.
49 Oral communication from R. Gilbert in Ascona, 23 April 1973.
50 Eisler, *Musik und Politik*, pp. 57f.
51 On the July conflict in Vienna (15–18 July 1927) cf. E. Fischer, *Erinnerungen und Reflexionen*, Hamburg 1969, pp. 161ff.
52 *Chronik zur Geschichte der deutschen Arbeiterbewegung*, vol. II, p. 211.
53 The 11th Party Conference of the KPD took place in Essen from 2 to 7 March, that of the SPD in Kiel from 22 to 27 May.
54 cf. Hannes Heer, *Thälmann*, Hamburg 1975, p. 106.

55 S. Tretiakov, 'Woher und Wohin?' in *Ästhetik und Kommunikation*, 4, 1971, p. 86.
56 *ibid.*, p. 87.
57 cf. E. Simons, 'Der BPRS und sein Verhältnis zur KPD' in *Literatur der Arbeiterklasse. Aufsätze über die Herausbildung der deutschen sozialistischen Literatur (1918–1933)*, Berlin-DDR 1971, p. 122.
58 cf., above all, the contributions to the *Arbeiter-Illustrierte-Zeitung* (AIZ) in *Ästhetik und Kommunikation*, 10, 1973.
59 Bruno Frei, *Der Papiersäbel*, Frankfurt am Main 1971, p. 131.
60 Eberhard Knödler-Bunte, 'Fragen an Theo Pinkus über seine Arbeit bei der AIZ' in *Ästhetik und Kommunikation*, 10, 1973, p. 69.
61 Quoted from Ludwig Hoffmann and Daniel Hoffmann-Ostwald (eds.), *Deutsches Arbeitertheater 1918–1933*, vol. I, Berlin 1972, p. 241.
62 *ibid.*, p. 251.
63 *ibid.*, p. 243.
64 *ibid.*, p. 253.
65 Boris Arvatov, *Kunst und Produktion*, Munich 1972, postscript by H. G. and K. Hielscher, pp. 116ff. See also R. Tietze, Introduction to V. Meyerhold, *Theaterarbeit 1917–1930*, Munich 1974, pp. 7ff.
66 Ludwig Hoffmann and Daniel Hoffmann-Ostwald (eds.), *op. cit.*, p. 298.
67 *ibid.*, p. 299.
68 Of Eisler's militant songs, the 'Kominternlied' was the quickest in achieving international use. The various translations of the text differ considerably from each other.
69 Eisler, *Musik und Politik*, pp. 32f. ('On modern music'.)
70 *ibid.*, p. 160.
71 cf. Mayer, 'Über die musikalische Integration des Dokumentarischen', pp. 351ff.
72 cf. H. Lethen, *Neue Sachlichkeit 1924–1932*, Stuttgart 1970.
73 Already in 'Naturbetrachtung' (op. 13) Eisler has the chorus sing: '. . . Witty fellows: artists and scholars./They speak volumes about the marvels of technology./It is easy for them to talk about the work of our hands.' (*Lieder und Kantaten*, vol. V, p. 162.)
   During 1928 Eisler more than once formulated similar ideas, as in his discussion of Hindemith's *Cardillac* (which Eisler regarded as representative of 'Neue Sachlichkeit in music'): 'Modern man certainly affirms all the technological achievements of the present day. He uses them. He loves the big city and its noise, and he is enamoured of the precise rhythms of machines. Only the people

who serve these machines do not interest him.' (*Musik und Politik*, p. 80.) 'Do not forget that the machines are there solely to satisfy the needs of people. When, as you compose, you open the window, remember that the noise of the street is not an end in itself and is produced by people ... Choose texts and subjects that are as suitable as possible.' (*Musik und Politik*, p. 92.)

Some years later, Adorno criticized Hindemith's 'trivial musicianship' in particular as being reactionary: 'In the reality in which we live, there is no question of happily living for the moment in a natural state in the way that musicians play for the moment: one has to see through reality ... The musicians want to create enclaves in rationalized society where the power of reason will give way to feeble naturalness; and on the other hand they want to promulgate and glorify the blind process of rationalization itself as a myth of unspoilt nature in the guise of the "tempo of the times". They want to take away from man what is good in reason and persuade us that what is bad in the existing order is natural.' In *Impromptus*, Frankfurt am Main 1968, p. 69.

74 *Kunst und Gesellschaft: Hanns Eisler*, pp. 27 and 92.
75 Theodor W. Adorno, *Einleitung in die Musiksoziologie. Zwölf theoretische Vorlesungen*, Hamburg 1968, pp. 77f.
76 Ernst Bloch, *Experimentum Mundi. Fragen, Kategorien des Herausbringens, Praxis. Dem Andenken Rosa Luxemburgs*, Frankfurt am Main 1975, p. 124.
77 Notowicz, *Gespräche*, p. 147.
78 *Lieder und Kantaten*, vol. V, pp. 155ff.
79 Notowicz, *Gespräche*, p. 54.
80 *Musik und Politik*, p. 58.
81 cf. *Kunst und Gesellschaft: Hanns Eisler*, pp. 82ff.
82 *Die Rote Fahne*, 7 August 1929 and 30 January 1929.
83 Quoted from *Kulturwille* (Leipzig), 3, March 1929.
84 H. F. Redlich, 'Neue Probleme der Chorkomposition' in *Anbruch*, October 1929, pp. 302ff.
85 Arnold Schoenberg, *Harmonielehre*, Vienna 1922, pp. 207f. (Trans. Roy E. Carter, *Theory of Harmony*, London 1978.)
86 S. Tretiakov, 'Hanns Eisler' in *Sinn und Form: Sonderheft*, p. 118.
87 Printed in *Kunst und Gesellschaft: Hanns Eisler*, p. 60.
88 *Kunst und Gesellschaft: Hanns Eisler*, p. 55; *Kampfmusik*, 3, 1931, p. 4.
89 cf. Walter Benjamin, *Illuminationen: Ausgewählte Schriften*, Frankfurt am Main 1961, p. 407.

90 On this, see C. Zetkin, quoted in Hannes Heer, *Thälmann*, Hamburg 1975, p. 104.

91 *Kunst und Gesellschaft: Hanns Eisler*, p. 97.

92 In the original version of the text, on which the gramophone recording of 1932 is based – it arose in conjunction with the film *Week-end Kuhle Wampe* – Brecht tried to introduce the question of the critical housing situation: 'Come out of your hole/That they call a house/ And a grey week/Will be followed by a red weekend.'

93 Bunge, *Gespräche*, p. 53.

94 Eisler tells of his first collaboration with Busch in Notowicz, *Gespräche*, pp. 176ff. Busch died in 1980.

95 *Lieder und Kantaten*, vol. V, p. 55.

96 Klemm, 'Über Eislers Balladen' in *Arbeitshefte*, p. 47.

97 Kurt Tucholsky, *Lerne lachen ohne zu weinen, Auswahl 1928– 1929*, Berlin 1972, p. 505.

98 Walter Benjamin, 'Linke Melancholie' in *Lesezeichen, Schriften zur deutschsprachigen Literatur*, Leipzig 1972, pp. 255f.

99 David Drew, Foreword to Drew, ed., *Über Kurt Weill*, Frankfurt am Main 1975, p. xiii. cf. also Bunge, *Gespräche*, p. 256.

100 Bunge, *Gespräche*, p. 294.

101 Tucholsky, *op. cit.*, p. 343.

102 Bunge, *Gespräche*, p. 129; Notowicz, *Gespräche*, pp. 192f.; Völker, *Brecht-Chronik*, Munich 1971, p. 48.

103 Brecht, *Gesammelte Werke* 19, p. 336.

104 His memories of this – in conversation with Notowicz (*Gespräche*, pp. 181f.) – must be imperfect.

105 Oral communication from Marta Feuchtwanger in Pacific Palisades, 24 September 1973.

106 Even so, already in 1928 Brecht was writing: 'The Neue Sachlichkeit is reactionary.' (*Gesammelte Werke* 15, p. 161.) On this matter, cf. also his satire on the idolization of technology, '700 Intellektuelle beten einen Öltank an' [700 intellectuals pray to an oil tank]: '. . . God has come again/In the form of an oil tank./Thou ugly one/Thou art the loveliest!/Ravish us/Thou objective one!/Snuff out our ego!/ Make us collective!/For it is not our will/But Thine . . .' *Gesammelte Werke* 8, pp. 316f.

107 The phrase 'Change the world: it needs it!' was taken up by Brecht and Eisler in *Die Massnahme* (*Gesammelte Werke* 2, p. 652). These lines provided the title for Günter Lippmann's outstanding television film about Eisler, Berlin-DDR, 1973.

108 *Musik und Politik*, p. 224.

109 *ibid.*

110 Hildegard Brenner, editorial to 'Grosse und kleine Pädagogik. Brechts Modell der Lehrstücke' in *Alternative*, 78/79, 1971, pp. 101ff.

111 Walter Benjamin, 'Was ist das epische Theater?' in *Lesezeichen*, pp. 281f.

112 Brecht, *Gesammelte Werke* 17, p. 1024.

113 S. Tretiakov, in *Sinn und Form: Sonderheft*, p. 122.

114 *Musik und Politik*, p. 168.

115 M. Grabs, in Bertolt Brecht, *Die Massnahme*, critical edition by R. Steinweg, Frankfurt am Main 1972, p. 214.

116 *ibid.*, p. 82. Eisler set the third version of the text, which Brecht printed in his 'Versuchen'. cf. Hanns Eisler, *Die Massnahme. Lehrstück von Bert Brecht. op. 20*, piano arrangement by Erwin Ratz, Vienna 1931 (Universal Edition).

117 *Musik und Politik*, p. 161.

118 *loc. cit.*

119 *ibid.*, p. 129.

120 Lenin's well-known essay first appeared in German in 1920 in Leipzig as a commission from the publisher Franckes Verlag GmbH. It originally bore the title 'Der "Radikalismus" – die Kinderkrankheit des Kommunismus' ['Radicalism' – communism's childhood disease]. cf. also R. Steinweg, 'Brechts "Die Massnahme" – Übungstext, nicht Tragödie' in *Alternative*, 78/79, 1971, pp. 137ff.

121 cf. Bunge, *Gespräche*, p. 95.

122 Firstly as a speaking chorus, then in two parts, both times accompanied only by percussion. cf. Grabs, *op. cit.*, pp. 222f.

123 *Musik und Politik*, p. 225. cf. 'Zeugnisse der Rezeption' in Brecht, *Die Massnahme*, critical edition by R. Steinweg, pp. 319ff.

124 *ibid.*, pp. 326, 331, 346.

125 *ibid.*, pp. 338, 366.

126 cf. the reports collected by Steinweg, *ibid.*, pp. 237ff.

127 *Chronik zur Geschichte der deutschen Arbeiterbewegung*, vol. II, pp. 251f.

128 cf. E. Simons, 'Der BPRS und sein Verhältnis zur KPD', in *Literatur der Arbeiterklasse*, pp. 118ff.

129 Brecht, in Wolfgang Gersch and Werner Hecht (eds.), *Kuhle Wampe oder Wem gehört die Welt. Protokoll*, Leipzig 1971, pp. 98f.

130 *ibid.*, p. 109.

131 *ibid.*, pp. 33f.; cf. *Lieder und Kantaten*, vol. II, pp. 153f.
132 A. Betz, 'Dynamisierung des Widerspruchs. Über Eisler und Brecht' p. 76.
133 *Kunst und Gesellschaft: Hanns Eisler*, p. 52.
134 *Musik und Politik*, p. 260; cf. also Notowicz, *Gespräche*, pp. 230f.
135 Walter Benjamin, 'Ein Familiendrama auf dem epischen Theater' in *Lesezeichen*, p. 286.
136 Brecht, *Gesammelte Werke* 2, p. 895.
137 Benjamin, *op. cit.*, p. 288.
138 Later Eisler changed the title to 'Lob des Sozialismus' [In Praise of Socialism]; cf. Bunge, *Gespräche*, pp. 229f. Both versions are present in the edition *Lieder und Kantaten* (vol. I, p. 6 and vol. VII, p. 54). During his final years in East Germany, Eisler repeatedly drew attention in conversations to the fact that history had been divided into erroneous periods, that 'communism' was an inappropriate term at a time of economic shortage and that in general socialism was still very much in the early days of its development.
139 Klemm, *Hanns Eisler – für Sie porträtiert*, p. 19.
140 *ibid.*, p. 18.
141 Brecht, *Gesammelte Werke* 15, p. 479.
142 *Musik und Politik*, p. 131.
143 Knepler, '. . . was des Eislers ist', p. 36.
144 Bunge, *Gespräche*, p. 219.
145 *Musik und Politik*, pp. 171ff.; Joris Ivens, *Die Kamera und ich. Autobiographie eines Filmers*, Hamburg 1974, pp. 52ff.
146 Klemm, *op. cit.*, p. 21.
147 The *Illustrierte Rote Post* (19, 1932, supplement, p. 7) reported this in an announcement: ' "Tretiakov and Eisler write an opera": The well-known Soviet Russian poet S. Tretiakov is writing an opera with Hanns Eisler, which is to be performed in January 1933 at the "Little Opera House" in Leningrad. It is to be a political opera, dealing with circumstances in capitalist Germany. Tretiakov assembled the materials for it whilst travelling through Germany last year. Eisler has just gone to Moscow to make a start on his work there.' Some references to it can be found in letters of Tretiakov to Brecht from the years 1932–5. (In the Bertolt Brecht Archive, Berlin.)
148 Brecht, *Gesammelte Werke* 19, p. 327. Brecht continues: 'New problems appear and require new methods. Reality is changing; in order to represent it, the representation must change.'
149 'Die Erbauer einer neuen Musikkultur' [The builders of a new

musical culture] (1931) may be reckoned Eisler's most important essay during the Weimar Republic. (*Musik und Politik*, pp. 140ff.)
150 cf. H. Huppert, in *Zur Tradition der sozialistischen Literatur in Deutschland. Eine Auswahl von Dokumenten*, Berlin 1967, p. 512.
151 *Musik und Politik*, p. 159.
152 S. Tretiakov, 'Das Theater der Attraktionen' in *Ästhetik und Kommunikation*, 13, 1973, p. 79.
153 Brecht, *Gesammelte Werke* 19, p. 336.
154 Eisler, *Reden und Aufsätze*, p. 55.

3. Fifteen years of exile

1 Eisler-Fischer, 'Eisler in der Emigration', p. 70. On the performance of *Die Massnahme* in Vienna, there exists a report recalling the event by Josef Toch (Hanns Eisler Archive, Berlin).
2 cf. 'Lieder, Gedichte, Chöre', Brecht, *Gesammelte Werke* 9, p. 435, also p. 429.
3 Letter to Brecht from Paris (undated, probably March 1934), copy in the Hanns Eisler Archive, Berlin.
4 *Lieder und Kantaten*, vol. I, pp. 100ff.
5 ibid., vol. V, p. 53.
6 ibid., vol. V, p. 101.
7 Eisler-Fischer, *op. cit.*, p. 70.
8 Oral communication from Prévert in Paris, 9 December 1971.
9 Copy in the Hanns Eisler Archive, Berlin.
10 Joris Ivens, *Die Kamera und ich*, Hamburg 1974, p. 75.
11 ibid., p. 76.
12 loc. cit.
13 E. Klemm, Postscript to Hanns Eisler, *Präludium und Fuge über B-A-C-H* for string trio op. 46.
14 E. Krenek, 'Eigenzitat aus: Brief an T. W. Adorno' in *Zeugnisse, T. W. Adorno zum 60. Geburtstag*, Frankfurt am Main 1963.
15 Quoted from G. Mayer's sleeve note for the recording of Eisler's *Kleine Sinfonie* and Suites (Nova, No. 885043).
16 Letter from Moscow, 20 July 1935 (Hanns Eisler Archive, Berlin).
17 Werner Mittenzwei, *Bertolt Brecht. Von der 'Massnahme' zu 'Leben des Galilei'*, Berlin-DDR 1973, p. 164.
18 On the occasion of his visit to Moscow in 1935, Brecht said in an interview: 'The play I wrote with Hanns Eisler, "Rundköpfe und Spitzköpfe", deals with this theme [racism] and I believe that the heart of this problem of such great importance was clearly revealed

with the help of the new method . . . In the play it emerges that classification by heads instead of by the content of people's purses is better for rich people than for the poor.' Quoted from W. Hecht (ed.), *Brecht im Gespräch*, Frankfurt am Main 1975, p. 201.

19 Marx–Engels, *Werke*, Berlin-DDR 1964, vol. 23, p. 16. On the widespread weakness of dependants to personalize problems and thereby to isolate themselves from the centre of these problems, Brecht speaks at the beginning of the play: 'This Iberian knows: the people/Not very well versed in abstraction, and whom need/ Has made impatient, seek to lay the blame for such/Collapse on a familiar being/With mouth and ear and running on two legs . . .' *Gesammelte Werke* 3, p. 920.

20 Brecht, *Gesammelte Werke* 17, p. 1087.

21 Brecht, *Gesammelte Werke* 18, p. 161.

22 Brecht, *Gesammelte Werke* 15, p. 480.

23 Eisler, Preface to the score of *Rundköpfe*, Hanns Eisler Archive, Berlin.

24 Letter from London, October 1936, Hanns Eisler Archive, Berlin.

25 Mittenzwei, *op. cit.*, p. 154, and Klaus Völker, *Brecht-Chronik*, Munich 1971, p. 67.

26 Letter from Paris of 24 May 1934, Hanns Eisler Archive, Berlin.

27 Letter from London, around August 1934, Hanns Eisler Archive, Berlin.

28 Bunge, *Gespräche*, p. 70.

29 Eisler, *Musik und Politik*, pp. 243f.

30 Oral communication from M. Bauman in Stockbridge, Mass., 26 August 1973.

31 Letter from New York of 19 January 1935, Hanns Eisler Archive, Berlin.

32 Bauman, now a professor at the Brooklyn College in New York, had just completed his training at the Juilliard School. He was the first American performer of Eisler's songs, and shortly afterwards also of the songs of Charles Ives. Oral communication, see note 30.

33 With songs from *Die Mutter*, the 'Solidarity Song' and the 'United Front Song'.

34 Report of the German Consulate General in San Francisco, 21 March 1935 ('Musical Performance by the Composer Hanns Eisler'). Original in the National Archive, Koblenz, R 18/1009/fol. 166–72.

35 Including, amongst others, 'History of the German workers' music movement from 1848' in *Music Vanguard* (New York), April 1935.

The journal's editor was the musicologist Charles Seeger, father of Pete Seeger. There was also a special publication *The Crisis in Music*, issued by the Downtown Music School in Manhattan. See Eisler, *Musik und Politik*, pp. 211ff., 362ff., 370ff.

36 Copy in the Hanns Eisler Archive, Berlin.

37 Lammel, 'Hanns Eislers Wirken für die Einheitsfront', p. 9.

38 Copy in the Hanns Eisler Archive, Berlin.

39 Brecht, *Gesammelte Werke* 18, p. 246.

40 Bunge, Gespräche, p. 231. cf. also J. K. Lyon (ed.), 'Der Briefwechsel zwischen Brecht und der New Yorker Theater Union von 1935' in *Brecht-Jahrbuch 1975*, pp. 136ff.

41 *New York Herald Tribune*, 1 December 1935.

42 Letter to Benjamin in Paris, copy in the Bertolt Brecht Archive, Berlin.

43 *Lieder und Kantaten*, vol. III, pp. 225ff.; Brecht, *Gesammelte Werke* 9, pp. 633ff.

44 The best known was to be 'Das Lied vom 7. Januar' to a text by Ludwig Renn. See *Lieder und Kantaten*, vol. V, p. 103. There is a report on Eisler in Spain by Carlos Palacio in *Arbeitshefte der Akademie der Künste der DDR: Hanns Eisler heute*, pp. 67f.

45 Grabs, 'Über Hanns Eislers Kammerkantaten', p. 446.

46 The two works were not performed until twenty years later in East Germany.

47 *Lieder und Kantaten*, vol. III, pp. 220ff.; Brecht, *Gesammelte Werke* 9, pp. 689ff.

48 G. Knepler, Postscript to Hanns Eisler, *Lenin-Requiem*, Leipzig 1970. cf. also Siegmund-Schultze, 'Zu einigen Grundfragen der Musikästhetik', pp. 167f.

49 Letter of 20 July 1935, Hanns Eisler Archive, Berlin.

50 Eisler talks about his *Deutsche Sinfonie* in a radio interview with Leah Plotkin (Station WQXR, New York) of 22 April 1938. Transcript in the possession of J. Schumacher, Woodbury, Conn.

51 In an (undated) catalogue of works – evidently drawn up by himself – in the Hanns Eisler Archive, Berlin.

52 Drew, 'Eisler and the Polemic Symphony'.

53 *Lieder und Kantaten*, vol. 3, pp. 93ff.

54 Bunge, *Gespräche*, p. 231. On 9 April 1937, Grete Steffin wrote from Svendborg to Benjamin in Paris: 'Eisler has gone to Skovbostrand again and has taken a furnished, very attractive house right on the sound and 5 minutes away from Brecht. Brecht is often working on his new novel, but in general he is working on an opera with

Eisler: GOLIATH.' (Copy in the Bertolt Brecht Archive, Berlin.) It
seems that Brecht was to consider taking up the project once again,
at the end of 1944, but again it came to nothing. cf. *Arbeitsjournal*,
p. 701.

55 Oral communication from E. Bloch in Tübingen, 27 May 1973.
About his relationship with Eisler, Bloch said: 'I probably first got to
know him in Berlin, in around 1932, at a coffee-house; there were
three of us, the other being Adorno. At the time Adorno was still
entirely pro-Communist. We then saw him in Prague (1937) and
this was not just a meeting in a coffee-house, but a more protracted
interchange. And it was then that I got to know him as a man who
could formulate ideas with the greatest liveliness, wit and precision,
utterly exceptional in this precision and verbal wit, in conjuring up
fine and relevant images, and also in self-criticism and in criticism of
the Party . . .' (transcribed from a tape recording).

56 Eisler/Bloch in Eisler, *Musik und Politik*, pp. 397ff.

57 Neither gives a central place to the one *or* the other, but to the
difficulties of *mediation*, and hence the true crux of the matter.

58 Hans-Jürgen Schmitt (ed.), *Die Expressionismusdebatte, Materialien zu einer marxistische Realismuskonzeption*, Frankfurt am
Main 1973, p. 50.

59 Eisler/Bloch, in Eisler, *Musik und Politik*, p. 409.

60 *ibid.*, pp. 408f.

61 cf. Mayer/Knepler, 'Hätten sich Georg Lukács und Hanns Eisler in
der Mitte des Tunnels getroffen?', pp. 358ff., above all pp. 368f.

62 *Musik und Politik*, p. 410.

63 Ernst Bloch, *Erbschaft dieser Zeit*, Frankfurt am Main 1973,
p. 269.

64 Eisler knew Lukács in Berlin through the BPRS; from 1931 on,
Lukács published items in *Linkskurve*. Bloch already knew Lukács
before the First World War, the two having been students together
for a time in Heidelberg.

In his essay 'Es geht um den Realismus', in which he attempted to
sum up the debate over Expressionism, Lukács countered Bloch and
Eisler particularly sharply. He was not afraid to make insinuations.
Thus, for instance: '. . . (we) see that, *despite* the "German predicament", this popular and realistic literature has given rise to such
powerful masterpieces as, say, the *Simplizissimus* of Grimmelshausen. It can be left to the Eislers to estimate the value of dissected
pieces of this masterpiece for purposes of montage; for living German literature it will survive as a living and topical whole in all its

greatness (and with all its limitations).' Hans-Jürgen Schmitt, *op. cit.*, p. 226.)

Grimmelshausen had previously been mentioned by none of the participants. Eisler, who was allergic to Lukács' style, was particularly annoyed – according to Bloch (oral communication, see note 55) – that he was up against 'a type, rather than an individual' (cf. *Musik und Politik*, 'Antwort an Lukács', pp. 433f.). Arising from this, Brecht wrote his 'Small emendation': 'In the debate over Expressionism in *Das Wort*, something happened in the heat of the battle which requires a small emendation.

'Lukács has rather swept the floor with my friend Eisler – whom few will see as a pure aesthete – because in giving his testimony about his inheritance he did not show the expected pious emotions. He rummaged around, so to speak, and refused to take possession of *everything*. Now, possibly, as an exile, he is in no position to carry so much around with him.

'But may I be permitted a few lines about the formalities of the affair. There is talk here of "the Eislers" who should or should not do something or other. In my opinion the Lukácses should completely abandon the use of such a plural, as long as there is in fact only one Eisler amongst our musicians. The millions of workers, whether their skins be white, yellow or black, who have inherited the mass songs of Eisler will certainly share my opinion in this. But also all manner of professional musicians familiar with Eisler's work which, as I am told, contributes to a continuing heritage of German music in a magnificent way, would be disconcerted if the German émigrés – in contrast to the seven Greek cities who contested the honour of having produced a Homer – were to get so carried away as to boast of having seven Eislers.' (Brecht, *Gesammelte Werke* 19, pp. 337f.)

65 Brecht, *Arbeitsjournal*, p. 27.
66 Important elements of this controversy appear to have been anticipated – a century before – in Heine's confrontation with Goethe's aesthetic ideas. cf. Albrecht Betz, *Ästhetik und Politik. Heinrich Heines Prosa*, Munich 1971, pp. 12ff.
67 Werner Mittenzwei, *Brechts Verhältnis zur Tradition*, Berlin-DDR 1973, p. 52.
68 Mittenzwei, quoted from Fritz J. Raddatz, Foreword to Raddatz (ed.), *Marxismus und Literatur. Eine Dokumentation*, vol. I, Hamburg 1969, p. 40.
69 It is not possible to discuss here the extent to which Eisler and Brecht

were also subliminally affected by an aversion to Lukács as a man of the nineteenth century whose cultural values were still dominated by high bourgeois antecedents.

70 cf. A. Stephan, 'Georg Lukács' erste Beiträge zur marxistischen Literaturtheorie' in *Brecht-Jahrbuch 1975*, pp. 79ff.

71 Ernst Bloch, *Erbschaft dieser Zeit*, Frankfurt am Main 1973, p. 228.

72 At that time Joris Ivens was President of the Association of Documentary Film Producers in New York. Eisler's association with Ivens, which dated back to their collaboration on *Die Jugend hat das Wort* in 1932, stood him in good stead. His first film music in the USA was written for Ivens' film on China (see below).

73 Joachim Radkau, *Die deutsche Emigration in den USA*, Düsseldorf 1971, p. 366.

74 cf., amongst others, Horst Duhnke, *Die KPD von 1933–1945*, Vienna 1974, pp. 260ff.; Ernst Fischer, *Erinnerungen und Reflexionen*, Hamburg 1969, pp. 373ff.

75 Ottwalt, a member of the KPD and of the BPRS, emigrated to the Soviet Union in 1933, and until 1937 was on the editorial staff of *Internationale Literatur*, which was published in Moscow.

76 Undated, probably late 1938. Copy in the Bertolt Brecht Archive, Berlin.

77 Eisler, *Musik und Politik*, p. 452.

78 cf. Eric Bentley, *Thirty Years of Treason. Excerpts from Hearings before the House Committee on Un-American Activities, 1938–1968*, New York 1971, p. 107.

79 Letter from the Executive Secretary of the American Guild to Eisler of 23 April 1938. Original in the German Library, Frankfurt am Main, Abt. IX Exil-Literatur 1933–45 (EB 70/117).

80 Radkau, *op. cit.*, p. 187.

81 *ibid.*, pp. 35f.

82 *ibid.*, p. 37.

83 A copy of the lecture was placed at my disposal by Harry Robin.

84 Letter from H. W. Hays to the author (dated 26 December 1973).

85 Radkau, *op. cit.*, p. 276.

86 *loc. cit.*

87 Hans Gutmann, 'Der tönende Film' in *Melos*, January 1928, p. 9.

88 Letter from Helen van Dongen to the author (dated 2 October 1974).

89 Oral communication from Harry Robin in Los Angeles, 26 September 1973.

90 Joris Ivens, *Die Kamera und Ich*, Hamburg 1974, p. 140.

91 Oral communication from Ivens in Paris, 15 December 1971.
92 Letter from Eisler in New York to Lombardo Toledano in Mexico City of 9 March 1939. Copy in the Hanns Eisler Archive, Berlin.
93 Letter from H. W. Hays to the author (see note 84 above).
94 Letter from Eisler to Piscator of 19 August 1939.
95 Oral communication from Lou Eisler-Fischer, 31 December 1973.
96 Letter from Alvin Johnson to John Marshall of 1 November 1939. Original in The Rockefeller Foundation Archives, New York.
97 Ivens, *op. cit.*, p. 77.
98 Eisler wrote a first draft for the forthcoming project in October 1939: 'Research program on the relation between music and film'. This already contains in embryonic form the principal concerns of the subsequent book *Composing for the Films*.
99 Bunge, *Gespräche*, p. 16.
100 Adorno/Eisler, *Komposition für den Film*, pp. 57f.
101 *ibid.*, pp. 65f.
102 *ibid.*, p. 68.
103 *ibid.*, pp. 162 and 167.
104 cf., amongst others, Theodore Strauss' report in the *New York Times* of 30 November 1941, 'Musical Marathon/In the Score for "The Forgotten Village" Hanns Eisler set a Record of Sorts'.
105 Adorno/Eisler, *Komposition für den Film*, pp. 41f.
106 According to Eisler's 'Final report' on the project, dated 31 October 1942. Quoted from the original in The Rockefeller Foundation Archives, New York.
107 cf. Adorno/Eisler, *Komposition für den Film*, pp. 213f.
108 Joachim Radkau, *Die deutsche Emigration in den USA*, Düsseldorf 1971, pp. 107ff.
109 Letter from Eisler in Woodbury, Conn., to Piscator of 11 August 1941.
110 Brecht, *Arbeitsjournal*, p. 498.
111 *ibid.*, p. 313.
112 *ibid.*, p. 422.
113 These were: *Hangmen also Die* (Fritz Lang), 1943; *None but the Lonely Heart* (Odets), 1944; *Spanish Main* (Borzage), 1945; *Jealousy* (Machate), 1945; *Deadline at Dawn* (Clurman), 1946; *A Scandal in Paris* (Sirk), 1946; *Woman on the Beach* (Renoir), 1947; *So well Remembered* (Dmytrik), 1947.
114 cf. Brecht, *Arbeitsjournal*, pp. 463ff.
115 The première, with Charles Laughton in the title role, took place at the Coronet Theatre in Beverly Hills on 31 July 1947. Serge Hovey,

a composition pupil of Eisler's at the University of Southern California, acted as musical assistant.

116 Ratz, 'Hanns Eisler zum 50. Geburtstag', p. 1024.

117 Brecht, *Arbeitsjournal*, p. 406.

118 cf. Hennenberg, 'Zur Dialektik des Schliessens in Liedern von Hanns Eisler', p. 224.

119 Betz, ' "Komm! Ins Offene, Freund!" Zum Verhältnis von Text und Musik in Kompositionen von Gedichten Hölderlins und Heines', p. 662.

120 Bunge, *Gespräche*, p. 23.

121 Brecht, *Arbeitsjournal*, p. 523.

122 *Lieder und Kantaten*, vol. II, p. 138; Bunge, *Gespräche*, p. 22.

123 *Lieder und Kantaten*, vol. II, pp. 138ff.

124 Brecht, *Arbeitsjournal*, p. 497.

125 Bunge, *Gespräche*, p. 224.

126 *ibid.*, p. 293.

127 *ibid.*, p. 292.

128 *ibid.*, p. 293.

129 L. von Sonnleithner in *Schubert, Die Erinnerungen seiner Freunde*, ed. O. E. Deutsch, Leipzig 1966, pp. 135f.

130 Oral communication from Marta Feuchtwanger in Pacific Palisades, 24 September 1973.

131 Letter to Odets of 17 December 1945. The papers of Clifford Odets are at Stockbridge, Mass., and have been used by Margaret Brenman-Gibson as the basis of a biography.

132 Letter to Odets of 3 February 1946.

133 Letter to Odets of 23 April 1946.

134 cf. Klaus Kochmann and Harald Möller, 'Von der Kriegskoalition zur offen antikommunistischen Politik' in *Alternative*, 87, 1972, pp. 226ff.

135 Ernst-Ulrich Huster, *Determinanten der westdeutschen Restauration, 1945–1949*, Frankfurt am Main 1972, pp. 9f.

136 Joachim Radkau, *Die deutsche Emigration in den USA*, Düsseldorf 1971, p. 272.

137 Salka Viertel, *The Kindness of Strangers*, New York 1969, p. 302.

138 Oral communication from Lou Eisler-Fischer (see note 95 above).

139 Eisler, *Musik und Politik*, p. 499.

140 Bentley, *Thirty Years of Treason*, p. 73 (see note 78 above).

141 Kochmann/Möller, *op. cit.*, pp. 227f.

142 McCann, *Hanns Eisler Hearings*, p. 4. *The Hollywood Reporter* of 28 April 1947 stressed: 'The announced investigation of Hanns

Eisler, brother of Gerhart, will only incidentally concern Hollywood . . . but names of *prominent persons in Washington will be pulled in*.'

143 In *Los Angeles Examiner* of 26 April 1947.

144 Frederic Ewen, *Bertolt Brecht, His Life, his Art and his Times*, New York 1967, p. 416.

145 *Los Angeles Times*, 13 May 1947; also *Los Angeles Examiner, San Francisco Examiner*, etc. The entire Californian press – which was predominantly right-wing – took up the case.

146 Eisler in *Sinn und Form: Sonderheft*, p. 26.

147 Eric Bentley later adapted parts of the hearings as a play, giving it the title *Are you now or have you ever been* (New York 1972).

148 *Hearings Regarding Hanns Eisler*, Washington 1947 (Government Printing Office), p. 25.

149 McCann, *Hanns Eisler Hearings*, p. 16.

150 Bunge, *Gespräche*, pp. 60f.

151 Thomas Mann, *Briefe 1937–1947*, Berlin 1965, pp. 591 and 595f.

152 In *Sinn und Form: Sonderheft*, pp. 28f.

153 On this, see Alvah Bessie, *Inquisition in Eden. One of the Hollywood Ten*, New York 1965. The 'Ten' were the film directors and writers who had refused to answer the question about membership of the Communist Party, invoking the First Amendment of the American Constitution. Already this was considered suspicious. The Hollywood Ten were sentenced to an average of a year's imprisonment, most of them being released somewhat earlier 'for good conduct'. They were: Alvah Bessie, Herbert Bibermann, Lester Cole, Edward Dmytrik, Ring Lardner Jr., John Howard Lawson, Albert Maltz, Samuel Ornitz, Adrian Scott and Dalton Trumbo. cf. also D. Trumbo, *The Time of the Toad*, a *Study of Inquisition in America*, Los Angeles 1949.

154 Ewen, *op. cit.*, p. 415.

155 The reviewer for the *New York Times* (29 February 1948) was Olin Downes, and for the *New York Herald Tribune* (1 March 1948) Virgil Thomson. Already a week before the concert the *New York Times* had published a major report on Eisler – 'Musician's Case' – by S. L. M. Barlow (22 February 1948).

156 Eisler arranged the Second Septet from sketches for music for Charlie Chaplin's silent film *Circus* in 1947.

157 Thomson in the *New York Herald Tribune* (see note 155 above).

158 Eisler, *Musik und Politik*, pp. 529f. (In the original English.) Thomas Mann's Statement for the Committee for the First Amendment

closed with these words: 'I testify, moreover, that to my mind the
ignorant and superstitious persecution of the believers in a political
and economic doctrine which is, after all, the creation of great
minds and great thinkers – I testify that this persecution is not only
degrading for the persecutors themselves but also very harmful to
the cultural reputation of this country. As an American citizen of
German birth, I finally testify that I am painfully familiar with
certain trends. Spiritual intolerance, political inquisitions, and declining legal security, and all this in the name of an alleged "state of
emergency" . . . that is how it started in Germany. What followed
was fascism and what followed fascism was war.' (Printed as the
Foreword to G. Kahn, *Hollywood on Trial*, New York 1948.)

4. The final decade

1 Quoted from the original in the papers of L. Feuchtwanger, Pacific
  Palisades.
2 Eisler, *Materialien*, p. 196.
3 Oral communication from Lou Eisler-Fischer, 31 December 1973.
  cf. also Ratz, 'Hanns Eisler zum 50. Geburtstag'.
4 Eisler, *Materialien*, p. 193.
5 Note on single sheet in the Hanns Eisler Archive, Berlin.
6 The poem, so far unpublished, exists in Catherine Duncan's English
  version under the title 'Visit to Berlin (The Survivor)'. Hanns Eisler
  Archive, Berlin.
7 Brecht, *Arbeitsjournal*, p. 883.
8 Brecht, *Gesammelte Werke* 17, p. 1154 and 16, p. 907.
9 Andrej Zhdanow, *Über Kunst und Wissenschaft*, Berlin-DDR
  1951, p. 70.
10 Bunge, *Gespräche*, p. 312.
11 Brecht, *Arbeitsjournal*, p. 870.
12 *ibid.*, p. 910.
13 Eisler, 'Hörer und Komponist' in *Europäisches Tagebuch*, 6, 1949,
   p. 9.
14 In a toned-down continuation of what had been common practice
   after 1933, nothing was said of the political motives, and instead the
   compositions were written off as *a priori* aesthetically inferior.
15 Quoted from Klemm, *Hanns Eisler – für Sie porträtiert*, p. 32.
16 Brecht, *Gesammelte Werke* 19, p. 528.
17 Johannes R. Becher, *Tagebuch 1950*, Berlin 1952, pp. 450 and 469.
18 Eisler, *Materialien*, p. 227.

19 *ibid.*, pp. 204ff.
20 As early as 1949, this perspective led him to start work on a version of Lenz's *Hofmeister*, '. . . the earliest – and extremely sharp – portrayal of the German predicament' (*Arbeitsjournal*, p. 915). A little later he wanted to show the intellectual above all as a charlatan in Goethe's *Urfaust*. To a lesser extent, his version of Molière's *Don Juan* and his third version of *Galilei* both also belong in the same context.
21 Brecht, 'Thesen zur Faustus-Diskussion' in *Sinn und Form* (Berlin-DDR), V/3–4, 1953, p. 196. Reprinted in *Gesammelte Werke 19*, pp. 535f.
22 Letter from Thomas Mann to Eisler of 5 November 1952, printed in *Sinn und Form: Sonderheft*, p. 247.
23 Eisler, *Materialien*, p. 210.
24 Fischer, 'Doktor Faustus und der deutsche Bauernkrieg', p. 63.
25 Eisler-Fischer, 'Faust in der DDR. Dokumente, betreffend Hanns Eisler, Bertolt Brecht und Ernst Fischer', p. 567.
26 *ibid.*, p. 565.
27 W. Ulbricht in *Chronik zur Geschichte der deutsche Arbeiterbewegung* (Berlin-DDR 1967–), vol. IV, p. 604. Quoted from W. Zobl, 'Die Auseinandersetzung um Eislers revolutionäre Umfunktionierung des Dr. Faustus' in *Das Argument: Hanns Eisler*, AS 5, Berlin 1975, p. 251.
28 Brecht, *Gesammelte Werke 19*, pp. 545f.
29 Eisler-Fischer, 'Faust in der DDR', p. 567.
30 Eisler, *Materialien*, pp. 231ff.
31 Brecht, *Gesammelte Werke 19*, p. 547.
32 Transcription of a discussion in the Akademie der Künste der DDR on 14 May 1956, Hanns Eisler Archive, Berlin.
33 Note on single sheet in the Hanns Eisler Archive, Berlin.
34 Eisler in Herbert Knust (ed.), *Materialien zu Bertolt Brechts 'Schweyk im Zweiten Weltkrieg'*, Frankfurt am Main 1973, p. 300.
35 *Lieder und Kantaten*, vol. III, pp. 182ff. The draft letter quoted previously on a single sheet in the Hanns Eisler Archive, Berlin.
36 Bunge, *Gespräche*, p. 286.
37 Gagarin's flight in space on 12 April 1961.
38 Bunge, *Gespräche*, p. 142.
39 *Lieder und Kantaten*, vol. X, p. 28. The text of the 'Epilogue' is by Stephan Hermlin.
40 Arnold Schoenberg, *Style and Idea*, New York 1950, p. 73.
41 Friedrich Hölderlin, *Sämtliche Werke und Briefe*, vol. I, ed. G.

Mieth, Munich 1970, pp. 241 and 196. The following analysis is
taken from an essay I wrote in honour of my teacher at the Collège
de France (Paris), Robert Minder. (cf. A. Betz, ' "Komm! Ins Offene,
Freund!" ', pp. 363 ff.)

42 Conversation with H. Bunge in *Sinn und Form: Sonderheft*, p. 314.
43 Grabs, ' "Wir, so gut es gelang, haben das Unsre gatan." Zur
Aussage der Hölderlin-Vertonungen Hanns Eislers', pp. 57f.

5. Eisler's modernity

1 Bunge, *Gespräche*, pp. 45 and 319.
2 David Drew, 'A composer of Revolution' in *New Statesman*, 14
September 1962.
3 Bunge, *Gespräche*, p. 189.
4 Heinrich Heine, *Sämtliche Werke*, ed. E. Elster, Leipzig, Berlin and
Vienna 1887–90, vol. VII, p. 409.

Bibliography

Primary sources

Eisler, Hanns, *Werke in Einzelausgaben*, Universal Edition (Vienna)
1924–, opp. 1–21, opp. 60–5
Lieder und Kantaten, vols. I–X, VEB Breitkopf & Härtel Musikverlag,
Leipzig 1955–
Gesammelte Werke (Serie I), VEB Deutscher Verlag für Musik, Leipzig
1968–; Bärenreiter, Kassel 1968–
Ausgewählte Lieder, vols. I–V, VEB Deutscher Verlag für Musik,
Leipzig 1971–2
Instrumentalmusik, VEB Deutscher Verlag für Musik, Leipzig 1973–
Instrumentalmusik in Einzelausgaben, Verlag Neue Musik, Berlin-
DDR 1959–
Petits Morceaux pour les enfants opp. 31/32, Heugel, Paris 1934
Vierzehn Arten, den Regen zu beschreiben op. 70, Edition Peters/
Collection Litolff, Leipzig 1960

Eisler, Hanns, *Johann Faustus* (libretto), Aufbau, Berlin-DDR 1952
Reden und Aufsätze, ed. W. Höntsch, Reclam, Leipzig 1961
Musik und Politik: Schriften 1924–1948, VEB Deutscher Verlag für
Musik, Leipzig 1973; Rogner & Bernhard, Munich 1973
Materialien zu einer Dialektik der Musik, Reclam, Leipzig 1973
and Theodor W. Adorno, *Komposition für den Film*, Rogner &
Bernhard, Munich 1969 (first published as Hanns Eisler, *Composing for the Films*, Oxford University Press, New York/London
1947)

Bunge, Hans, *Fragen Sie mehr über Brecht, Hanns Eisler im Gespräch*,
Rogner & Bernhard, Munich 1970
Notowicz, Nathan, *Wir reden hier nicht von Napoleon. Wir reden von
Ihnen! Gespräche mit Hanns Eisler und Gerhart Eisler*, Verlag Neue
Musik, Berlin-DDR 1971

Secondary sources

Bibliographies

Klemm, Eberhardt, 'Chronologisches Verzeichnis der Kompositionen von Hanns Eisler', *Beiträge zur Musikwissenschaft*, XV/1, Berlin-DDR 1973
Hanns Eisler 1898–1962, Kulturbund der DDR, Berlin 1973 (The first attempt at a chronological catalogue, by no means complete. A fuller version appears in *Beiträge zur Musikwissenschaft* XV/1.)
Hanns Eisler–für Sie porträtiert, Leipzig 1973
Notowicz, Nathan and Elsner, Jürgen, *Hanns Eisler–Quellennachweise*, Leipzig 1961

Special issues of periodicals

Alternative: Materialistische Kunsttheorie II, Hanns Eisler, 69, Berlin 1969
Arbeitshefte der Akademie der Künste der DDR: Hanns Eisler heute, 19, Berlin 1974 (proceedings of Eisler Colloquium at Akademie der Künste, November 1973)
Beiträge zur Musikwissenschaft: Hanns Eisler 1898–1962, XV/1, Berlin-DDR 1973
Das Argument: Hanns Eisler, AS 5, Berlin 1975
Kunst und Gesellschaft: Hanns Eisler, Musik im Klassenkamp, 20/21, Berlin 1973
Sinn und Form: Sonderheft Hanns Eisler, Berlin-DDR 1964

Books, Articles, Reviews

Adorno, Theodor W., 'Hanns Eisler, Duo für Violine und Violoncello op. 7, Nr. 1', *Musikblätter des Anbruch*, Vienna 1925, pp. 422f.
'Hanns Eisler, Klavierstücke op. 3', *Die Musik* (Stuttgart), July 1927, pp. 749f.
'Hanns Eisler, Zeitungsausschnitte. Für Gesang und Klavier, op. 11', *Anbruch*, Vienna 1929, pp. 219f.
Betz, Albrecht, 'Dynamisierung des Widerspruchs. Über Eisler und Brecht', *Bertolt Brecht I, Text und Kritik*, Munich 1972, pp. 72ff.
' "Komm! Ins Offene, Freund!" Zum Verhältnis von Text und Musik in Kompositionen von Gedichten Hölderlins und Heines', *Hom-*

mages à Robert Minder, Revue d'Allemagne, V/3, Strasbourg 1973, pp. 649ff.

'Parabel vom Missbrauch des Intellekts', Materialien zu Hanns Eislers 'Johann Faustus', Tübingen 1974

Blake, David, 'Hanns Eisler', The Listener, 15 September 1966

Boehmer, Konrad, 'Zu Eislers Text "Die Erbauer einer neuen Musikkultur"', Kunst und Gesellschaft (Tübingen), 5/6, 1971, pp. 31ff.

Brecht, Bertolt, Gesammelte Werke, Frankfurt am Main 1967

Arbeitsjournal, Frankfurt am Main 1973

'Thesen zur Faustus-Diskussion', Sinn und Form (Berlin-DDR), V/3-4, 1953, pp. 194ff.

'Zum Geleit', Hanns Eisler, Lieder und Kantaten, vol. I, Leipzig 1955

'Die Musik zur "Massnahme"', Schriften zum Theater, vol. II, Berlin and Weimar 1964

'Über die Verwendung von Musik für ein episches Theater', Schriften zum Theater, vol. III, Berlin and Weimar 1964

Brockhaus, Heinz Alfred, Hanns Eisler, Leipzig 1961

Bukofzer, Manfred, 'Revolutionäre Musik', Melos, 9, 1930, p. 443

Drew, David, 'Eisler and the Polemic Symphony', The Listener, 4 January 1962

Eisler, Georg, 'Mein Vater', Neues Forum (Vienna), September 1972

Eisler, Hilde, 'Erinnerungen an Hanns Eisler. Zum 10. Todestag des Komponisten', Deutsche Lehrerzeitung (Berlin-DDR), 34, 1972, p. 6

Eisler-Fischer, Louise, 'Faust in der DDR. Dokumente, betreffend Hanns Eisler, Bertolt Brecht und Ernst Fischer', Neues Forum (Vienna), October 1969, pp. 561ff.

'Eisler in der Emigration', Neues Forum (Vienna), October 1972, pp. 70ff.

Elsner, Jürgen, 'Die Majakowski-Vertonungen', Musik und Gesellschaft (Berlin-DDR), XVIII, 1968, pp. 345ff.

'Einiges zur Entwicklung Hanns Eislers in den zwanziger Jahren', Sammelbände zur Musikgeschichte der DDR, vol. I, Berlin 1969, pp. 9ff.

Zur vokalsolistischen Vortragsweise der Kampfmusik Hanns Eislers, Leipzig 1971

Fischer, Ernst, 'Doktor Faustus und der deutsche Bauernkrieg', Sinn und Form (Berlin-DDR), IV/6, 1952, pp. 59ff.

'Hanns Eisler und die Literatur', Überlegungen zur Situation der Kunst, Zurich 1971, pp. 77ff.

'Hanns Eisler', Wiener Tagebuch, 9 September 1972, pp. 26f.

Goldschmidt, 'Gedanken über Hanns Eisler', *Musik und Gesellschaft* (Berlin-DDR), VIII, 1958, pp. 352ff.

Grabs, Manfred, 'Über Hanns Eislers Kammerkantaten', *Musik und Gesellschaft* (Berlin-DDR), XVIII, 1968, pp. 445ff.

'Film- und Bühnenmusik im sinfonischen Werk Hanns Eislers', *Sammelbände zur Musikgeschichte der DDR*, vol. I, Berlin 1969, pp. 20ff.

' "Wir, so gut es gelang, haben das Unsre getan." ' Zur Aussage der Hölderlin-Vertonungen Hanns Eisler', *Beiträge zur Musikwissenschaft* (Berlin-DDR) XV/1, 1973, pp. 49ff.

Harris, Dave, 'Anmerkungen zu den Verhören', *Alternative* (Berlin), 87, 1972

Haug, Wolfgang Fritz, 'Hans Faust und Hans Wurst in Eislers Version der Faust-Sage', *Materialien zu Hanns Eislers 'Johann Faustus'*, Tübingen 1974

Hennenberg, Fritz, 'Zur Dialektik des Schliessens in Liedern von Hanns Eisler', *Sammelbände zur Musikgeschichte der DDR*, vol. II, Berlin 1971, pp. 181ff.

Herbort, Heinz Josef, 'Hanns Eisler – Porträt eines Nonkonformisten', *Die Zeit* (Hamburg), 14 June 1968

Jungheinrich, Hans-Klaus, 'Musik und Realismus – einige Aspekte bei Hanns Eisler', *Musik zwischen Engagement und Kunst, Studien zur Wertungsforschung* 3, Graz 1972, pp. 69ff.

Klemm, Eberhardt, 'Bemerkungen zur Zwölftontechnik bei Eisler und Schönberg', *Sinn und Form* (Berlin-DDR), XVI, 1964, pp. 771ff.

Postscript to Hanns Eisler, *Präludium und Fuge über B-A-C-H* for string trio op. 46, Leipzig 1973

'Über Eislers Balladen' in *Arbeitshefte der Akademie der Künste der DDR*, 19, 1974

Knepler, Georg, 'Hanns Eisler und das "Neue" in der Musik', *Musik und Gesellschaft*, VIII, 1958, pp. 344ff.

'Erinnerungen an Hanns Eisler', *Beiträge zur Musikwissenschaft* (Berlin-DDR), XI, 1969

'. . . was des Eislers ist', *Beiträge zur Musikwissenschaft* (Berlin-DDR), XV/1, 1973, pp. 29ff.

and Notowicz, Nathan, 'Diskussion mit Eberhardt Klemm', *Sinn und Form* (Berlin-DDR), XVII, 1965, pp. 261ff.

Lammel, Inge, 'Hanns Eisler und die proletarisch-revolutionäre deutsche Musik der zwanziger Jahre', *Musik und Gesellschaft* (Berlin-DDR), XIII, 1963, pp. 25–8

'Eislers Wirken für die Einheitsfront in der Internationalen revolutionären Musikbewegung', *Arbeitshefte der Akademie der Künste der DDR*, 19, 1974, pp. 61ff.

Lombardi, Luca, 'Zur Eisler-Rezeption in der BRD', *Arbeitsheft der Akademie der Künste der DDR*, 19, 1974, pp. 213ff.

Lück, Hartmut, 'Adorno als Geist, Eisler als Praktikus. Filmmusik und die Ursachen', *Neues Forum* (Vienna), January 1970, pp. 37ff.

Lukács, Georg, 'In memoriam Hanns Eisler', *Alternative* (Berlin), 69, 1969, pp. 220ff.

Mainka, Jürgen, 'Musikalische Betroffenheit. Zum Begriff des Gestischen', *Beiträge zur Musikwissenschaft* (Berlin-DDR), XV/1, 1973

Mayer, Günter, 'Die Kategorie des musikalischen Materials in den ästhetischen Anschauungen Hanns Eislers' (Dissertation), Humboldt University, Berlin-DDR, 1969

'Über die musikalische Integration des Dokumentarischen', *Bericht über den Internationalen Musikwissenschaftlichen Kongress, Leipzig 1966*, Kassel and Leipzig 1970, pp. 351ff.

'Historischer Materialstand. Zu Hanns Eislers Konzeption einer Dialektik der Musik', *Deutsches Jahrbuch der Musikwissenschaft für 1972*, Leipzig 1973

'Zum Verhältnis von politischem und musikalischem Fortschritt. Zu Hanns Eislers Konzeption einer Dialektik der Musik', *Beiträge zur Musikwissenschaft* (Berlin-DDR), XV/1, 1973

and Knepler, Georg, 'Hätten sich Georg Lukács und Hanns Eisler in der Mitte des Tunnels Getroffen? Zur Polemik zwischen gegensätzlich Gleichgesinnten', *Dialog und Kontroverse mit Georg Lukács*, ed. W. Mittenzwei, Leipzig 1975, pp. 358ff.

McCann, David, *The Hanns Eisler Hearings: Hollywood, Washington & Beyond* (Workshop), University of California at Los Angeles 1971

Mayer, Hans, 'An aesthetic debate of 1951: Comment of a text by Hanns Eisler', *New German Critique* 2, Wisconsin 1974, pp. 58ff.

Notowicz, Nathan, 'Eisler und Schönberg', *Deutsches Jahrbuch der Musikwissenschaft für 1963*, Leipzig 1964, pp. 7ff.

Pozner, Vladimir, 'Hanns Eisler', *Vladimir Pozner se souvient*, Paris 1972, pp. 171ff.

Ratz, Erwin, 'Hanns Eisler', *Musikblätter des Anbruch* (Vienna), VI, 1924, pp. 381ff.

'Hanns Eisler zum 50. Geburtstag', *Europäische Rundschau* (Vienna), 22, 1948

Rebling, Eberhardt, 'Ein Blick in ein grosses Werk. Zum Liedschaffen

Hanns Eislers', *Musik und Gesellschaft* (Berlin-DDR), VII, 1957, pp. 5ff.

Schönewolf, Karl, 'Hanns Eislers Musik' (Zu "Die Mutter")', *Theaterarbeit – 6 Aufführungen des Berliner Ensembles*, Berlin-DDR 1966, pp. 152ff.

Siegmund-Schultze, Walther, 'Zu einigen Grundfragen der Musikästhetik', *Wissenschaftliche Zeitschrift der Martin-Luther-Universität Halle/Wittenberg*, XI/2, 1962, pp. 167ff.

Stephan, Rudolf, 'Kleine Beiträge zur Eisler-Kritik', *Studien zur Wertungsforschung* 3, Graz 1973, pp. 53ff.

Stuckenschmidt, Hans Heinz, 'Hanns Eisler', *Musikblätter des Anbruch* (Vienna), X, 1928, pp. 163ff.

'Politisch Lied? Der Komponist Hanns Eisler im Streit der Meinungen', *Frankfurter Allgemeine Zeitung*, V, 16 March 1965

'Hanns Eisler', *Die grossen Komponisten unseres Jahrhunderts*, Munich 1971, pp. 99ff.

Völker, Klaus, 'Der positive und der negative Faust', *Materialien zu Hanns Eislers 'Johann Faustus'*, Tübingen 1974

Zobl, Wilhelm, 'Hanns Eisler', *Neues Forum* (Vienna), December 1971, pp. 63ff.

'Kritik der westlichen Avantgarde und ihrer ökonomischen Widersprüche – ausgehend von Hanns Eislers Überlegungen', *Musik zwischen Engagement und Kunst, Studien zur Wertungsforschung* 3, Graz 1972, pp. 80ff.

List of works

compiled by David Blake

In the nine volumes of Lieder und Kantaten issued by the Deutsche Akademie
de Künste, DDR, many of the dates of composition were provided by
Eisler from memory. Subsequent research has shown most of these to be
inaccurate, in some cases extremely so. The order of works here is only
approximately accurate. Dates are only given where, as the result of the
researches of Eberhardt Klemm, they can be relied upon.

A. Vocal works

1. Solo, chorus and orchestra

Opus	Title	Text	Date of compo- sition
16	*Tempo der Zeit* Cantata for alto, bass, speaker, chorus and small orchestra	David Weber (David Weber and Robert Winter were pseudonyms of Robert Gilbert)	1929
20	*Die Massnahme* Lehrstück for tenor, 3 speakers, male chorus, mixed chorus and small orchestra 　1　Lob der UdSSR 　2　Lob der illegalen Arbeit 　3　Gesang der Reiskahnschlepper 　4　Lenin-Zitat (a cappella) 　5　Streiklied 　6　Lied des Händlers 　7　Ändere die Welt, sie braucht es 　8　Lob der Partei 　9　Wir sind der Abschaum der Welt	Brecht	1930
25	Lieder, Balladen und Chöre from *Die Mutter* 　1　Wie die Krähe 　2　Lied von der Suppe 　3　Der zerrissene Rock	Brecht	1931

276

Opus	Title	Text	Date of composition
	4 Bericht vom 1. Mai		
	5 Lob des Kommunismus (also: Lob des Sozialismus)		
	6 Lob des Lernens		
	7 Lob eines Revolutionärs		
	8 Im Gefängnis zu singen		
	9 Lob der Wlassowas		
	10 Lob der dritten Sache		
	11 Grabrede über einen Genossen, der an die Wand gestellt wurde		
	12 'Steh auf, die Partei ist in Gefahr!'		
	13 Lob der Dialektik		

The *Mutter* score also exists in a
cantata version accompanied by two
pianos: some numbers, including
nos. 1 and 8, were arranged for a New
York performance in 1935. The
arrangement was completed in 1968
by members of the Deutsche
Akademie der Künste.

Opus	Title	Text	Date of composition
47	*Kalifornische Ballade* Cantata version of music for a radio production for alto, baritone, chorus and orchestra	Ernst Ottwalt	1934
	1 Ballade vom eigenen Frieden		
	2 Gross sind die Schätze der Erde		
	3 Ballade ('Auf, Jungen, auf')		
	4 Ballade vom Zug nach dem Westen		
	5 Der Ruf nach dem Westen		
	6 Die Vernichtung		
50	*Deutsche Sinfonie* for soli, chorus and orchestra	Brecht	1935–9
	1 Präludium ('Oh Deutschland, bleiche Mutter')		
	2 An die Kämpfer in den Konzentrationslagern		
	3 Etüde 1 for orchestra		
	4 Potsdam		
	5 In Sonnenburg		
	6 Etüde 2 for orchestra		

278   List of works

Opus	Title	Text	Date of composition
7	Begräbnis des Hetzers im Zinksarg		
8	Bauernkantate	Eisler after Julius Bittner	
9	Das Lied vom Klassenfeind (Arbeiterkantate) see also A 3 op. 41/4)		
10	Allegro for orchestra (see also B)		
11	Epilog ('Seht, unsre Söhne')		1959

Lenin-Requiem
Cantata for soli, chorus and orchestra — Brecht — 1936–7

Mitte des Jahrhunderts
Cantata for soprano, chorus and orchestra — Johannes R. Becher — 1950
  1 Präludium
  2 Dank euch, Ihr Sowjetsoldaten
  3 Du grosses Wir

Bilder aus der 'Kriegsfibel'
for soli, male chorus and orchestra — Brecht — 1957

2. Voice and orchestra

Drei Lieder — Li-Tai-Pe, Geisha song, trans. Klabund — before 1923

Glückliche Fahrt
for soprano and orchestra — Goethe — 1946

Das Vorbild
Triptych for alto and small orchestra — Goethe — 1952

Die Teppichweber von Kujan-Bulak
Cantata for soprano and orchestra — Brecht — 1957

Music to *Wilhelm Tell* — Schiller — 1961
  Vorspiel
  Gesang 'Es lächelt der See'
  for soprano, tenor and orchestra

Ernste Gesänge — 1962
  for baritone and strings
  Vorspiel und Spruch — Hölderlin
    1 Asyl — Hölderlin fragment — 1936

Opus	Title	Text	Date of composition
2	Traurigkeit (Chanson allemande) (see A 5)	Berthold Viertel	1955
3	Verzweiflung	Leopardi	1955
4	An die Hoffnung (see A 5)	Hölderlin fragment	1943
5	XX Parteitag	after Helmut Richter	1962
6	'Komm! ins Offene, Freund!'	Hölderlin fragment	
7	Epilog	Stephan Hermlin	1961

3. Voice and small orchestra

The majority of these songs exist in versions with piano. Some, like the 'Solidaritätslied', have accompaniments for full orchestra, wind band, folk bands etc. It has not been considered necessary to specify these. Some songs have a choral refrain, often optional.

	Gesang des Abgeschiedenen five songs for alto and chamber orchestra	Japanese or Chinese	before 1923
	'Sehr leises Gehn im lauen Wind' for alto and chamber orchestra		before 1923
	Drum sag der SPD ade	Robert Winter	1928
	Lied der roten Matrosen	Erich Weinert	1928
18	Sechs Balladen		1929–30
	1 Ballade von der Krüppelgarde	David Weber	
	2 Ballade zum § 218	Brecht	
	3 Anrede an den Kran 'Karl'	Brecht	
	4 Song von Angebot und Nachfrage (Lied des Händlers from *Die Massnahme*)	Brecht	
	5 Lied vom Trockenbrot (for piano only) (from *Der Kaufmann von Berlin*)	Walter Mehring	
	6 Ballade vom Nigger Jim	Weber	
22	Vier Balladen for male chorus or solo and small orchestra		1930
	1 Lied der Baumwollpflücker	Bruno Traven	
	2 Ballade von der Wohltätigkeit	Kurt Tucholsky	

Opus	Title	Text	Date of composition
3	Lied der Bergarbeiter (from *Heer ohne Helden*)	Wiesner-Gmeyner	
4	Ballade von den Säckeschmeissern	Julian Arendt	
	Lied der roten Flieger	Kirsanow	1931
	From *Niemandsland*	Leonhard Frank	1931
	1 Arbeitslied		
	2 Montage über den Krieg		
	3 Negerlied		
	4 Der heimliche Aufmarsch	Weinert	
27	From *Kuhle Wampe*	Brecht	1931
	1 Solidaritätslied		
	2 Die Spaziergänge		
	3 'Wir wollten ein Obdach haben' (subsequently cut from the film)		
28	Sechs Lieder		1929–31
	1 Der rote Wedding	Weinert	
	2 Der heimliche Aufmarsch	Weinert	
	'Arbeiter, Bauern' (see also above)		
	3 Kampflied für die IAH		
	4 Lied des Kampfbundes		
	5 Lied der Arbeitslosen (Stempellied)	Weber	
	6 Kominternlied	Jahnke/Vallentin	
	Lied der Werktätigen (Kominternlied with new text – 1949)	Stephan Hermlin	1929–31
	Der neue Stern	Weinert	
	Ballade von den Seeräubern	Brecht	
37	From *Das Lied vom Leben*		
	1 Anrede an ein neugeborenes Kind also	Mehring	1931
	2 Matrosensong		
	3 Kesselsong		
	From *Kamerad Kasper*		
	Lied der Mariken	Brecht	
39	Ballade vom Soldaten (or Ballade vom Weib und dem Soldaten)	Brecht	1932

Opus	Title	Text	Date of compo-sition
	From *Die Jugend hat das Wort* Magnito-Komsomolzenlied (Lied vom Ural)	Tretjakow	1932
	Das Lied vom vierten Mann		
	Streiklied ('Fischer von St Barbara')		
	Lied der deutschen Rotarmisten	Weinert	
41	Vier Balladen 1 Das Lied vom SA-Mann 2 Ballade vom Baum und den Ästen 3 Das Lied vom Anstreicher Hitler 4 Das Lied vom Klassenfeind (see also *Deutsche Sinfonie*, A 1)	Brecht	1931–2
	From *Dans les rues* 'Mon oncle a tout repeint'	Nohain	1933
42	Die Ballade von der Billigung der Welt	Brecht	1934
43	Spartakus 1919		
45	Lieder, Songs und Balladen from *Die Rundköpfe und die Spitzköpfe* 1 Hymne des erwachenden Jahoo 2 Lied eines Freudenmädchens (Nanna's Lied) 3 Lied von der Tünche 4 Sichellied (Bauernlied) 5 Die Ballade vom Knopfwurf 6 Kavatine der Isabella 7 Was-man-hat-das-hat-man-Lied 8 Chorlied von der nützlichen Missetat (Das neue Iberinlied) 9 Lied von der belebenden Wirkung des Geldes 10 Die Ballade vom Wasserrad 11 Lied der Kupplerin (Kuppellied) 12 Duett (Nanna–Isabella) 13 Lied eines Grossen (Terzett) 14 Das 'Vielleicht–Lied' (Rundgesang der Pachtherren)	Brecht Julius Bittner	1934–6

Opus	Title	Text	Date of composition
48	Zwei Lieder 　1 Bankenlied 　2 Ein neues Stempellied	 Clément/Mehring Weber	1931–2
	Das Einheitsfrontlied	Brecht	1934
	Sklave, wer wird dich befreien	Brecht	1934
	Das Saarlied	Brecht	1934
	Ballade von der Judenhure Marie Sanders	Brecht	1934
	Lied gegen den Krieg	Brecht	1934
	From *Abdul Hamid* 　Friedenssong	 Ernst Schoen	1937
	Marsch des 5. Regiments (Spanienlied)	Petero	
	Brother Patriot (refrain as in above)		
	Close the ranks		
	Dictator's Song		
	Song of Light		
	Musik zu *Schweyk im zweiten Weltkrieg* Songs accompanied by two pianos; nos. 1, 6 and 13 by 8 cellos, 8 basses and timpani; nos. 3, 8, 9, 12, 16 scored for full orchestra 　1 Erste Szene: In den höheren Regionen 　2 Das Lied vom Weib des Nazi-soldaten 　3 Intermezzo: Schweyks Rückkehr 　　　von der Gestapo 　4 Das Lied vom kleinen Wind 　5 Schwarzer Rettich 　6 Zweite Szene: In den höheren Regionen 　7 'Heinrich schlief bei seiner 　　　Neuvermählten' (unacc.) 　8 Intermezzo 　9 Beseda Polka 　10 Lied der Anna 　11 Lied von der Moldau	Brecht	1943–59

Opus	Title	Text	Date of composition
12	Vorspiel zur dritten Szene		
13	Dritte Szene: In den höheren Regionen		
14	'Bei der Kanone dort'		
15	Kälbermarsch		(1932–3)
16	Intermezzo		
16a	Überleitung		
17	'Als wir nach Jaromersch zogen'		
18	Lied vom Kelch		
19	Deutsches Miserere		
20	Schweyks Abgesang		
21	Schlussgesang (Also 3 Entr'actes)		
	Musik, zu *Leben des Galilei* for soli, SSA chorus (female and boys), flute/piccolo, clarinet, harpsichord	Brecht	1946
	Musik zu *Die Geschichte der Simone Machard*	Brecht	1946
1	Erste Szene des Engels		
2	Der zweite Traum		
3	Dritter Gesang des Engels		
4	Lied der Simone und Marsch		
	Lied über die Gerechtigkeit	Walter Fischer	1948
	Lied über den Frieden ('Krieg ist kein Gesetz der Natur')	Walter Fischer	1949
	Hymne der Deutschen Demokratischen Republik ('Auferstanden aus Ruinen')	Becher	1949
	Lieder from *Die Tage der Commune*	Brecht	1950
1	Geneviève: 'Ostern ist Ball sur Seine'		
2	Père Josèphe		
3	Geneviève: 'Margot ging auf den Markt heut früh'		
4	Resolution ('In Erwägung, dass')		1934
	Kinderlieder	Brecht	1950–1
1	Die Pappel vom Karlsplatz		
2	'Anmut sparet nicht noch Mühe' Festlied der Kinder		
3	Das Lied vom kriegerischen Lehrer		
4	Willem hat ein Schloss		

Opus	Title	Text	Date of composition
	5 Die Vogel warten im Winter auf Futter		
	6 Friedenslied	Pablo Neruda/Brecht	
	From *Frauenschicksale* Das Lied vom Glück	Brecht	1952
	Music from the film *Herr Puntila und sein Knecht Matti* 1 Storch, Storch, Steiner . . . Volkslied für Kinder oder Frauenchor a cappella 2 Die Gräfin und der Förster 3 Puntila-Lied	Brecht	1955
	Vier Szenen auf dem Lande for children's or female voices 1 Starr stand der Frost 2 Die Sonne steigt 3 Das Korn wird reif 4 Herbst engt die Sicht nicht ein	Erwin Strittmatter	1956
	Lied der Tankisten	Weinert	1957
	Regimenter gehn	Majakowski	1957
	From *Das Schwitzbad* Marsch der Zeit	Majakowski	1957
	Lieder from *Sturm* 1 Linker Marsch 2 Läuse-Lied 3 Lied vom Subbotnik	Majakowski Peter Hacks Majakowski	1957
	Sputnik-Lied 'Herr Dulles möcht so gerne' for voice and jazz ensemble (see also A 5)	Kuba	1957
	Am 1. Mai (Kinderlied)	Brecht	1958
	Lied der Pflastersteine	Weinert	1961

Opus	Title	Text	Date of composition

4. Voice and chamber ensemble

	Die Mausefalle for high voice, piano (or chamber orchestra), violin 1 Palmström hat nicht Speck im Haus 2 Morgen kommt vom Kopf	Christian Morgenstern	before 1923
	Wenn es nur einmal so ganz still wäre for alto, violin, viola, cello	Rilke	before 1923
5	Palmström Studies on twelve-note rows for sprech-stimme, flute, clarinet, violin/viola, cello 1 Venus Palmström 2 Notturno 3 L'art pour l'art 4 Galgenbruders Frühlingslied 5 Couplet von der Tapetenblume	Morgenstern	1924
9	Tagebuch des Hanns Eisler Cantata for female trio, tenor, violin, piano	Eisler	1926
	Ulm 1592 for voice and string quartet	Brecht	1934
	Bettellied for voice, violin, cello	Brecht	1935
	Neun Kammerkantaten 1 Die Gott-sei-bei-uns-Kantate Kinderkantate for solo, chorus, string quartet (also version with piano)	Brecht	1937
	2 Die Weissbrotkantate for voice, two clarinets, viola, cello (also version with piano)	after Silone	
60	3 Die römische Kantate for voice, two clarinets, viola, cello Version with piano	after Silone	
	4 'Man lebt von einen Tage zu dem andern'–Kantate im Exil for voice, two clarinets, viola, cello	after Silone	

Opus	Title	Text	Date of composition
62	Version with piano		
	5 *Kriegskantate*	after Silone	
	for voice, two clarinets, viola, cello		
65	Version with piano		
	6 *Nein*	after Silone	
	for voice and string quartet		
	7 *'Die den Mund auf hatten'*	after Silone	
	for voice, two clarinets, viola, cello		
	8 *Kantate auf den Tod eines Genossen*	after Silone	
	for voice, flute, clarinet, viola, cello		
64	Version with piano		
	9 *Zuchthauskantate*	Eisler	
	for voice, two clarinets, viola, cello		

Kantate zu Herrn Meyers erstem Geburtstag   1938
for voice, viola, piano

Zwei Sonette   Brecht   1939
for voice and two clarinets
    1 Sonett über Goethes Gedicht:
       'Der Gott und die Bajadere'
    2 Sonett über Schillers Gedicht:
       'Die Bürgschaft'

Drei Kinderlieder
for voice and viola
    1 'Schlafe, mein Kindchen'
    2 'Hab ein Vöglein gefunden'
    3 'Büble, nimm den Ziegenbock'

Zu Brechts Tod 'Die Wälder atmen noch'   1956
for voice and four horns

5. Voice and piano

Zwei Lieder   before
                                                  1923

    1 Der müde Soldat   Schi-King
    2 Die rote und die weisse Rose   Li-Tai-Pe

'Vielleicht dass ich durch schwere Berge gehe'   Rilke

Tod   Mikula

Opus	Title	Text	Date of composition
	'O, nimm mir'		
	Leise an verschlossener Türe		
	Lass alle Spannung der Freude	Rabindranath Tagore	
	Zwei Kinderlieder 1 Mädele bind den Geissbock an 2 Kindchen, mein Kindchen	Des Knaben Wunderhorn	
	Immer wieder nahst Du, Melancholie		
	Von der Armut und vom Tode 1 'Du der du weis' und dessen weites Wissen' 2 'Betrachte sie und sieh, was ihnen gleiche' 3 'Und ihre Hände sind wie die von Frauen' 4 'Sie sind so still, fast gleichen sie den Dingen' 5 'Und wenn sie schlafen, sind sie wie an alles' 6 'Ihr Mund ist wie der Mund' 7 'Und ihre Stimme kommt von ferne her' (male chorus) 8 'Und weh' (female chorus) 9 'Und sieh, ihr Leib ist wie ein Bräutigam'	Rilke	
	Drei Lieder 1 Ausblick 2 Trinklied 3 Ständchen	Kramer Fischart Falcke	
	Nachtgruss	Eichendorff	
	Totenopfer	Eichendorff	
	Unter Feinden	Nietzsche	

Opus	Title	Text	Date of composition
	Galgenlieder von Morgenstern	Morgenstern	
	1 Idylle		
	2 Die beiden Flaschen		
	3 Die beiden Trichter		
	4 Philantropisch		
	5 Galgenbruders Frühlingslied		
	6 Die Würfel		
	'Auf einer grünen Wiese'		
	Von der Langeweile		
	'Eines Morgens im Blumengarten'	Tagore	
	Zwei Lieder		
	1 Herbst	Trakl	
	2 Wenn Du es so haben willst	Tagore	
	Ich habe die Ladung gehabt	Tagore	
	Nach dem Traum		
	'Jetzt bleibt mir nur'		
	'Wenn der Tag vorbei'	Tagore	
	'Es war im Mai'	Tagore	
	'Was ist die Traurigkeit'		
	'Nun ist ein Tag zu Ende'		
	'Dunkler Tropfe'	Morgenstern	
	Tanzlied der Rosetta ('Leonce und Lena')	Büchner	
	Zwei Lieder		
	1 Nenn ich dich Aufgang oder Untergang	Rilke	
	2 Im Frühling	Trakl	
	Im Licht des Sakeflusses	Geisha song trans. Klabund	

Opus	Title	Text	Date of composition
	Zwei Lieder		
	1 Bitte an den Hund	Japanese	
	2 Rondell	Trakl	
	Oh könntest du meine Augen sehen		
2	Sechs Lieder		1922
	1 'So schlafe nun, du Kleine'	Claudius	
	2 An den Tod	Claudius	
	3 Das Alter	Japanese trans. Bethge	
	4 'Erhebt euch, Freunde'	Klabund	
	5 'Der Mond wird oft noch'	Klabund	
	6 'Ich habe nie vermeint'	Klabund	
11	*Zeitungsausschnitte*		1925–6
	1 Mariechen		
	2 Kinderlied aus dem Wedding		
	3 Liebeslied eines Kleinbürgermädchens–Heiratsannonce		
	4 Kriegslied eines Kindes Aus einer Enquête		
	5 Die Sünde		
	6 Mutter und Vater		
	7 Der Tod		
	8 Liebeslied des Grundbesitzers–Heiratsannonce		
	9 Aus einer Romanbeilage–'Schweyk' Predigt des Feldkuraten	Hašek	
	10 Frühlingsrede an einen Baum im Hinterhaushof		
	Lustige Ecke		1925–6
	1 Noblesse Oblige		
	2 'Der kleine Kohn'		
12	Pantomime	Bela Balázs	
	Kumpellied		
	Roter Matrosensong	Grau	
	Couplet vom Zeitfreiwilligen		

Opus	Title	Text	Date of composition
	Zeitungssohn		
	Auch ein Schumacher	Brecht	
	'Was möchtst du nicht'	Des Knaben Wunderhorn	
	Wir sind das rote Sprachrohr		1928
	Mit der IFA marschiert	Slang	
	Ein Rotarmistenlied		
	Lenin ist eingeschreint		
	Sergeant Waurich	Kästner	
	O Fallada, da du hangest – Ein Pferd beklagt sich (also version for small orchestra)	Brecht	1932
33	Vier Wiegenlieder für Arbeitermütter 1 'Als ich dich in meinem Leib trug' 2 'Als ich dich gebar' 3 'Ich hab' dich ausgetragen' 4 'Mein Sohn, was immer auch'	Brecht	1932–3
	Und es sind die finstern Zeiten	Brecht	
	Kälbermarsch (used in *Schweyk*. See A 3)	Brecht	1932–3
	Ballade von den Ossegger Witwen	Brecht	1934
	Hammer und Sichel	Brecht	1934
	Zwei Songs 1 Bucket-Song 2 Mother Bloor	Hunter	
	Der Pflaumenbaum (also with harmonium)	Brecht	
	Der Räuber und sein Knecht	Brecht	1935

Opus	Title	Text	Date of composition
	Deutsches Lied 1937 'Marie weine nicht' (also for flute, clarinet, bassoon, strings)	Brecht	1937
	Spanisches Liedchen 1937	Brecht	1937
	Das Lied vom 7. Januar Spanienlied for voice and accordion	Ludwig Renn	1937
	Wie könnten wir je vergessen	Spanish song	
	Wir sind der Freiheit Soldaten	Stern	
	Deutsches Kriegslied	Brecht	
	Zwei Elegien 1 'In die Städte kam ich' 2 An die Überlebenden 'Ihr, die ihr auftauchen werdet'	Brecht	1937
	Zwei Lieder nach alten deutschen Texten 1 'Es geht eine dunkle Wolk' herein' 2 'Ich weiss ein Blümelein blaue'	Old German	
	Der Zweck der Musik	Latin proverb	
	Lied einer deutschen Mutter	Brecht	
	Lieder aus Svendborger Gedichte VI 1 Spruch 1939 'In den finsteren Zeiten wird da noch gesungen werden' 2 Über die Dauer des Exils a 'Schlage keinen Nagel in die Wand' b 'Sieh den Nagel in der Wand' 3 Zufluchtsstätte 4 Elegie 1939 'Wirklich, ich lebe in finsteren Zeiten'	Brecht	1939
	Über den Selbstmord	Brecht	
	Shakespeare Sonett Nr. 66	Shakespeare	1939
	Gruss an die Mark Brandenburg	Robert Gilbert	
	An den Schlaf	Mörike	

Opus	Title	Text	Date of composition
	Der Schatzgräber	Goethe	
	Die Hollywood-Elegien		1942
1	'Unter den grünen Pfefferbäumen'	Brecht	
2	'Die Stadt ist nach den Engeln genannt'	Brecht	
3	'Jeden Morgen mein Brot zu verdienen'	Brecht	
4	Hollywood	Brecht	
5	'In den Hügeln wird Gold gefunden'	Brecht	
6	'The rat men accused me'	Eisler	
7	'I saw many friends'	Brecht	
8	'Über die vier Städte kreisen'	Brecht	
	Winterspruch	Brecht	1942
	Zwei Lieder	after Blaise Pascal	
1	Despite these miseries		
2	The only thing		
	Lieder aus *Steffinische Sammlung*	Brecht	1942
1	Spruch 'Das ist nun alles'		
2	Frühling I 'Heute, Ostersonntag früh'		
3	In den Weiden		
4	Der Kirschdieb		
5	Der Sohn 'Mein junger Sohn fragt mich'		
6	Hotelzimmer 1942 'An der weiss- getünchten Wand'		
7	Die Flucht 'Auf der Flucht vor meinen Landsleuten'		
8	An den kleinen Radioapparat		
9	Auf der Flucht 'Da ich die Bücher'		
10	Speisekammer 1942		
11	Panzerschlacht		
12	Gedenktafel für 4000 Soldaten, die im Krieg gegen Norwegen versenkt wurden		
13	Frühling II 'Fischreiche Wässer'		
	Lieder aus *Gedichte im Exil*	Brecht	1942–3
1	Die Maske des Bösen		
2	Vom Sprengen des Gartens		
3	Die Heimkehr 'Die Vaterstadt, wie find' ich sie doch?'		
4	Die Landschaft des Exils		
5	'Und ich werde nicht mehr sehen'		

Opus	Title	Text	Date of compo-sition
6	'In Sturmesnacht, in dunkler Nacht' Lied vom Juli 1942 (also version for flute, clarinet, bassoon, strings)		
	Die Mutter 'Wenn sie nachts lag'	Brecht	1943
	Fünf Anakreon-Fragmente 1 Geselligkeit betreffend 2 'Dir auch wurde Sehnsucht nach der Heimat tödlich' 3 Die Unwürde des Alterns 4 Später Triumph 5 In der Frühe	trans. Mörike	1943
	Aus der Heimat hinter den Blitzen rot	after Eichendorff	
	Sechs Hölderlin-Fragmente 1 An die Hoffnung 2 Andenken 3 Elegie 1943 4 Die Heimat 5 An eine Stadt 6 Erinnerung	Hölderlin	1943
	Das deutsche Miserere (used in *Schweyk*. See A 3)	Brecht	1943
	Lob des Weines	Brecht	
	Ardens sed virens		
	Printemps allemand	Karl Kraus	
	Der Butterräuber von Halberstadt	adap. Brecht	
	L'automne californien	Berthold Viertel	
	Rimbaud-Gedicht	Rimbaud	
	Eisenbahn		
	Neue Deutsche Volkslieder 1 Die alten Weisen	Johannes R. Becher	1950

Opus	Title	Text	Date of composition
2	Volkes eigen		
3	Die Welt verändern wir		
4	Wenn Arbeiter und Bauern		
5	Im Frühling		
6	Lied von der blauen Fahne		
7	Heimatlied		
8	Das ferne Lied		
9	Strasse frei!		
10	Hymne auf die UdSSR		
11	Lenin 'Er rührte an den Schlaf der Welt' (also for large orchestra)		
12	Deutschland		
13	Gesang vom Lernen		
14	Das Wunderland		
15	Zeit zum Wandern		
16	Wir reichen euch die Hand		
17	Weihnachtslied 1950		
18	Kinderlied zu Weihnachten		
	Du Sohn der Arbeiterschaft	Becher	
	From *Dr. Faustus*	Eisler	1952
1	Der Mensch		
2	Faustus Verzweiflung		
	Lied für Bukarest	Hermlin	1953
	Genesung	Becher	1954
	Von der Freundlichkeit der Welt	Brecht	1954
	Die haltbare Graugans	Brecht: after the American	1955
	Chanson allemande	Viertel	1955
	Die Götter	Xenophanes	1955
	Im Blumengarten	Brecht	1955
	L'automne prussien – Die Buckow-Kantate	Eisler	1955
	Wie der Wind weht	Brecht	1955

Opus	Title	Text	Date of composition
	Wiener Lied	Brecht	1955
	Und endlich	Peter Altenberg	1955
	Horatios Monolog	Shakespeare	1956
	Von Wolkenstreifen leicht befangen	Goethe fragment	1956
	Verfehlte Liebe	Heine	
	Legende von der Entstehung des Buches Taoteking	Brecht	1956
	Des Friedens Soldaten	Herzfelde	
	Weihnachtslied 1918 (also version for small orchestra)	Tucholsky	
	Ohne Kapitalisten geht es besser ('Zwei liebevolle Schwestern') (Different text for Sputnik-Lied. See A 3)	Kuba	1957
	Zwei Chansons 1 Lied vom guten Kern 2 Über die Elbe	Erich Brehm	1957
	Ballade vom Kreuzzug	Kuba	1957
	Steht auf!	Hermlin	1958
	Trommellied	Max Zimmering	
	Rezitativ und Fuge zum 60. Geburtstag von J. R. Becher	Becher	
	Um meine Weisheit unbekümmert	Hölderlin fragment	1959
	Motto – Auf einen chinesischen Theewurzellöwen	Brecht	1959
	Die Wasser fuhren zu Tale Kinderlied	Hermlin	1961

Opus	Title	Text	Date of composition
	Bleib gesund mir, Krakau	Gebirtig	
	Lieder nach Texten von Kurt Tucholsky (Nos. 1, 3 and 37 date from 1929–30)	Tucholsky	1959–61
	1 Feldfrüchte		
	2 In Weissensee		
	3 'Wenn die Igel in der Abendstunde' (Anna Luise)		
	4 Einkäufe		
	5 Immer raus mit der Mutter . . .!		
	6 Olle Kamellen		
	7 'Der schlimmste Feind'		
	8 Sehnsucht nach der Sehnsucht		
	9 Das Lied vom Kompromiss		
	10 Die freie Wirtschaft		
	11 Rückkehr zur Natur		
	12 Nach der Schlacht		
	13 Rosen auf den Weg gestreut		
	14 Revolutions-Rückblick		
	15 Die Unentwegten		
	16 Sommerlied		
	17 Marburger Studentenlied		
	18 Die weinenden Hohenzollern		
	19 Mutterns Hände		
	20 Heute zwischen gestern und morgen		
	21 Der Priem		
	22 Merkt ihr nischt?		
	23 Ruhe und Ordnung		
	24 Vor acht Jahren		
	25 Die Mäuler auf		
	26 Das alte Vertiko		
	27 Frohe Erwartung		
	28 Einigkeit und Recht und Freiheit		
	29 Der Smokingmann		
	30 Ideal und Wirklichkeit		
	31 Zuckerbrot und Peitsche		
	32 Couplet für die Bier-Abteilung		
	33 Gebet für die Gefangenen		
	34 Deutsches Lied		
	35 Weihnachten (also version for small orchestra)		
	36 Sozialdemokratischer Parteitag (also version for small orchestra)		

Opus	Title	Text	Date of composition
	37 Der Graben (also version for small orchestra) 38 An den deutschen Mond 39 Die Nachfolgerin		

6. Unaccompanied chorus

Opus	Title	Text	Date of composition
10	Drei Männerchöre 1 Tendenz (Sangesspruch) 2 Utopie 3 'Demokratie'	after Heine	1926
13	Vier Stücke für gemischten Chor 1 Vorspruch with speaker, side drum and cymbals ad lib. 2 Gesang der Besiegten 3 Naturbetrachtung 4 Kurfürstendamm		1928
14	Zwei Männerchöre 1 Bauernrevolution 2 Kurze Anfrage (Lied der Arbeitslosen)	after a song from the Peasants' Revolt 1525	1928
15	Auf den Strassen zu singen for mixed chorus and side drum	Weber	1928
17	Zwei Männerchöre 1 Der Streikbrecher 2 An Stelle einer Grabrede	Joe Hill/Ilse Kulcsar Weber	1929
19	Zwei Stücke für Männerchor 1 Ferner streiken: 50 000 Holzarbeiter 2 In den Militärbaracken	Kulcsar from the American First verse of a Bosnian soldiers' song	1929
21	Zwei Stücke für gemischten Chor 1 Liturgie vom Hauch 2 Über das Töten	Brecht Eisler	1930

Opus	Title	Text	Date of composition
35	Zwei Männerchöre		1933
	1 Kohlen für Mike	Brecht	
	2 Die erfrorenen Soldaten	Kraus	
51	*Gegen den Krieg*	Brecht	1936
	Cantata in variation form for mixed chorus		
	Kriegslied		
	for children's chorus		
	Fünf Kinderlieder	Brecht	
	1 Wo soll das hin		
	2 Die Mutter liegt im Krankenhaus		
	3 Kriegslied		
	4 Vom Kind, das sich nicht waschen wollte		
	5 Hoppeldoppel wopps Laus (Schauerballade)		
	Woodbury-Liederbüchlein	traditional	1941
	for 3-part children's or female choir		
	1 Evening talk		
	2 I had a little nut tree		
	3 Ah, hear the wind blow		
	4 The sick kitten		
	5 Nach einem Sprichwort (Cock crows in the morn)		
	6 Children's rhyme		
	7 Little Miss Muffat		
	8 Four and twenty tailors		
	9 Kanon (Little drop of water)		
	10 Hector Protector		
	11 The five toes		
	12 Pussy cat		
	13 The old woman from France		
	14 I had a little doggy		
	15 The old woman		
	16 An den Schlaf	after Mörike	
	17 Für Lou (zwei Sprüche)		
	18 Ode an die Langeweile (using Goethe and Schubert)	Eisler	
	19 Sommer adieu		
	20 On New Year's Day in the morning		

Opus	Title	Text	Date of composition
	Kanons		
1	Udarnik Kanon (a 2)		
2	From the Aeneid (a 4)	Virgil	
3	Oh endless is this misery (a 3 and cantus firmus)	Eisler	
4	Peace on earth (a 4)	Hermann Reichenbach	
5	Kanon für die zweite Parteikonferenz (a 4)	Brecht	
6	Kanon nach einem Volkslied (Duck dich, Hänschen) (a 2)	traditional	
7	Kanon ohne Text (a 4)		
8	'Eigenheiten, die werden haften' (a 3)	Goethe	
9	Charité-Kanon		

B. Orchestral works

Opus	Title	Date of composition
23	Suite No. 1 (from film *Opus III*)	1930
24	Suite No. 2 '*Niemandsland*' (from film)	1931
26	Suite No. 3 '*Kuhle Wampe*' (from film)	1931
29	*Kleine Sinfonie*	1932
30	Suite No. 4 '*Die Jugend hat das Wort*' (from film)	1932
35	Suite No. 5 '*Dans les rues*' (from film)	1933
40	Suite No. 6 '*Le grand jeu*' (from film)	1932
	Fünf Orchesterstücke (from film *400 Millionen*)	1938
	Allegro für Orchester (see also *Deutsche Sinfonie*)	1935–9
	Zwei Etüden für Orchester (see also *Deutsche Sinfonie* and film *Opus III*)	1935–9
	Scherzo mit solovioline (from film *400 Millionen*)	1938

Opus	Title	Date of composition
	Variationen über ein marschartiges Thema (*Der lange Marsch*) (from film *400 Millionen*)	1938
69	Kammersinfonie für 15 Instrumente (from film *Eis*)	1940
	Ouvertüre zu einem Lustspiel (Overture to *Höllenangst* (Nestroy) for small orchestra)	1948
	Rhapsodie für grosses Orchester with soprano solo to words from Goethe's *Faust* Pt II	1949
	Winterschlacht-Suite (from stage work)	1955
	Sturm-Suite (from stage work)	1957

C. Chamber music

Opus	Title	Date of composition
	Scherzo for string trio	1920
	Allegro moderato und Walzer for piano	before 1923
	Allegretto und Andante for piano	before 1923
	'Ich pflückte deine Blume' (Tagore) for viola, bass clarinet, harp, violin, cello	before 1923
	Scherzo for string quartet (incomplete)	
1	Sonata for piano (No. 1)	1923
3	Vier Klavierstücke	1923
4	Divertimento for wind quintet	1923
6	Sonata No. 2 for piano (in the form of variations)	1924
7	Duo for violin and cello	1924
8	Acht Klavierstücke	1925
31	Klavierstücke für Kinder	1932–3
32	Sieben Klavierstücke	1932–3

Opus	Title	Date of composition
44	Sonatine für Klavier (Gradus ad Parnassum)	1934
46	*Präludium und Fuge über B-A-C-H* for string trio	1934
49	Sonata for flute, oboe and harp	1935
	Sonata for violin and piano ('Reisesonate')	1937
75	String Quartet	1938
	Nonet No. 1 for flute, clarinet, bassoon, horn, string quartet, double bass	1939
92a	Septet No. 1 (Variations on American children's songs) (from film *Kinderfilm*) for flute/piccolo, clarinet, bassoon and string quartet	1940
70	*Vierzehn Arten, den Regen zu beschreiben* (from film *Regen*) Variations for flute, clarinet, violin/viola, cello, piano	1940
	Variations for piano	1940
	Nonet No. 2 (from film *Forgotten Village*) for flute, clarinet, bassoon, trumpet, percussion, 3 violins, double bass	1941
	Sonata No. 3 for piano	1943
	3 Fugues for piano	
	Septet No. 2 ('Zirkus') for flute/piccolo, clarinet, bassoon and string quartet	1947

In sections D and E cross reference has been made where details of individual songs are given or the music exists in other versions.

D. Theatre music

Title	Text	Date	Producer	Production and date where this differs from date of composition
Heimweh	Franz Jung	1927	Steckel	Berlin
Revue Hallo, Kollege Jungarbeiter		1928	Vallentin	Berlin
Kalkutta, 4 Mai	Lion Feuchtwanger	1928	Engel	Berlin
Die Bergarbeiter	Anna Gmeyner	1928	Dudow	Berlin
Maggie	Barrie	1928	Bild	Berlin
Der Kaufmann von Berlin (see A 3)	Walter Mehring	1929	Piscator	Berlin
Dantons Tod	Büchner	1929	K.-H. Martin	Berlin
Heer ohne Helden (see A 3)	Wiesner-Gmeyner	1930		Berlin
Die letzten Tage der Menschheit	Karl Kraus	1930		Berlin

302

Title	Author	Year	Director	Place
Das Gerücht	Munro or Charles Kirkpatrick	1930	K.-H. Martin	Berlin
Die Mutter (see A 1)	Gorky/Brecht	1931	Brecht	Berlin
Kamerad Kasper (see A 3)	Paul Schurek	1932	K.-H. Martin	Berlin
Rote Revue Wir sind ja sooo zufrieden	Brecht	1932	Brecht, Weinert, Weisenborn, Ottwalt	Berlin
Agitpropstück Bauer Baetz	Friedrich Wolf	1932		Berlin
Feuer aus den Kesseln	Ernst Toller	1934		Manchester and
Peace on Earth	Ernst Toller	1934		London
Die Rundköpfe und die Spitzköpfe (see A 3)	Brecht	1934–6	Brecht	Copenhagen 1936
Night Music	Clifford Odets	1939	Harold Clurman	New York
Medicine Show	Hofmann Hays	1941	Dassin	New York
Furcht und Elend des Dritten Reiches	Brecht	1945	Viertel	New York
Leben des Galilei (see A 3)	Brecht	1947	Joseph Losey	Los Angeles

Title	Text	Date	Producer	Production and date where this differs from date of composition
Höllenangst (see B)	Johann Nestroy	1948	Neubauer	Vienna
Eulenspiegel	Nestroy	1951	Stöhr	Vienna
Volpone	Ben Jonson	1953	Besson	Vienna
Lysistrata	Aristophanes	1954	W. Heinz	Vienna
Hamlet	Shakespeare	1954	W. Heinz	Vienna
Katzgraben	Erwin Strittmatter	1954	Brecht	Berlin
Winterschlacht (see B)	Becher	1955	Brecht	Berlin
Theatergeschichten	Nestroy	1955	Stöhr	Berlin
The Playboy of the Western World	Synge	1956	Wekwerth/Palitzsch	Berlin
Die erste Reiterarmee	Wsewolod Wischnewski	1956	Jung/Alsen	Berlin
Tage der Kommune (see A 3)	Brecht	1950	Wekwerth/Palitzsch	Karl-Marx Stadt 1956

Sturm (see A 3 and B)	Wladimir Bill-Belozerkowski	1957	Langhoff	Berlin
Die Geschichte der Simone Machard (see A 3)	Brecht	1957	Buckwitz	Frankfurt am Main
Schweyk im zweiten Weltkrieg (see A 3)	Brecht	1943–59	Theater der Polnischen Armee	Warsaw 1957
Lofter	Weisenborn	1958	Deutsches Fernsehzentrum	Berlin
Das Schwitzbad (see A 3)	Majakowski	1958		Berlin
Wilhelm Tell (see A 2)	Schiller	1961	Langhoff	Berlin 1962

E. Film music

Eisler re-used much of his film music in his symphonic and chamber works. The situation is very complex but where the adaptation is an obvious one, it appears in square brackets. The *Vierzehn Arten* and *Kammersinfonie* are unaltered film scores.

Title	Screenplay	Date	Producer	*Production and date where this differs from date of composition*
Opus III [Suite No. 1, Etüdes 1 and 2 from *Deutsche Sinfonie*]	Walter Ruttman	1927	Ruttman	Berlin

Title	Screenplay	Date	Producer	Production and date where this differs from date of composition
Niemandsland [Suite No. 2] (See also A 3)	Leonhard Frank	1931	Viktor Trivas	Berlin
Das Lied vom Leben (See A 3)	Walter Mehring	1931	Alexander Granowski	Berlin
Kuhle Wampe oder Wem gehört die Welt? [Suite No. 3] (See also A 3)	Brecht	1931	Ernst Ottwalt/ Slatan Dudow	Berlin
Die Jugend hat das Wort (Heldenlied or Magnitogorsk) [Suite No. 4] (See also A 3)	Tretjakow	1932	Joris Ivens	Moscow
Dans les rues [Suite No. 5] (See also A 3)	Trivas	1933	Trivas	Paris
Zuiderzee (Nouvelle terre, New Earth) Documentary	Ivens	1933	Ivens	Paris
Le grand jeu [Suite No. 6]	Charles Spaak	1934	Jacques Feyder	Paris
Abdul Hamid (The Damned) (See A 3)		1934	Grune	London
I Pagliacci (after Leoncavallo)		1936	Grune	London

306

Title	Writer	Year	Director	Location
400 Millionen Documentary on China [*Fünf Orchesterstücke, Variationen über ein marschartiges Thema, Scherzo mit solo violine*]		1938	Ivens	New York
Pete (Roleum) and his Cousins Puppet film for the World Exhibition		1939	Losey	New York
Kinderfilm Documentary [Septet No. 1]		1939	Losey	New York
Soil (Unser Acker) Educational film		1940	US Dept. for Agriculture	New York
Rain (Regen) Documentary [*Vierzehn Arten, den Regen zu beschreiben*]		1940	Ivens (1929)	New York
Forgotten Village [Nonet No. 2]	John Steinbeck	1941	Herbert Kline	New York
Hangmen also Die	Brecht	1942	John Wexley/ Fritz Lang	Hollywood
White Flood (Eis)		1943		
None but the Lonely Heart	Odets	1944	Odets	Hollywood
Spanish Main (Der Seeteufel von Cartagena)	Mankiewicz	1944–5	Frank Borzage	Hollywood

Title	Text	Date	Producer	Production and date where this differs from date of composition
Jealousy			Machate	Hollywood
Deadline at Dawn	Odets	1946	Clurman	Hollywood
A Scandal in Paris		1946	Sirk	Hollywood
So Well Remembered		1947	Edward Dmytrik	Hollywood
Woman on the Beach		1947	Jean Renoir	Hollywood
Treffass		1949	Geyer	Prague
Unser täglich Brot	Dudow	1949	Dudow	Berlin
Der Rat der Götter	Friedrich Wolf	1950	Kurt Maetzig	Berlin
Wilhelm Pieck–Das Leben unseres Präsidenten (Documentary)		1951	Andrew Thorndike	Berlin
Frauenschicksale (See A 3)	Dudow	1952	Dudow	Berlin
Schicksal am Lenkrad	Ruth Wieden	1953	Vergano	Vienna
Bel ami	Pozner	1955	Daquin	Vienna

Title	Author	Year	Director	City
Gasparone	Paryla	1955	Paryla	Vienna
Fidelio (after Beethoven)		1956	Walter Felsenstein	Vienna
Herr Puntila und sein Knecht Matti (See A 3)	Brecht/Pozner/Wieden	1955	Alberto Cavalcanti	Vienna 1956
Nuit et Brouillard (Documentary on Auschwitz)	Jean Vigo	1956	Alain Resnais	Paris
The Witches of Salem	Sartre	1957	Raymond Rouleau	Paris
Geschwader Fledermaus		1958	Erich Engel	Berlin
Trübe Wasser (after Balzac)		1959	Daquin	Paris
Globke (Documentary)		1961	Heynowski	Berlin
Spanien (Documentary)		1962	J. and K. Stern	Berlin
Esther (Television film)	Bruno Apitz	1962		Berlin

F. Arrangements

A selection as given in Notowicz and Elsner, *Hanns Eisler – Quellennachweise*

Drei deutsche Volkslieder
  1 Ich hab die Nacht geträumet
  2 Es fiel ein Reif
  3 Der Mai will uns mit Gunsten beweisen
	for voice and piano

Oh Susanna	for voice and small orchestra
Eugene Dennis	for voice and piano
Die Moorsoldaten	{ for voice and small orchestra { for voice and piano

Arrangements for wind band
  1 Volk outwaak
  2 Vaandellied (de Nobel)
  3 Unsterbliche Opfer (Trauermarsch)
  4 Brüder, zur Sonne
  5 Wir sind die junge Garde
  6 Chant du Départ (Méhul)

Die Internationale	for wind band
Dubinuschka	for wind band
Three Hebrew Dances	for chorus and small orchestra
Denk, daran, Marleen (Busch)	⎫
Ami go home (Busch)	⎬ for voice and piano
In allen Sprachen (Busch)	⎭

Chronology

1898 Hanns Eisler born in Leipzig, third child of the Austrian philosopher Rudolf Eisler (b. 1873) and Marie Ida Eisler (*née* Fischer, b. 1875).

1901 The Eisler family move from Leipzig to Vienna.

1904 Starts school.

1908–15 Attendance at the Staatsgymnasium No. 2 in Vienna. First attempts at composition.

1916 Soldier in a Hungarian regiment.

1917 Oratorio *Gegen den Krieg* (only fragments extant).

1918 Returns to Vienna from the front.

1919 Student of Karl Weigl at the New Viennese Conservatory. Start of a four-year period of private tuition with Schoenberg in Mödling near Vienna (autumn).

1920 Conductor of the Viennese workers' choirs 'Karl Liebknecht' and 'Stahlklang'.
Proofreader for Universal Edition (Vienna).

1921 Teacher at the Verein für volkstümliche Musikpflege.

1922 Six Songs for voice and piano op. 2 started.

1923 Sonata for piano op. 1 finished. First performance in Prague (10 April).
Composition of Piano Pieces op. 3 and the Divertimento for wind quintet op. 4.

1924 Publication of the first article on Eisler (Erwin Ratz in the October issue of *Musikblätter des Anbruch*).
First performance in Vienna of a work by Eisler (Sonata for piano op. 1, beginning of October).
Palmström (Christian Morgenstern) op. 5, Sonata No. 2 for piano op. 6 and Duo for violin and cello op. 7 written.

1925 Awarded the Art Prize of the City of Vienna (1 May).
Moves to Berlin.
First performance of the Songs op. 2 at the Donaueschingen Chamber Music Festival (July).
First performance of the Duo op. 7 at the International Chamber Music Festival in Venice (4 September).

Publication of pamphlets (by *Musikblätter des Anbruch*) Nos. 3 and 8 ('On old and new music' and 'Must the music-lover know anything about music theory?').

Piano Pieces op. 8 and Three Male Choruses (after Heine) op. 10 composed.

Work started on the *Zeitungsausschnitte* for voice and piano op. 11.

1926   Teacher at the Klindworth-Scharwenka Conservatory in Berlin.

Quarrel with Schoenberg (March).

Application for membership of the KPD.

Death of Eisler's father in Vienna (14 December).

The cantata *Tagebuch des Hanns Eisler* op. 9 composed.

1927   Eisler marries Charlotte (*née* Demant).

First performance of the *Tagebuch* op. 9 at the German Chamber Music Festival in Baden-Baden (July).

Music critic and columnist for *Die Rote Fahne*.

Starts work with the Agitprop group Das Rote Sprachrohr (November).

First performance of *Zeitungsausschnitte* op. 11 in Berlin (December).

Work on the opera *Moritz Meyer oder 150 Mark* (only partially extant) by David Weber (Robert Gilbert).

Music for Walter Ruttmann's film *Opus III*.

1928   Birth of Eisler's son Georg in Vienna.

Teacher at the Marxist School for Workers in Berlin.

Four Pieces for Mixed Chorus op. 13 and Two Male Choruses op. 14 written.

1929   Death of Eisler's mother in Vienna.

First performance of Walter Mehring's *Der Kaufmann Von Berlin* with music by Eisler (6 September).

First meeting with Ernst Busch.

First performance of the radio cantata *Tempo der Zeit* (David Weber) op. 16 at the German Chamber Music Festival in Baden-Baden (July).

Work on Werner Finck's cabaret *Die Katakombe* together with Ernst Busch (from the autumn). 'Lied der Arbeitslosen' (David Weber) written.

Performance of the militant song *Der rote Wedding* (Erich Weinert) from op. 28.

Auf den Strassen zu singen (Weber) for mixed chorus op. 15,

Two Male Choruses op. 17 and Two Pieces for male chorus op. 19 composed.

1930   Beginning of the working partnership and friendship with Bertolt Brecht.
First journey to the Soviet Union (November).
First performance of the Lehrstück *Die Massnahme* (Brecht) op. 20 in Berlin (13 December).
Two Pieces for mixed chorus (Brecht, Eisler) op. 21, Four Ballads (Traven, Kurt Tucholsky, Anna Wiesner-Gmeyner, Julian Arendt) op. 22 and Suite No. 1 for orchestra op. 23 written.

1931   The Eisler record 'Lied der Baumwollpflücker' (Traven) awarded first prize at the Leipzig Gramophone Exhibition.
Leader of the study group 'Dialectical materialism in music'.
Work on the journal *Kampfmusik* and in the Kampfgemeinschaft der Arbeitersänger (KdAS).
Travel in the Soviet Union (June–July).
Lecture in Düsseldorf 'The builders of a new music culture' (1 December).
Music for Victor Trivas' film *Niemandsland*. Suite No. 2 for orchestra op. 24 taken from this.
Music for the film *Kuhle Wampe* by Brecht, Ernst Ottwalt and Slaton Dudow (containing 'Solidaritätslied'). Suite No. 3 for orchestra taken from the *Kuhle Wampe* music.
Work on music for Brecht's stage play *Die Mutter* (op. 25).

1932   First public performance of the play *Die Mutter* in Berlin (16 January).
Journey to the Soviet Union for film work (2–26 May).
Public performances of the film *Kuhle Wampe* in Moscow (mid-May) and Berlin (30 May). Travel in the Soviet Union (September–October), chosen there as committee member for the International Music Bureau.
Music for Joris Ivens' film *Die Jugend hat das Wort*. Suite No. 4 for orchestra op. 30 taken from it.
Kleine Sinfonie op. 29 largely composed.

1933   Concert in Vienna (January). Beginning of exile.
Eisler in Czechoslovakia, Paris and London.
Piano Pieces for Children op. 31, Seven Piano Pieces op. 32 and Four Lullabies for Proletarian Mothers (Brecht) op. 33 finished.
Music for Ivens' film *Nouvelle terre*. Music for Trivas' film *Dans les rues*. Suite No. 5 for orchestra op. 34 taken from it.

1934   With Brecht in Denmark (February–March). *Lieder, Gedichte, Chöre* by Brecht/Eisler published in Paris (including in the Appendix, among other things, Four Ballads op. 41).
Eisler in Paris and London.
Music for Jacques Feyder's film *Le grand jeu*. Suite No. 6 for orchestra taken from this.
Sonatine for piano op. 44 and *Präludium und Fuge über B-A-C-H* for string trio op. 46 composed.
Work started on music for Brecht's stage play *Die Rundköpfe und die Spitzköpfe*.
Music for the radio story *Kalifornische Ballade*.
The 'Einheitsfrontlied' (Brecht) set to music (December).

1935   Lecture and concert tour in the USA (13 February to May).
First performance of the *Kleine Sinfonie* op. 29 given in London (BBC) by Ernest Ansermet (12 April).
Organizer of the first Workers' Music and Song Olympiad in Strasbourg (8–10 June).
President of the International Music Bureau.
Negotiations for the United Front at the Twelfth Festival of the ISCM in Prague (September).
Composition course and lectures at the New School for Social Research in New York (5 October to 18 January1936).
Participates with Brecht in the rehearsals for the New York performance of *Die Mutter* (November).
Sonata for flute, oboe and harp op. 49 composed.
Work started on the *Deutsche Sinfonie* (Brecht) op. 50.

1936   Eisler mainly in London.
Musical supervisor of the film of *I Pagliacci* in London.
First performance of *Die Rundköpfe und die Spitzköpfe* in Copenhagen (4 November).
Choral cantata *Gegen den Krieg* (Brecht) op. 51 written.

1937   Eisler in Spain (January), in Paris and with Brecht in Denmark (till the summer) and in Prague (October to December).
Collaboration with Ernst Bloch in Prague on political art.
Eisler marries Lou Jolesch (Anna-Louise *née* von Gosztonyi).
Lenin-Requiem (Brecht) finished.
Compositions: Two Elegies (Brecht) for voice and piano, Sonata for violin and piano, and nine chamber cantatas (Brecht, Ignazio Silone and others). (Several of them given first performance in Prague and Reichenberg on 3 and 5 December.)

1938   Moves to the USA (arrives 21 January).
       Welcoming concert for Eisler at the Concert Hall of the New
       School for Social Research in New York (27 February).
       Post as lecturer at the New School.
       String Quartet composed.
       Music for Ivens' documentary film on China *400 Millionen*.
       Five Orchestral Pieces taken from this.
1939   Guest Professor at the State Conservatory in Mexico City (May to
       September).
       Contract for a book with Oxford University Press in New York.
       Lieder from Brecht's *Svendborger Gedichten VI* and Two Sonnets
       (Brecht) for voice and two clarinets written.
       Composition of the Nonet No. 1.
1940   Stipendium from the Rockefeller Foundation for the film music
       project.
       Work started on the film music project (1 February).
       Music for the documentary film *White Flood* (identical to the
       Chamber Symphony for 15 instruments op. 69).
       Septet No. 1 op. 92a written.
1941   Compositions: *Vierzehn Arten, den Regen zu beschreiben* op. 70
       (after Ivens' film *Der Regen*), music for Herbert Kline's film
       Forgotten Village (after Steinbeck), Nonet No. 2, *Woodbury
       Liederbüchlein* and Variations for piano.
1942   Moves to Hollywood (20 April). Here renews his collaboration
       with Brecht. Teaching post at the University of Southern Califor-
       nia. Theodor W. Adorno becomes Eisler's co-author for the book
       Composing for the Films.
       Numerous works for voice and piano (*Hollywood-Elegien* and
       to texts from Brecht's *Steffinische Sammlung* and *Gedichte im
       Exil*).
1943   Compositions: *Fünf Anakreon-Fragmente* and *Sechs Hölderlin-
       Fragmente* for voice and piano, Sonata No. 3 for piano, and
       music for the film *Hangmen also Die* (Brecht, John Wexley and
       Fritz Lang).
       Work started on music for Brecht's play *Schweyk im zweiten
       Weltkrieg*.
1944   Work finished on *Composing for the Films* (summer).
       Music for Clifford Odets' film *None but the Lonely Heart*.
1945   Music for Brecht's play *Furcht and Elend des Dritten Reiches*.
1946   Music for Brecht's play *Leben des Galilei* and work started on the
       music for Brecht's *Die Geschichte der Simone Machard*.

Music for the film *Deadline at Dawn* by Odets and Harold Clurman.

1947   Summoned before the House Committee on Un-American Activities in Hollywood (spring).

The book *Composing for the Films* published by Oxford University Press in New York (autumn).

Hearing before the House Committee on Un-American Activities in Washington (24–6 September).

Septet No. 2 ('Zirkus') composed.

Music to Edward Dmytryk's film *So Well Remembered* and Jean Renoir's film *Woman on the Beach*.

1948   Deportation from the USA.

Farewell concert with music by Eisler in the New York Town Hall (28 February).

Participator in the Second International Congress of Composers and Music Critics in Prague (May), Lecture: 'Basic social questions of modern music'.

Eisler in Vienna.

Music for the play *Höllenangst* by Johann Nestroy.

1949   Guest in Berlin and Warsaw. Lecture at the Humboldt University, Berlin, 'Listener and composer' (22 January).

German edition of the film book (*Komposition für den Film*) published by Bruno Henschel und Sohn in Berlin.

Music for Geyer's film *Treffass* and Dudow's film *Unser Täglich Brot*.

Rhapsody for large orchestra.

National anthem of the German Democratic Republic (Johannes R. Becher) set to music.

1950   Moves to Berlin.

Member of the Deutsche Akademie der Künste. Holds master classes in composition.

Professor at the Deutsche Hochschule für Musik in Berlin.

Collaboration with Johannes R. Becher.

First performance of the *Neue Deutsche Volkslieder* (Becher) (22 May).

Performance of the Chamber Symphony at the Twenty-fourth Festival of the ISCM in Brussels (23 June).

National Prize, first class, of the DDR (7 October).

Composition of the Cantata *Mitte des Jahrhunderts* (Becher) and music to the film *Der Rat der Götter* by Friedrich Wolf and Kurt Maetzig.

1951 'Letter to West Germany' published in the journal *Sinn und Form*. The triptych *Das Vorbild* (to words by Goethe) and Children's Songs (Brecht) written.
Music to the play *Eulenspiegel* by Nestroy.

1952 Publication of the libretto to the opera *Johann Faustus*. Participation in the People's Congress for Peace in Vienna (12–19 December).
Music to Dudow's film *Frauenschicksale*.

1953 Eisler in Vienna.

1954 Music to the play *Katzgraben* by Erwin Strittmatter.
Lecture 'Schoenberg and his work' at the Deutsche Akademie der Künste (17 December).

1955 Publication of the first volume of *Lieder und Kantaten* in Leipzig.
Music to Becher's play *Winterschlacht*. *Winterschlacht-Suite* for orchestra taken from this.
Music for the films *Fidelio* by Walter Felsenstein and *Herr Puntila und sein Knecht Matti* by Brecht and Alberto Cavalcanti.

1956 Eisler in Paris and Vienna.
Music to Alan Resnais' documentary film on Auschwitz *Nuit et Brouillard* (Jean-Vigo prize).

1957 First performance of *Schweyk im zweiten Weltkrieg* in Warsaw (17 January).
Travel in the Soviet Union (summer).
Music for the film *Die Hexen von Salem* by Raymond Rouleau (screenplay: Jean-Paul Sartre).
Cantatas *Die Teppichweber von Kujan-Bulak* (Brecht) and *Bilder aus der Kriegsfibel* (Brecht) for soli, male chorus and orchestra.
Music to the play *Sturm* by Wladimir Bill-Belozerkowski. *Sturm-Suite* for orchestra put together from this.

1958 Eisler marries Stephanie (*née* Peschl).
Publication of 'On stupidity in music' in three issues of *Sinn und Form*.
National Prize, first class, of the DDR (7 October).
First performance of the *Lenin-Requiem* in Berlin (22 November).
Music to the film *Geschwader Fledermaus* by Erich Engel and the play *Das Schwitzbad* by Wladimir Majakowski.

1959 First performance of the *Deutsche Sinfonie* in Berlin (24 April).
Music to Louis Daquin's film *Trübe Wasser* (from *La Rabouilleuse* by Balzac).
Work started on the Tucholsky Lieder.

1960   Eisler in Vienna. First heart attack.
       Recuperation in Salzburg.
1961   Preparations for *Schweyk* performance in Milan (Piccolo-
       Teatro, G. Strehler). Afterwards in Ascona, Venice and Florence.
       In the autumn, preparations for *Schweyk* in Lyons and Paris (R.
       Planchon).
1962   Eisler in London. First English performance of the *Deutsche
       Sinfonie* (January).
       Lecture 'Content and Form' to the Society of German Composers
       and Musicologists in Berlin (9 March).
       Elected president of the Music Advisory Committee of the DDR
       (9 May).
       Ernste Gesänge for baritone and string orchestra finished.
       Dies in Berlin on 6 September.

The Chronology was compiled from: Eberhardt Klemm, 'Chronologisches Verzeichnis der Kompositionen Hanns Eislers' in *Beiträge zur
Musikwissenschaft* (Berlin-DDR), XV/1, 1973, pp. 93ff.

Index

by Frederick Smyth

page references given in italic refer to illustrations or their captions

Index